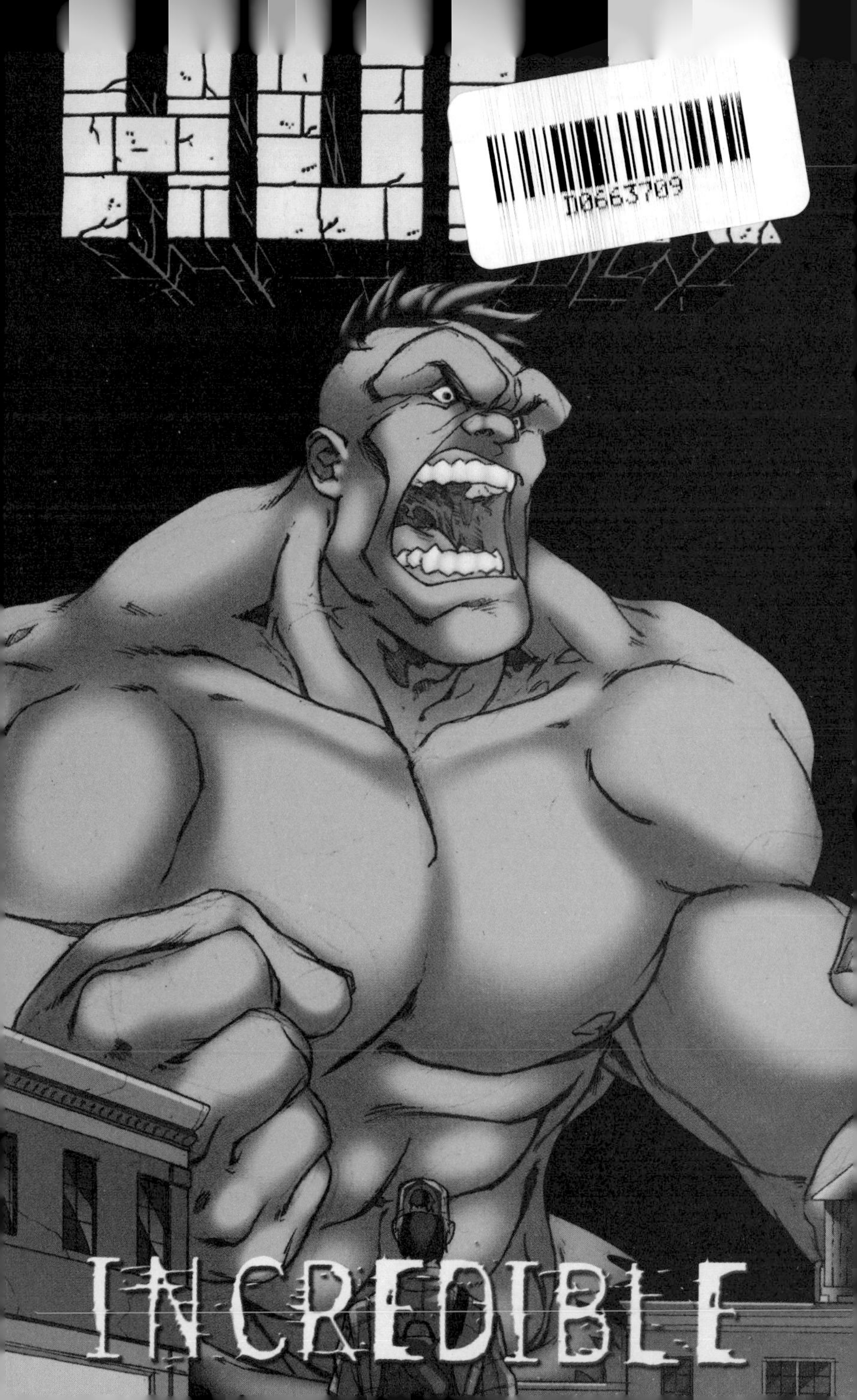
INCREDIBLE

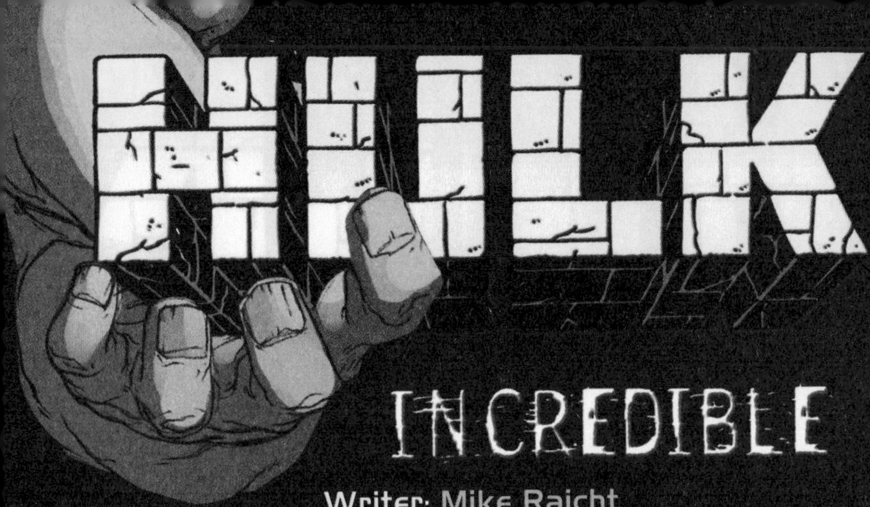
HULK
INCREDIBLE

Writer: Mike Raicht

Pencils: Joseph Dodd, Patrick Scherberger, Alex Sanchez & UDON's Ryan Odagawa

Colors: SotoColor's J. Rauch

Letters: Dave Sharpe

Cover Art: Shane Davis & SotoColor

Assistant Editor: John Barber

Editor: MacKenzie Cadenhead

Consulting Editor: C.B. Cebulski

Sales Manager: David Gabriel

Inspired by Stan Lee & Jack Kirby

Collections Editor: Jeff Youngquist

Assistant Editor: Jennifer Grünwald

Book Designer: Carrie Beadle

Creative Director: Tom Marvelli

Editor in Chief: Joe Quesada

Publisher: Dan Buckley

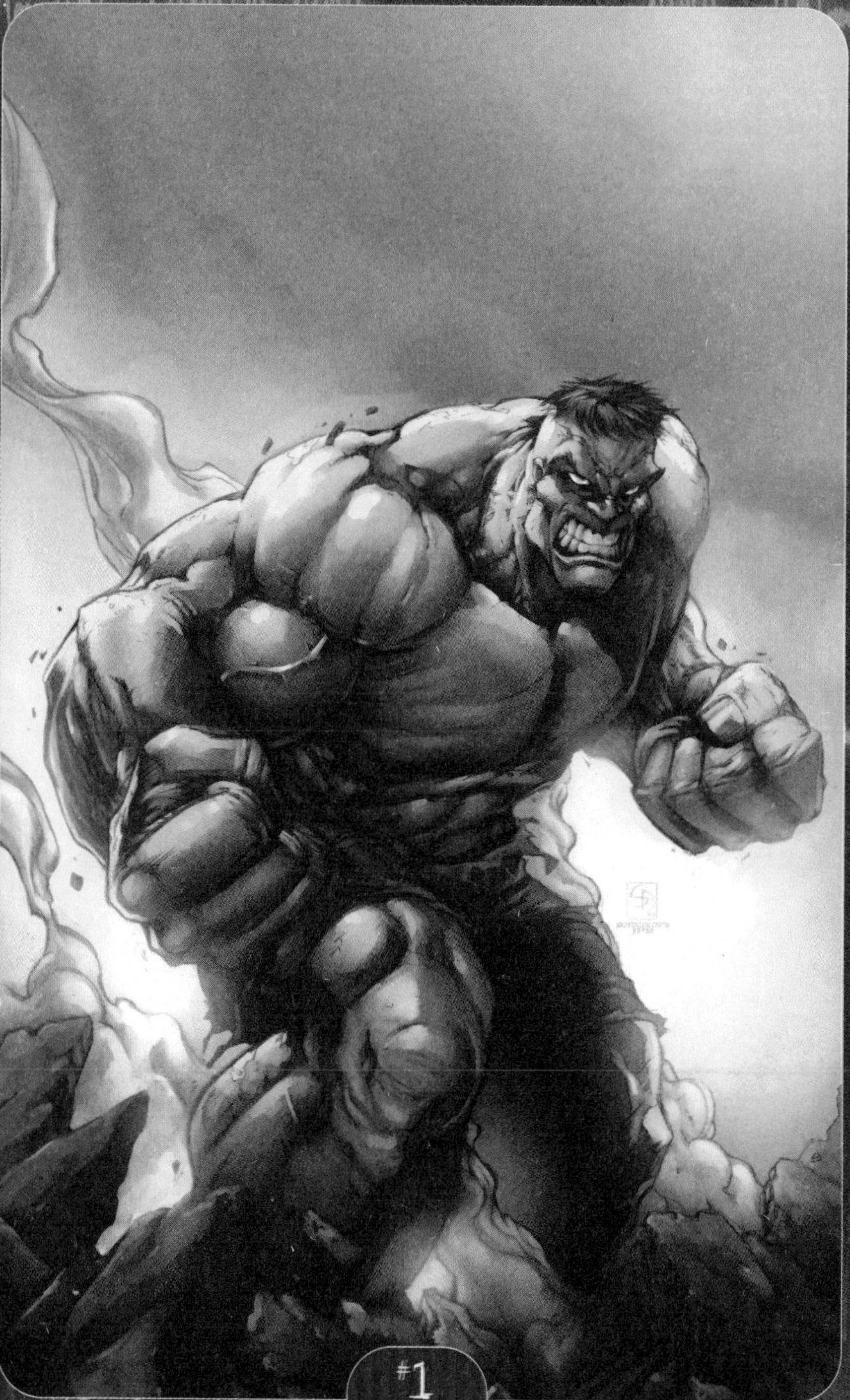

#1

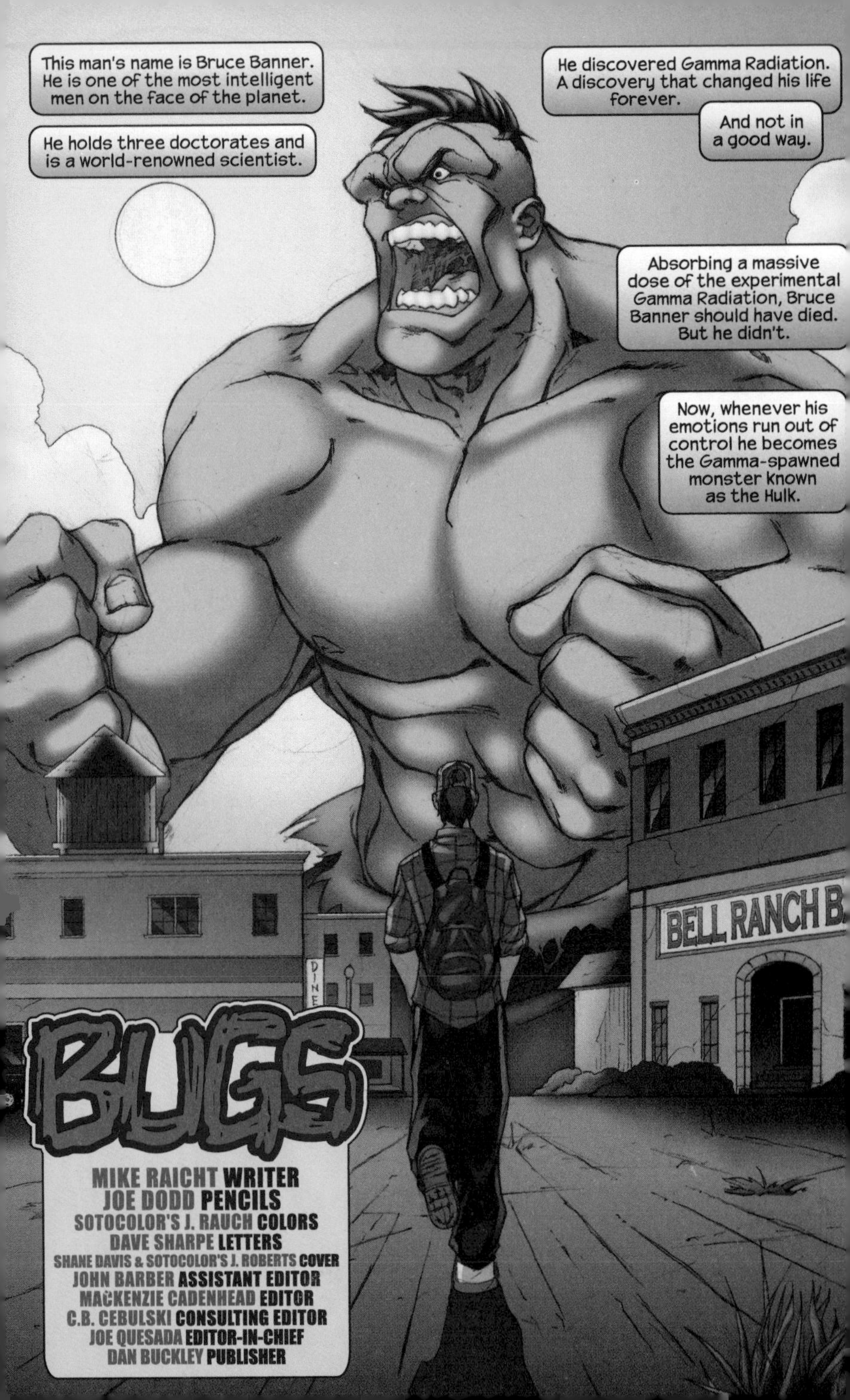
This man's name is Bruce Banner. He is one of the most intelligent men on the face of the planet.
He holds three doctorates and is a world-renowned scientist.
He discovered Gamma Radiation. A discovery that changed his life forever.
And not in a good way.
Absorbing a massive dose of the experimental Gamma Radiation, Bruce Banner should have died. But he didn't.
Now, whenever his emotions run out of control he becomes the Gamma-spawned monster known as the Hulk.
BELL RANCH B
BUGS
MIKE RAICHT WRITER
JOE DODD PENCILS
SOTOCOLOR'S J. RAUCH COLORS
DAVE SHARPE LETTERS
SHANE DAVIS & SOTOCOLOR'S J. ROBERTS COVER
JOHN BARBER ASSISTANT EDITOR
MACKENZIE CADENHEAD EDITOR
C.B. CEBULSKI CONSULTING EDITOR
JOE QUESADA EDITOR-IN-CHIEF
DAN BUCKLEY PUBLISHER

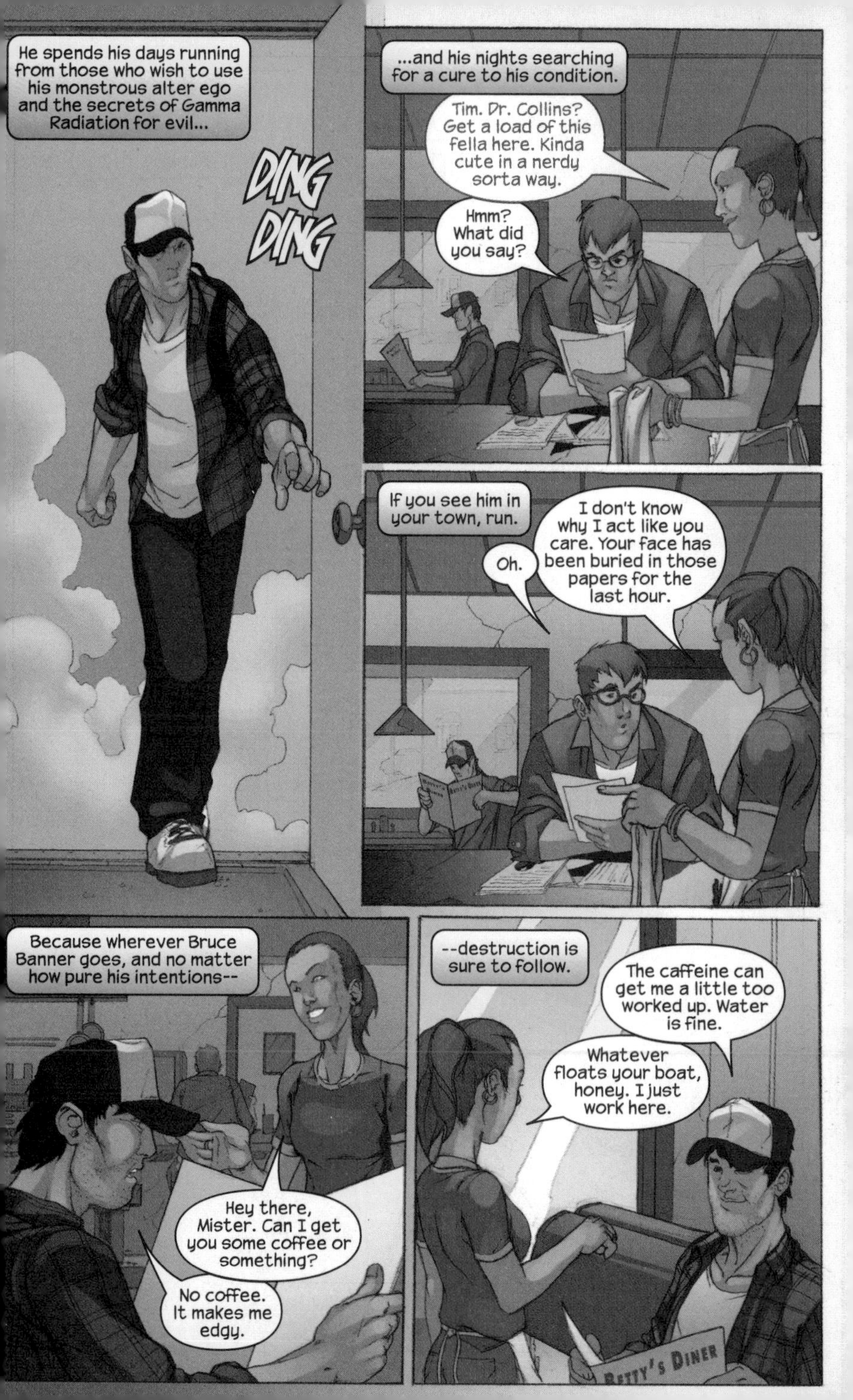
He spends his days running from those who wish to use his monstrous alter ego and the secrets of Gamma Radiation for evil...
DING DING
...and his nights searching for a cure to his condition.
Tim. Dr. Collins? Get a load of this fella here. Kinda cute in a nerdy sorta way.
Hmm? What did you say?
If you see him in your town, run.
I don't know why I act like you care. Your face has been buried in those papers for the last hour.
Oh.
Because wherever Bruce Banner goes, and no matter how pure his intentions--
Hey there, Mister. Can I get you some coffee or something?
No coffee. It makes me edgy.
--destruction is sure to follow.
The caffeine can get me a little too worked up. Water is fine.
Whatever floats your boat, honey. I just work here.
BETTY'S DINER

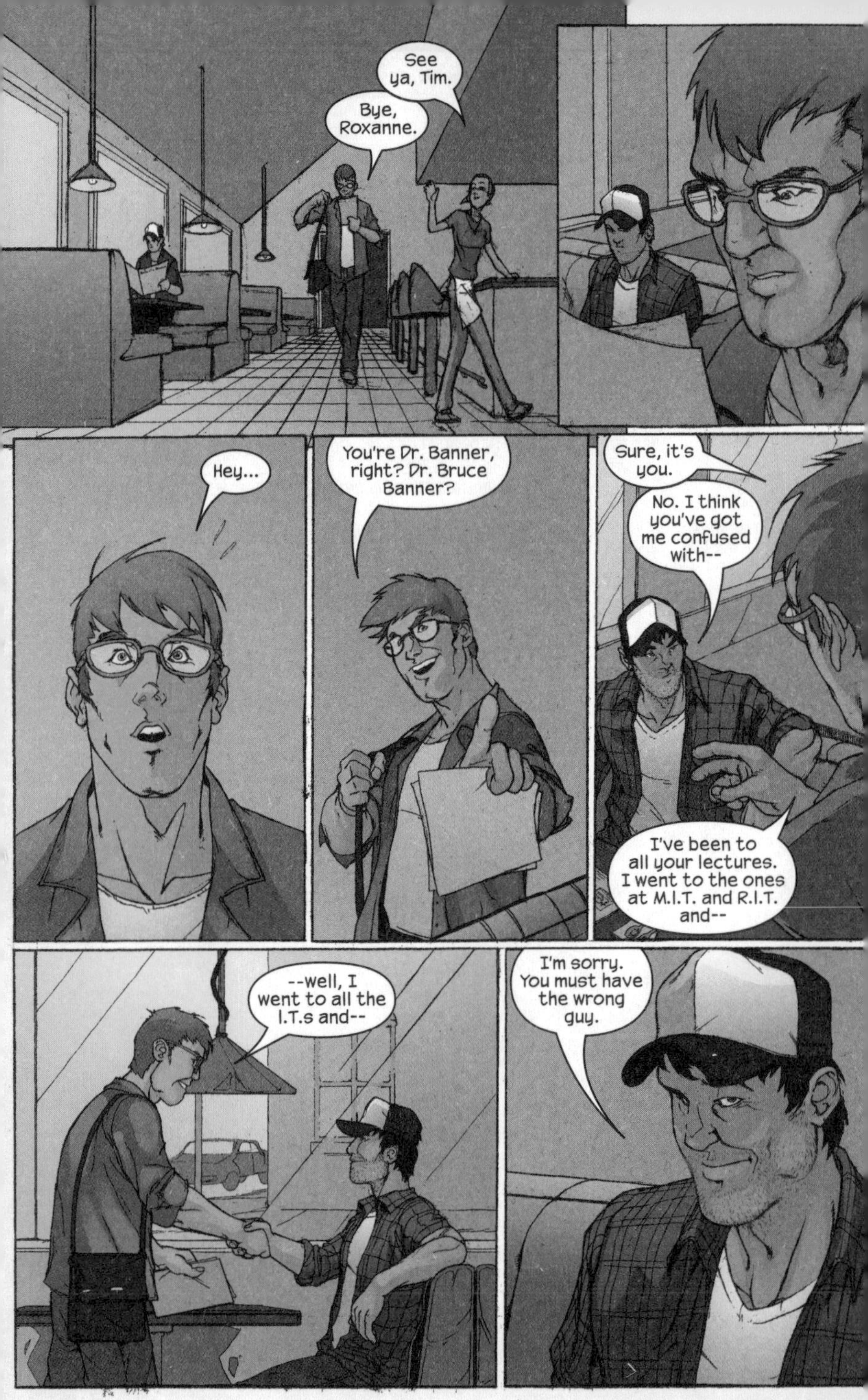

See ya, Tim.
Bye, Roxanne.
Hey...
You're Dr. Banner, right? Dr. Bruce Banner?
Sure, it's you.
No. I think you've got me confused with--
I've been to all your lectures. I went to the ones at M.I.T. and R.I.T. and--
--well, I went to all the I.T.s and--
I'm sorry. You must have the wrong guy.

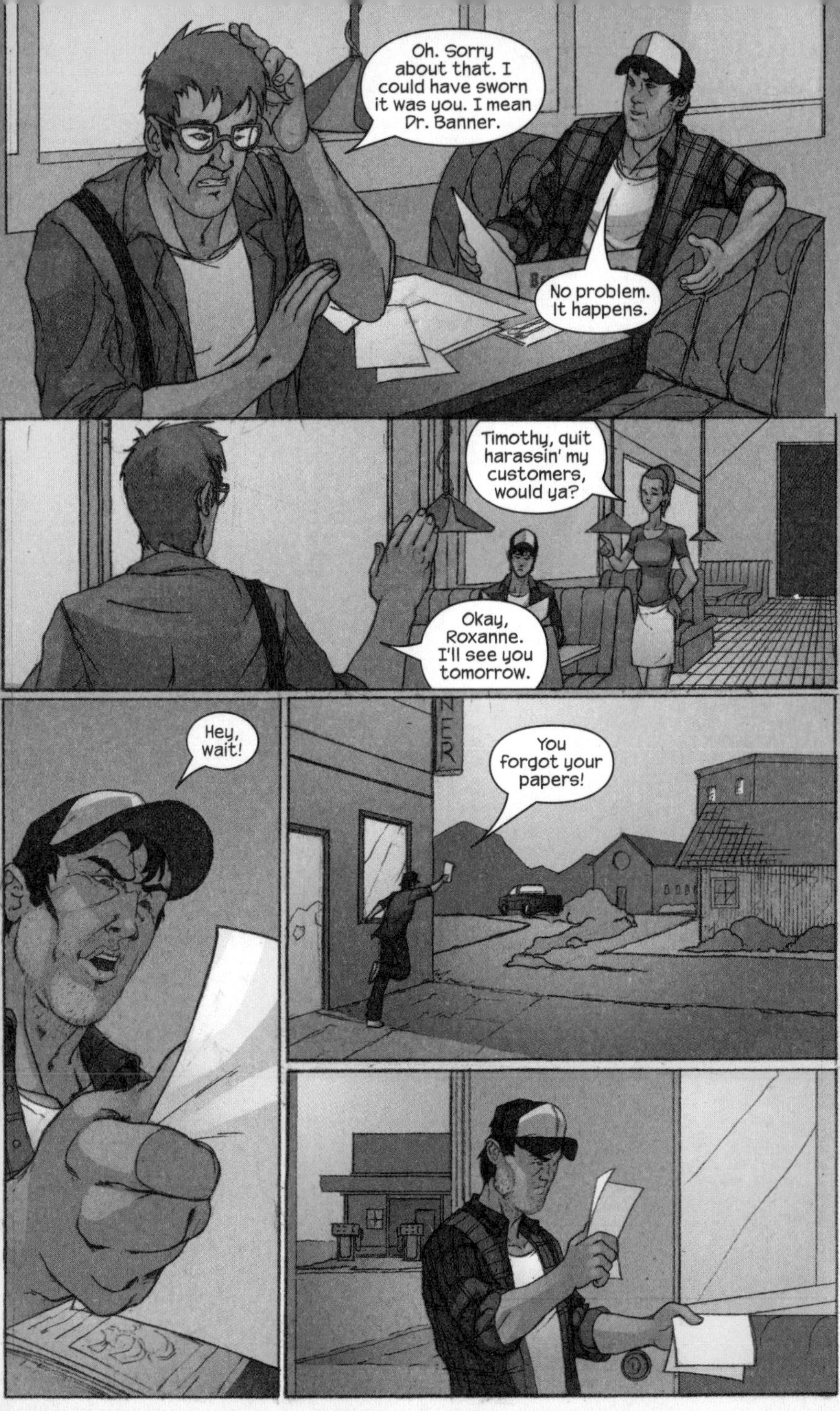

Oh. Sorry about that. I could have sworn it was you. I mean Dr. Banner.
No problem. It happens.
Timothy, quit harassin' my customers, would ya?
Okay, Roxanne. I'll see you tomorrow.
Hey, wait!
You forgot your papers!

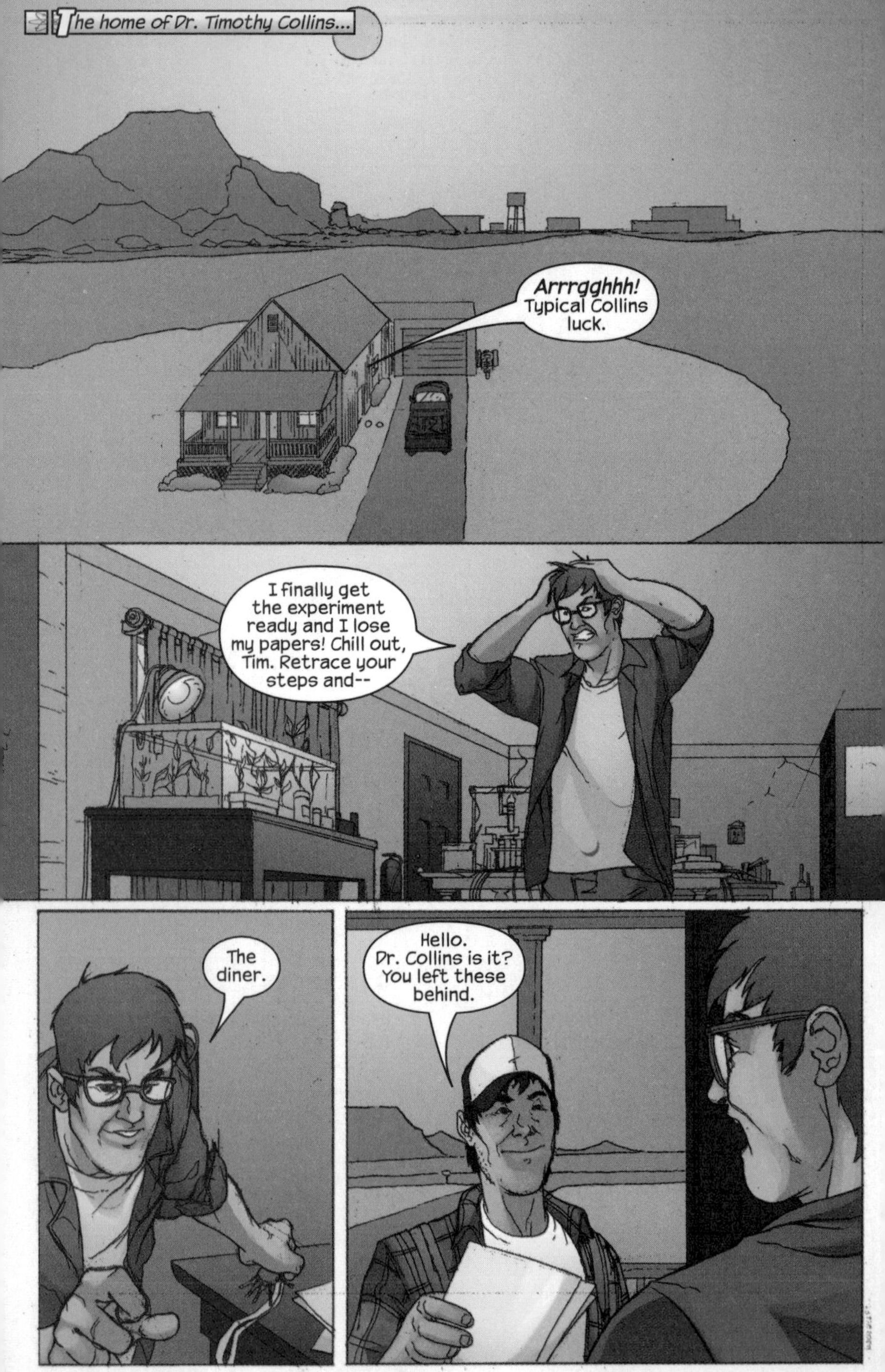
The home of Dr. Timothy Collins...
Arrrgghhh! Typical Collins luck.
I finally get the experiment ready and I lose my papers! Chill out, Tim. Retrace your steps and--
The diner.
Hello. Dr. Collins is it? You left these behind.

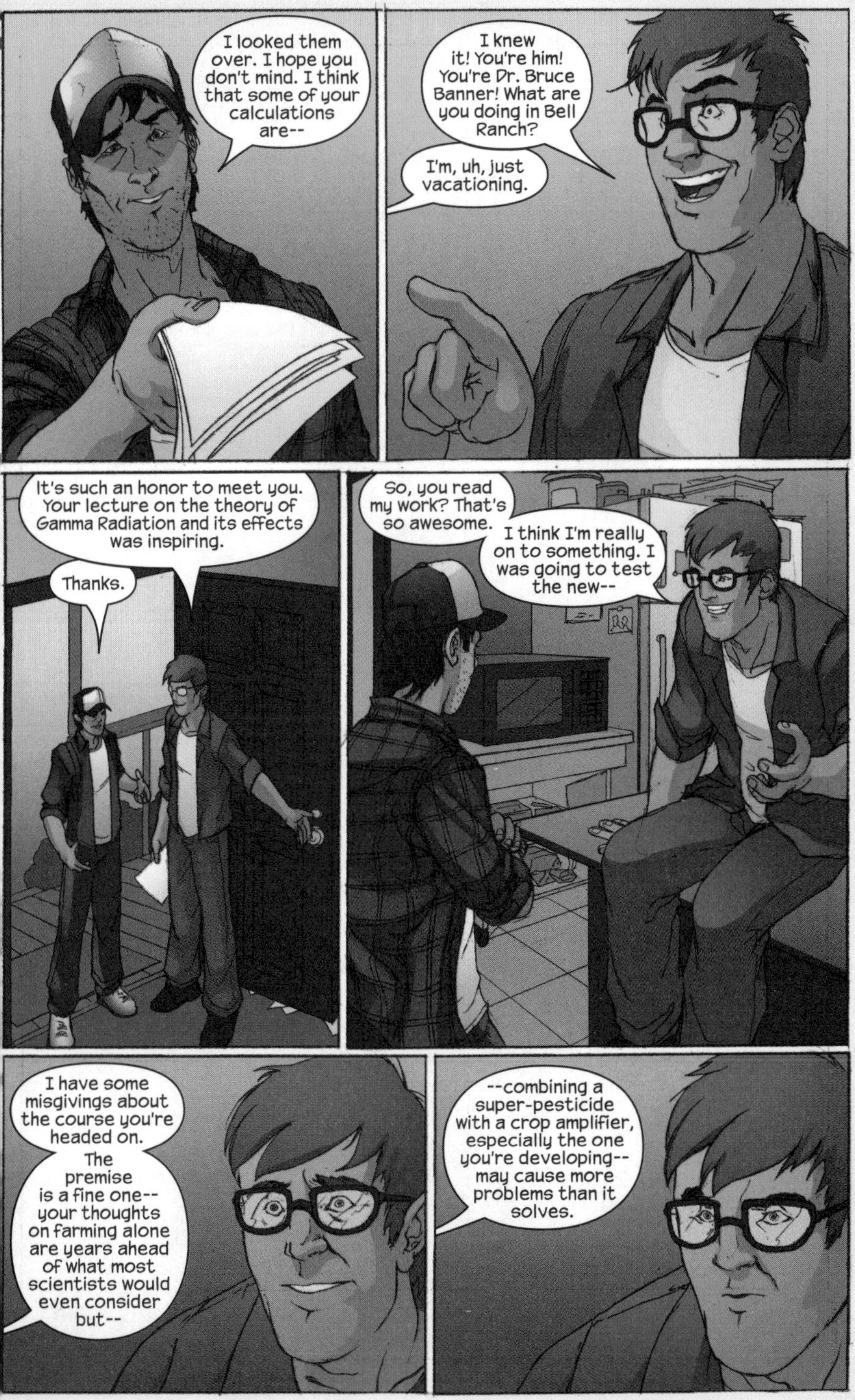
I looked them over. I hope you don't mind. I think that some of your calculations are--
I knew it! You're him! You're Dr. Bruce Banner! What are you doing in Bell Ranch?
I'm, uh, just vacationing.
It's such an honor to meet you. Your lecture on the theory of Gamma Radiation and its effects was inspiring.
Thanks.
So, you read my work? That's so awesome.
I think I'm really on to something. I was going to test the new--
I have some misgivings about the course you're headed on.
The premise is a fine one--your thoughts on farming alone are years ahead of what most scientists would even consider but--
--combining a super-pesticide with a crop amplifier, especially the one you're developing--may cause more problems than it solves.

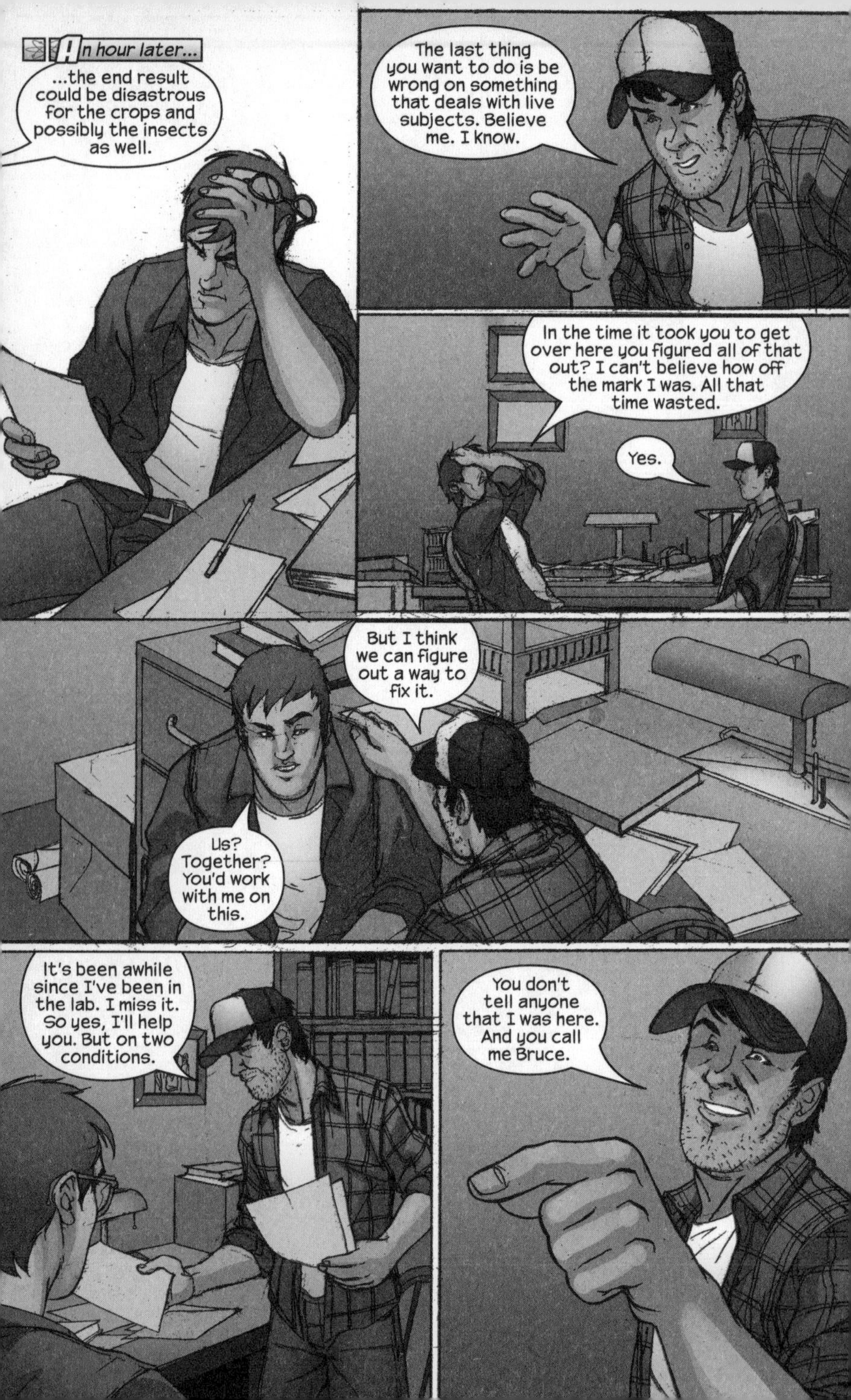
An hour later...
...the end result could be disastrous for the crops and possibly the insects as well.
The last thing you want to do is be wrong on something that deals with live subjects. Believe me. I know.
In the time it took you to get over here you figured all of that out? I can't believe how off the mark I was. All that time wasted.
Yes.
But I think we can figure out a way to fix it.
Us? Together? You'd work with me on this.
It's been awhile since I've been in the lab. I miss it. So yes, I'll help you. But on two conditions.
You don't tell anyone that I was here. And you call me Bruce.

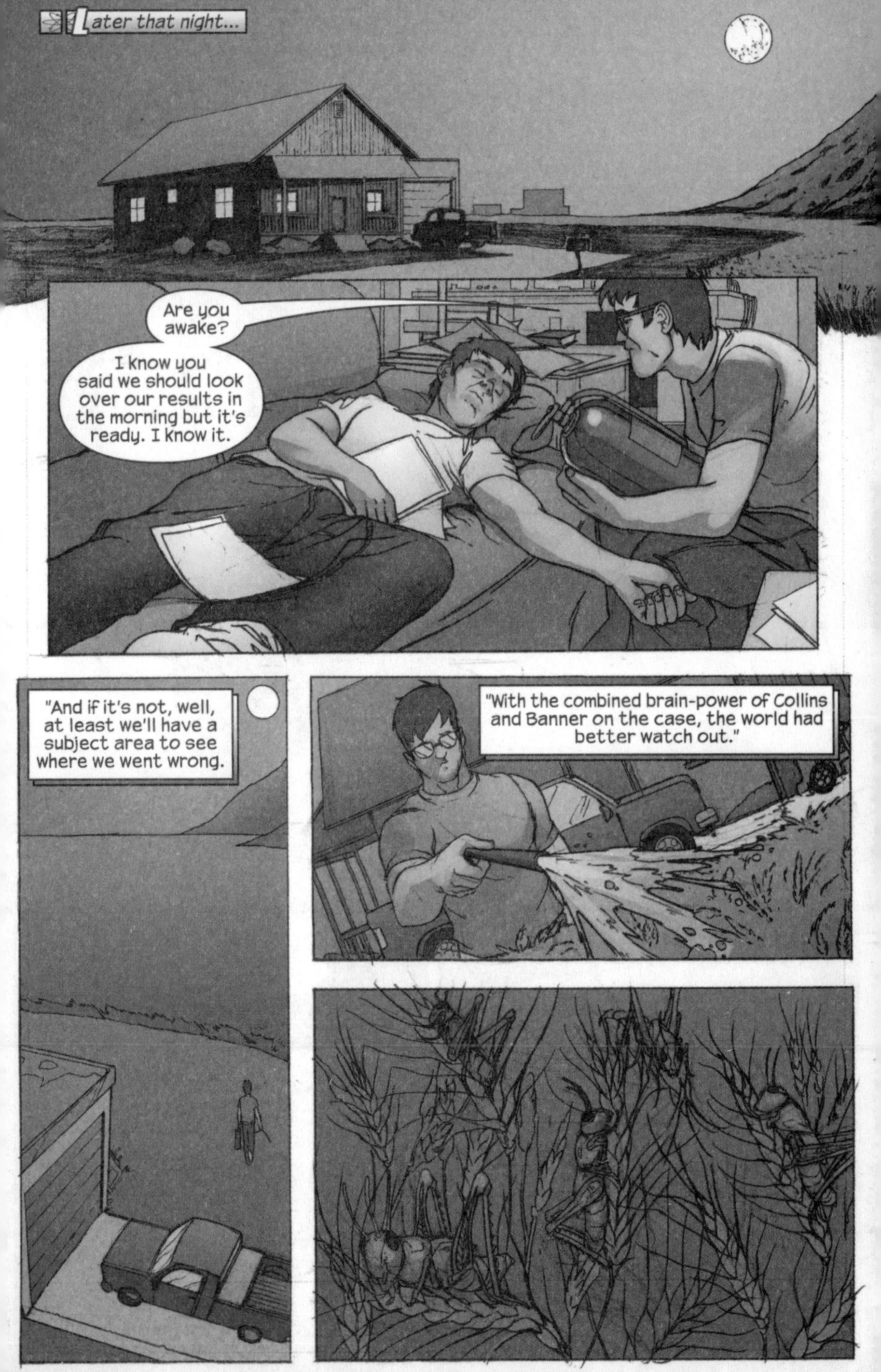
Later that night...
Are you awake?
I know you said we should look over our results in the morning but it's ready. I know it.
"And if it's not, well, at least we'll have a subject area to see where we went wrong.
"With the combined brain-power of Collins and Banner on the case, the world had better watch out."

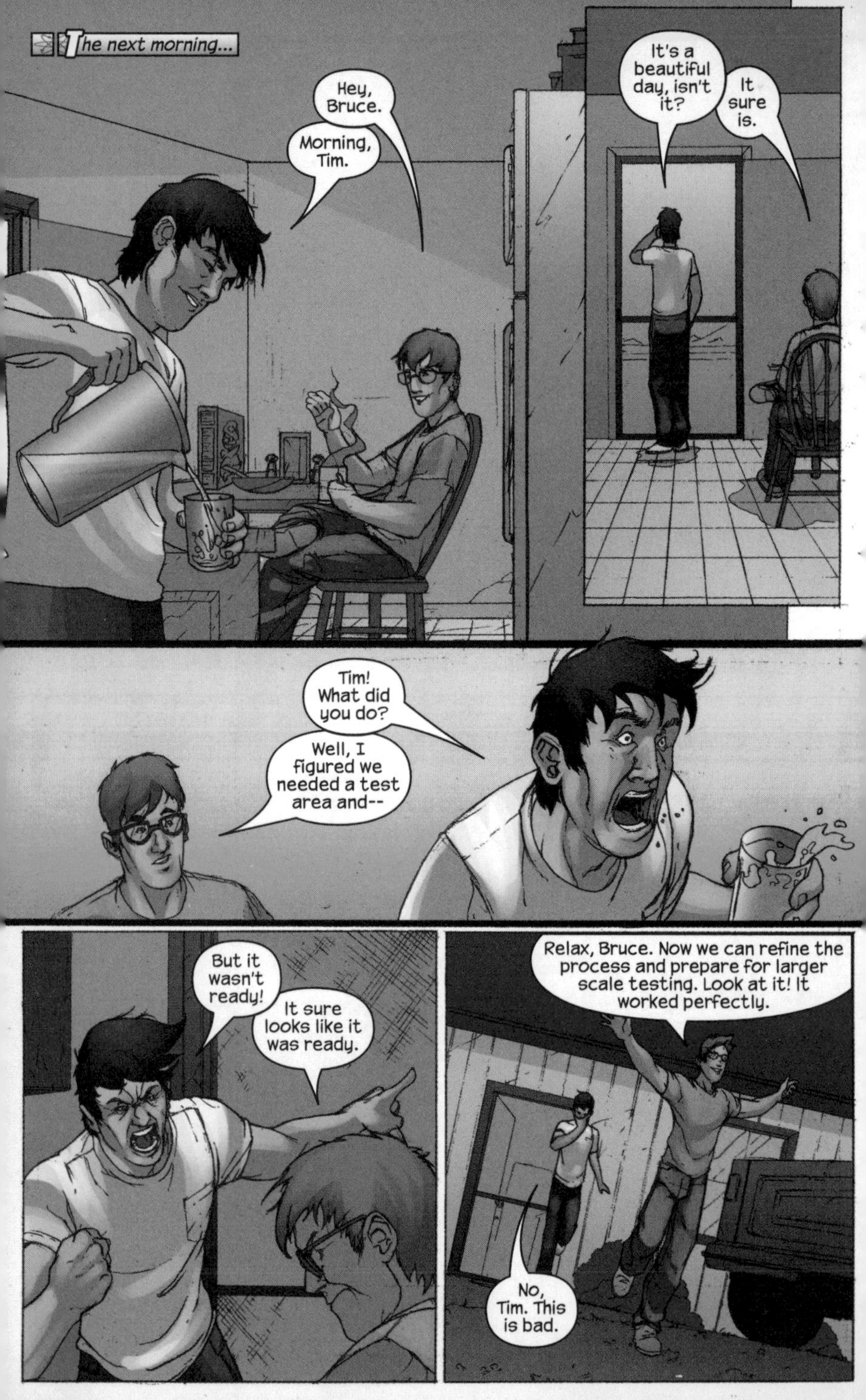
The next morning...
Hey, Bruce.
Morning, Tim.
It's a beautiful day, isn't it?
It sure is.
Tim! What did you do?
Well, I figured we needed a test area and--
But it wasn't ready!
It sure looks like it was ready.
Relax, Bruce. Now we can refine the process and prepare for larger scale testing. Look at it! It worked perfectly.
No, Tim. This is bad.

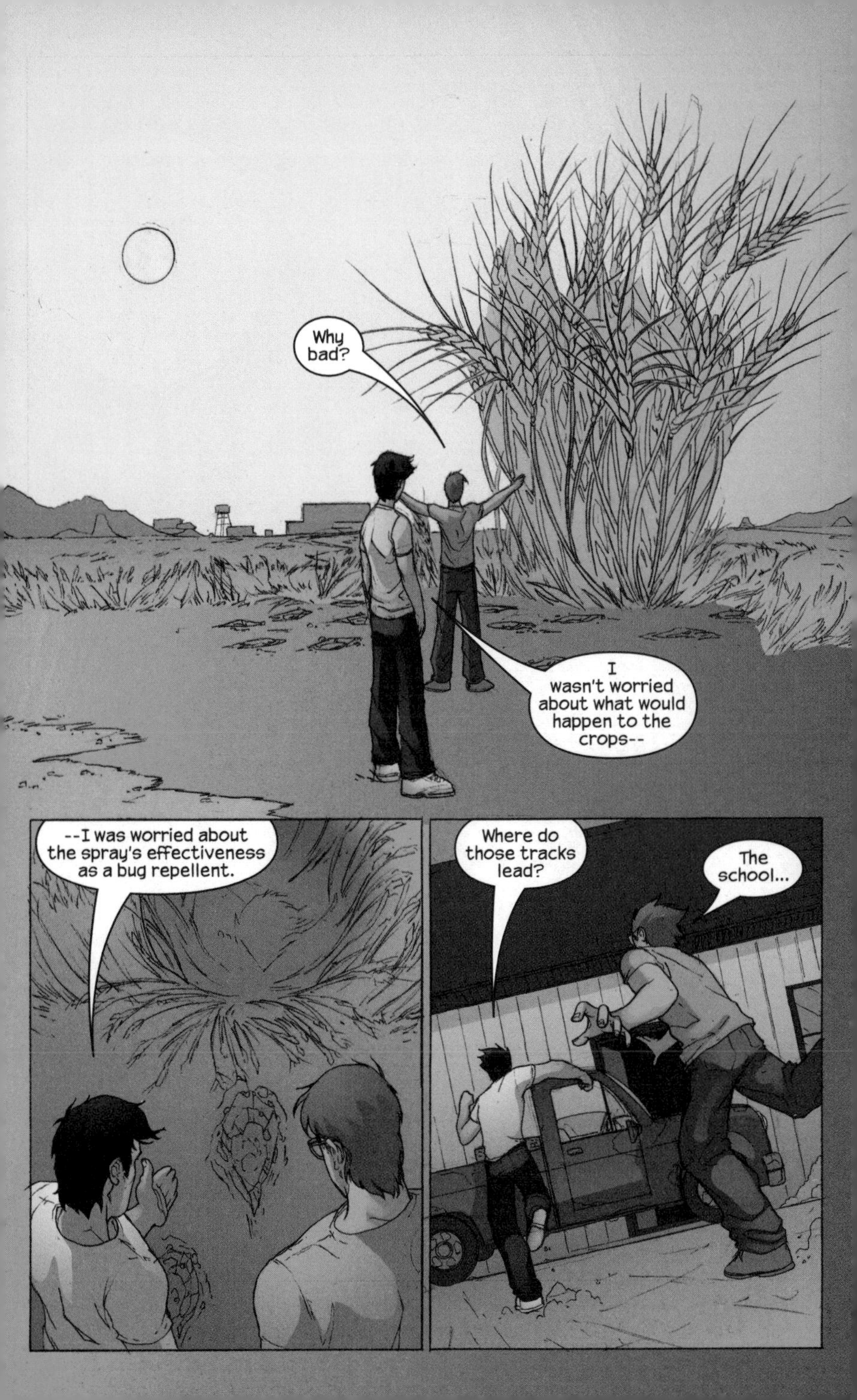
Why bad?
I wasn't worried about what would happen to the crops--
--I was worried about the spray's effectiveness as a bug repellent.
Where do those tracks lead?
The school...

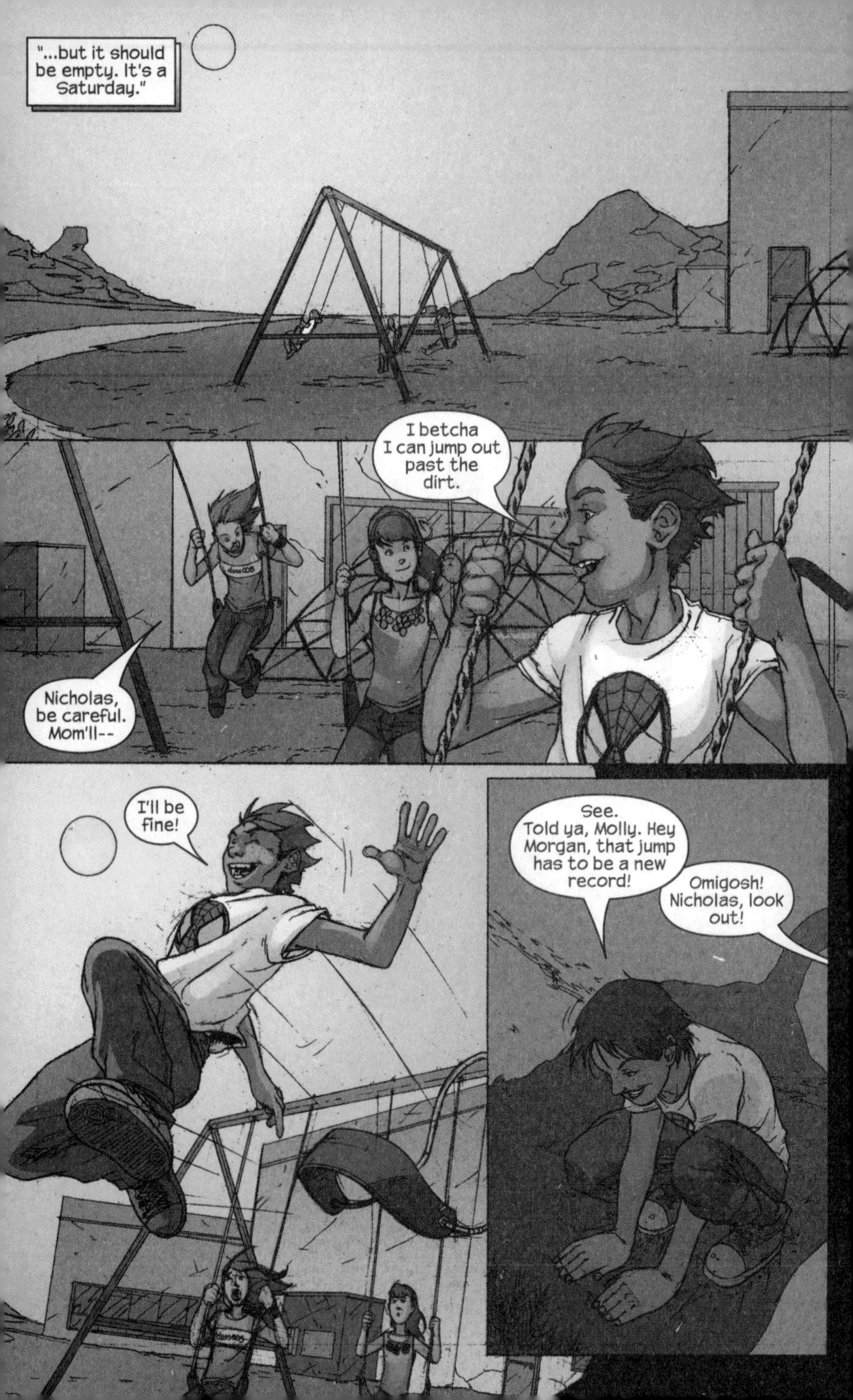
"...but it should be empty. It's a Saturday."
I betcha I can jump out past the dirt.
Nicholas, be careful. Mom'll--
I'll be fine!
See. Told ya, Molly. Hey Morgan, that jump has to be a new record!
Omigosh! Nicholas, look out!

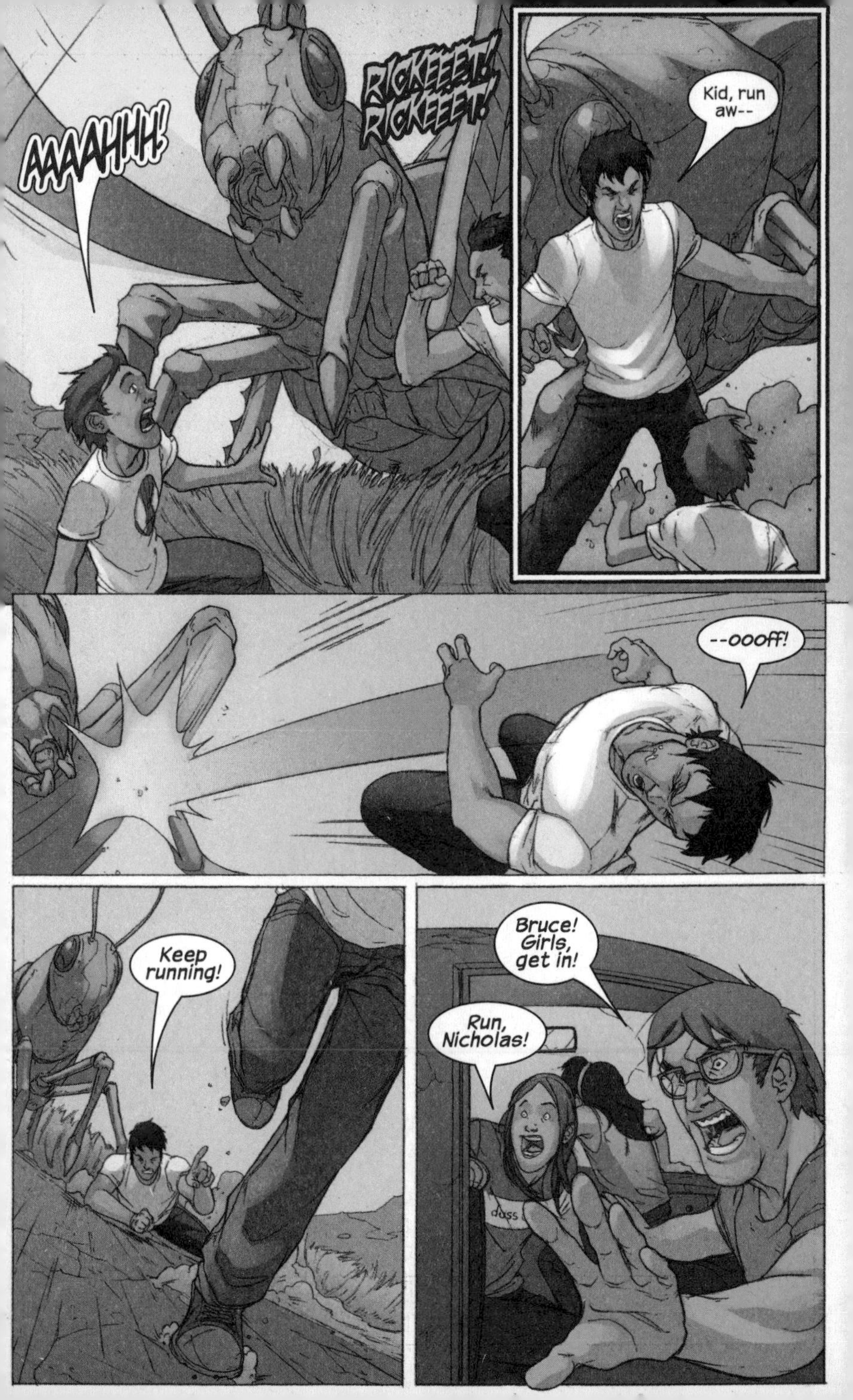
AAAAHHH!
RICKEEEET! RICKEEEET!
Kid, run aw--
--oooff!
Keep running!
Bruce! Girls, get in!
Run, Nicholas!

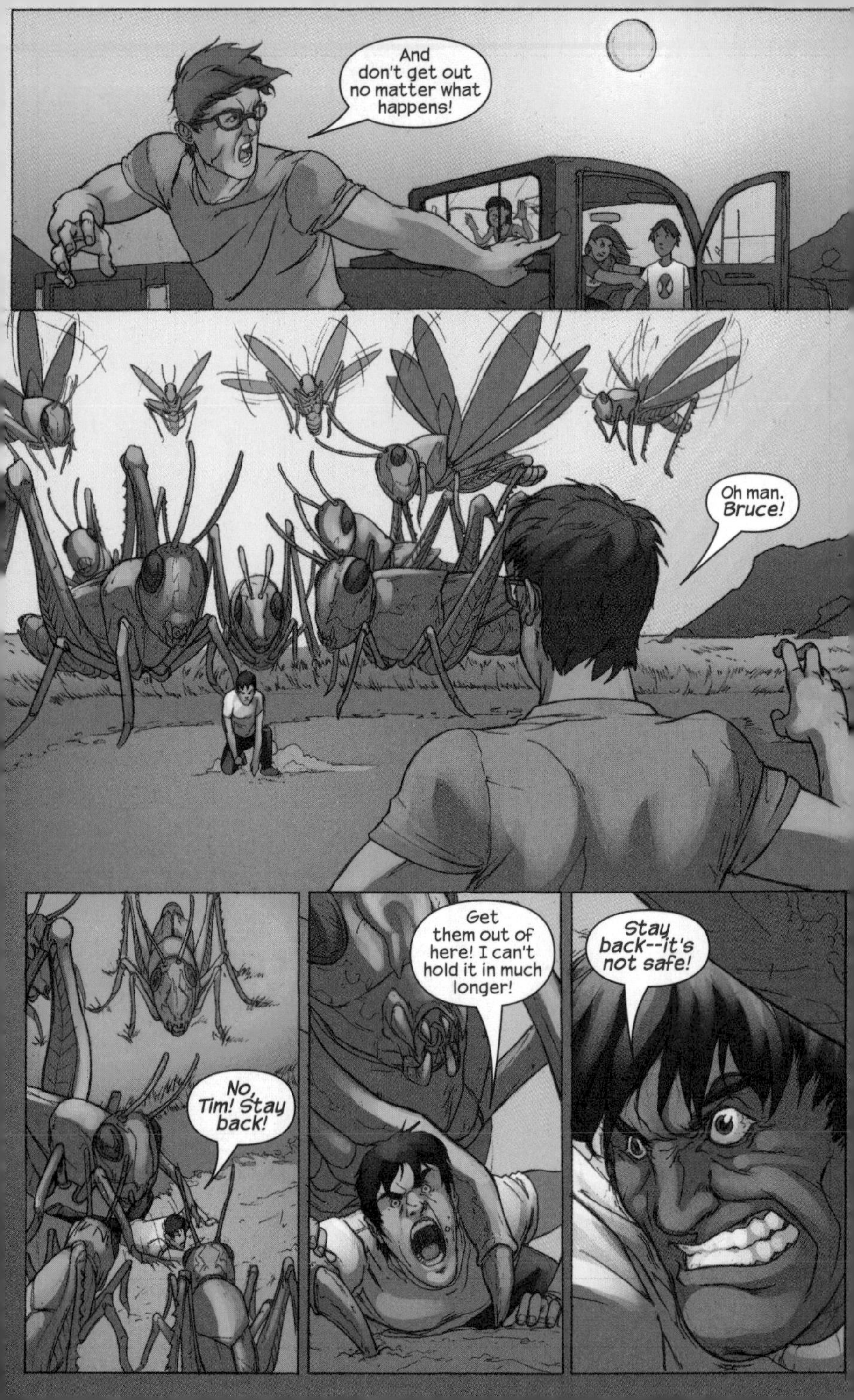
And don't get out no matter what happens!
Oh man. Bruce!
No, Tim! Stay back!
Get them out of here! I can't hold it in much longer!
Stay back--it's not safe!

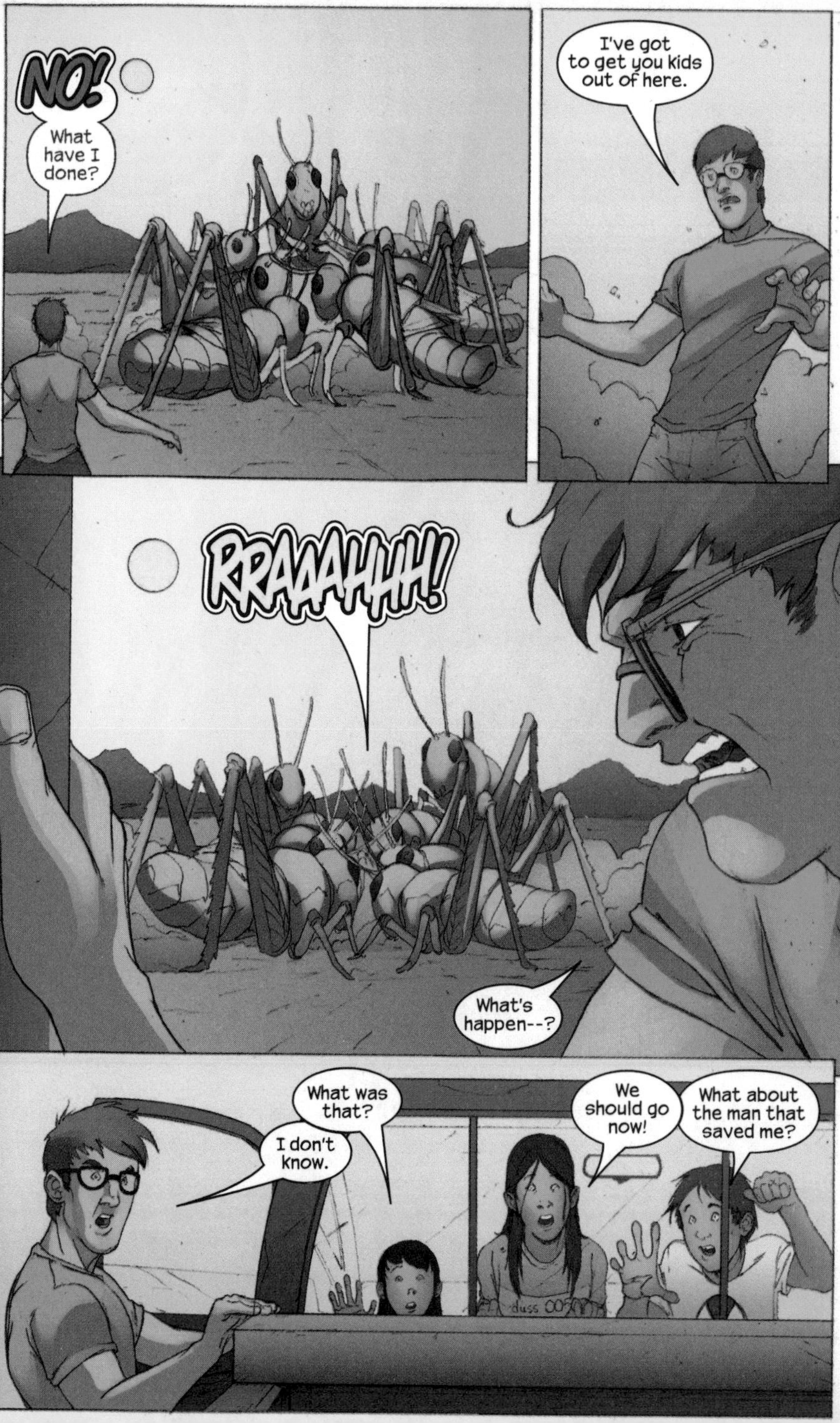
NO!
What have I done?
I've got to get you kids out of here.
RRAAAHHH!
What's happen--?
What was that?
I don't know.
We should go now!
What about the man that saved me?

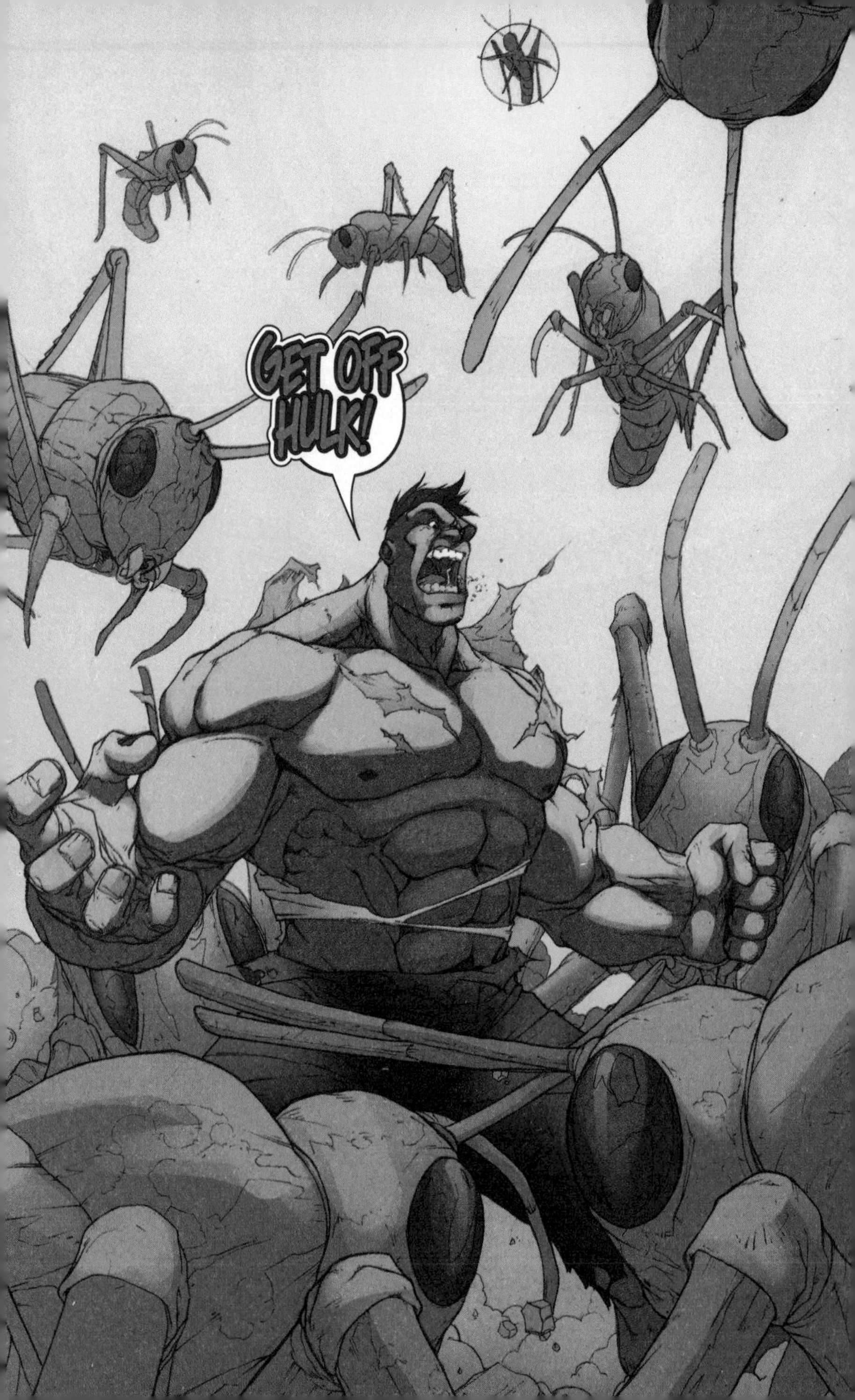
GET OFF HULK!

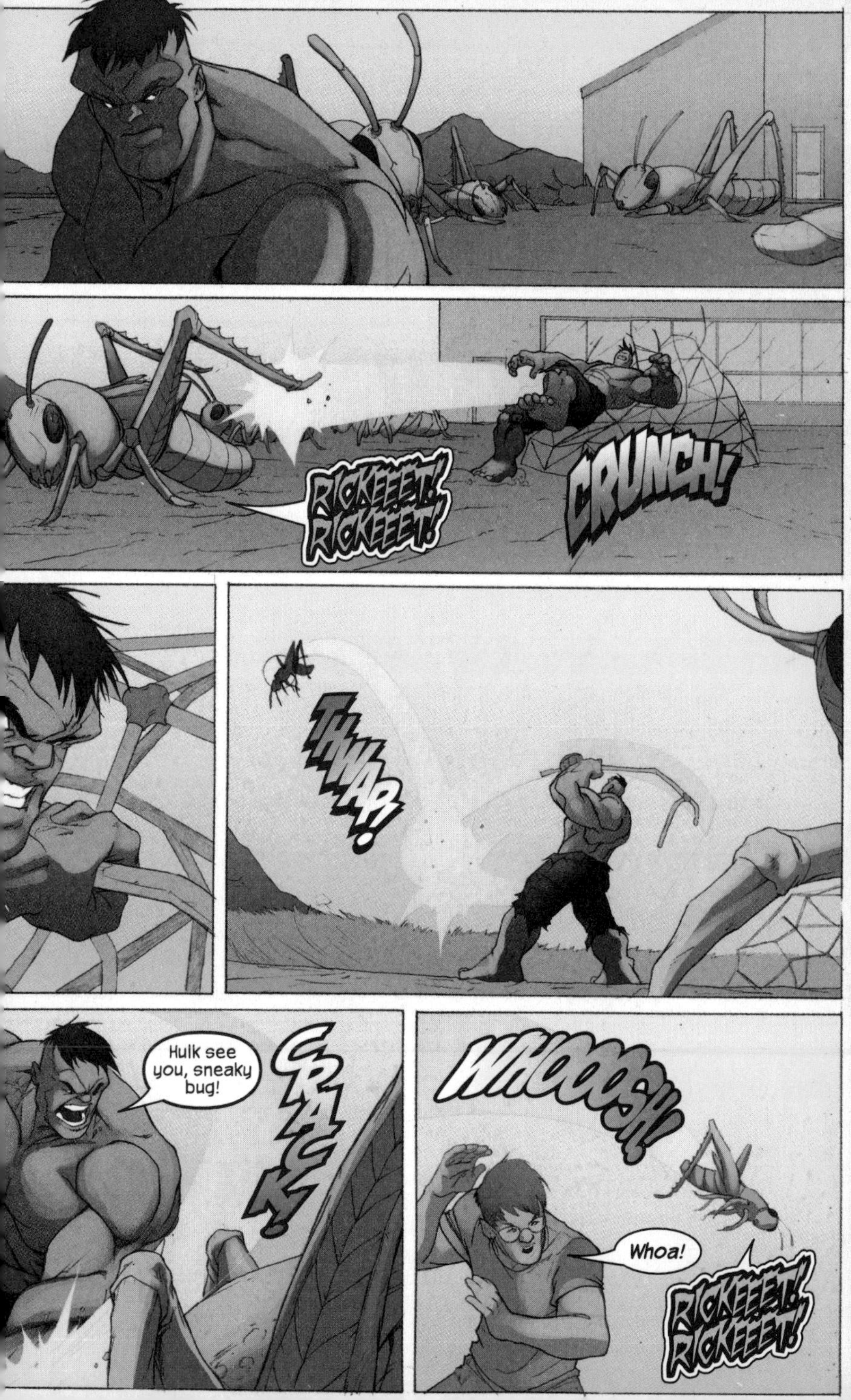
RICKEEET! RICKEEET!
CRUNCH!
THWAP!
Hulk see you, sneaky bug!
CRACK!
WHOOOSH!
Whoa!
RICKEEET! RICKEEET!

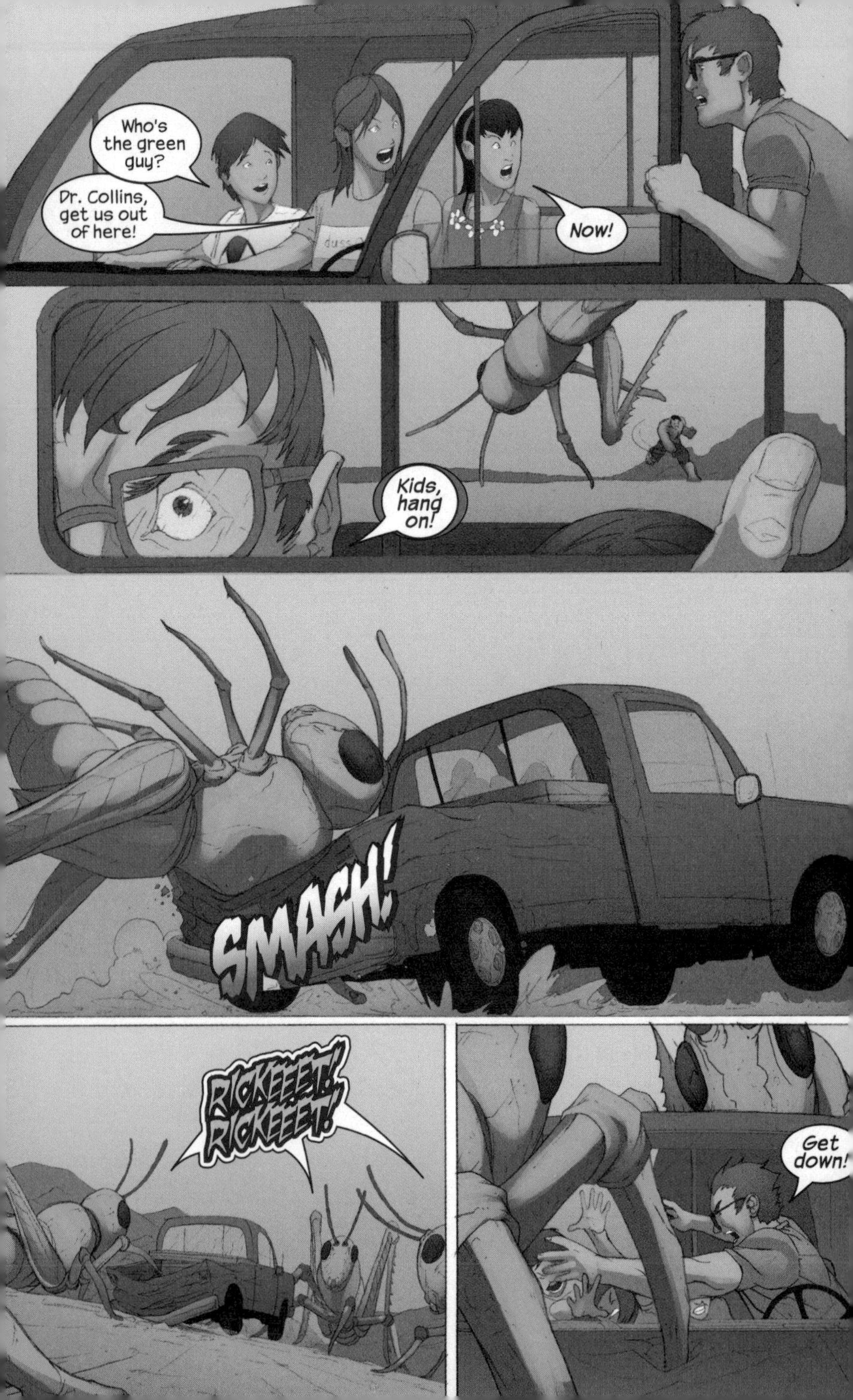
Who's the green guy?
Dr. Collins, get us out of here!
Now!
Kids, hang on!
SMASH!
RICKEEET! RICKEEET!
Get down!

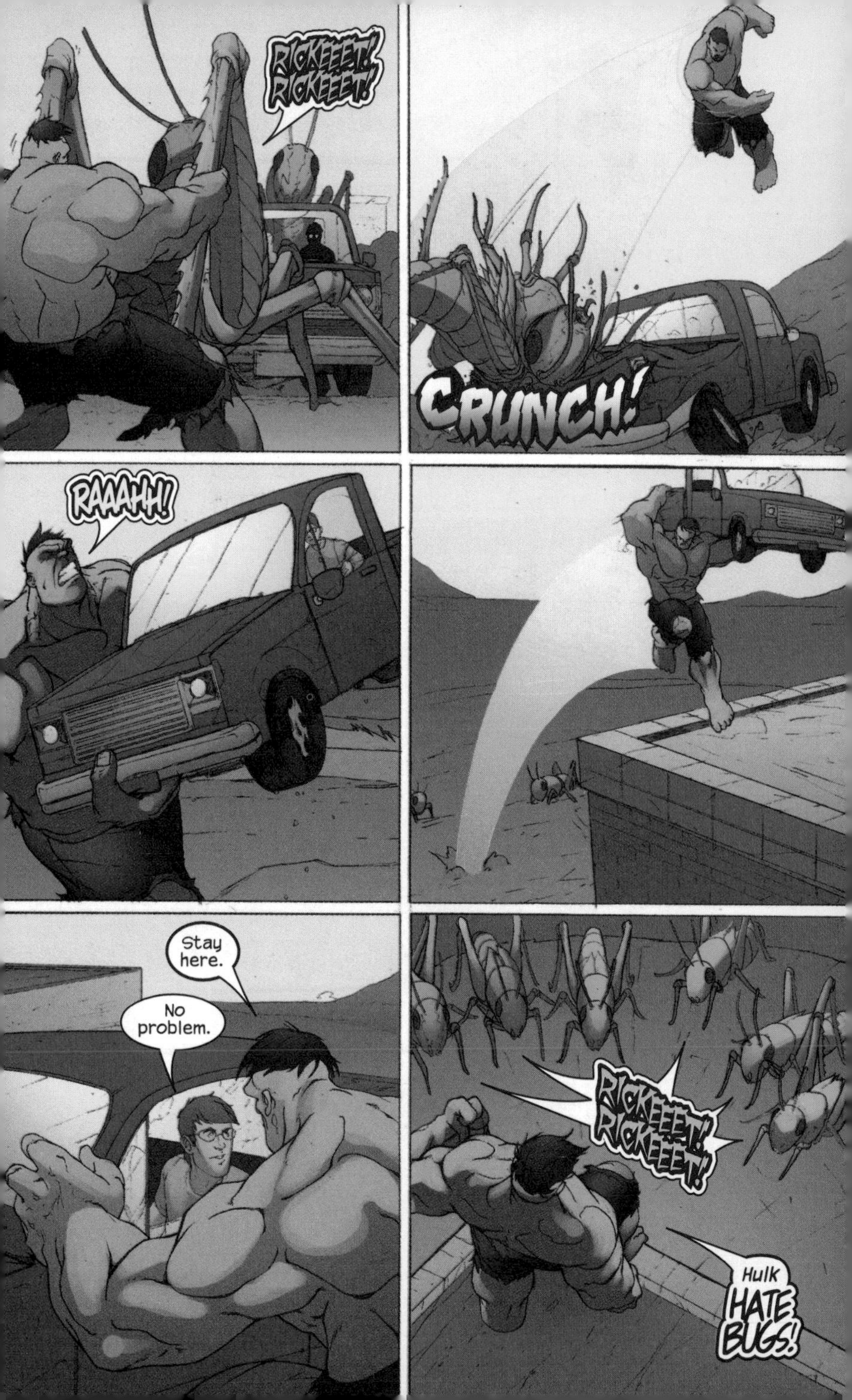
RICKEEET! RICKEEET!
CRUNCH!
RAAAHH!
Stay here.
No problem.
RICKEEET! RICKEEET!
Hulk HATE BUGS!

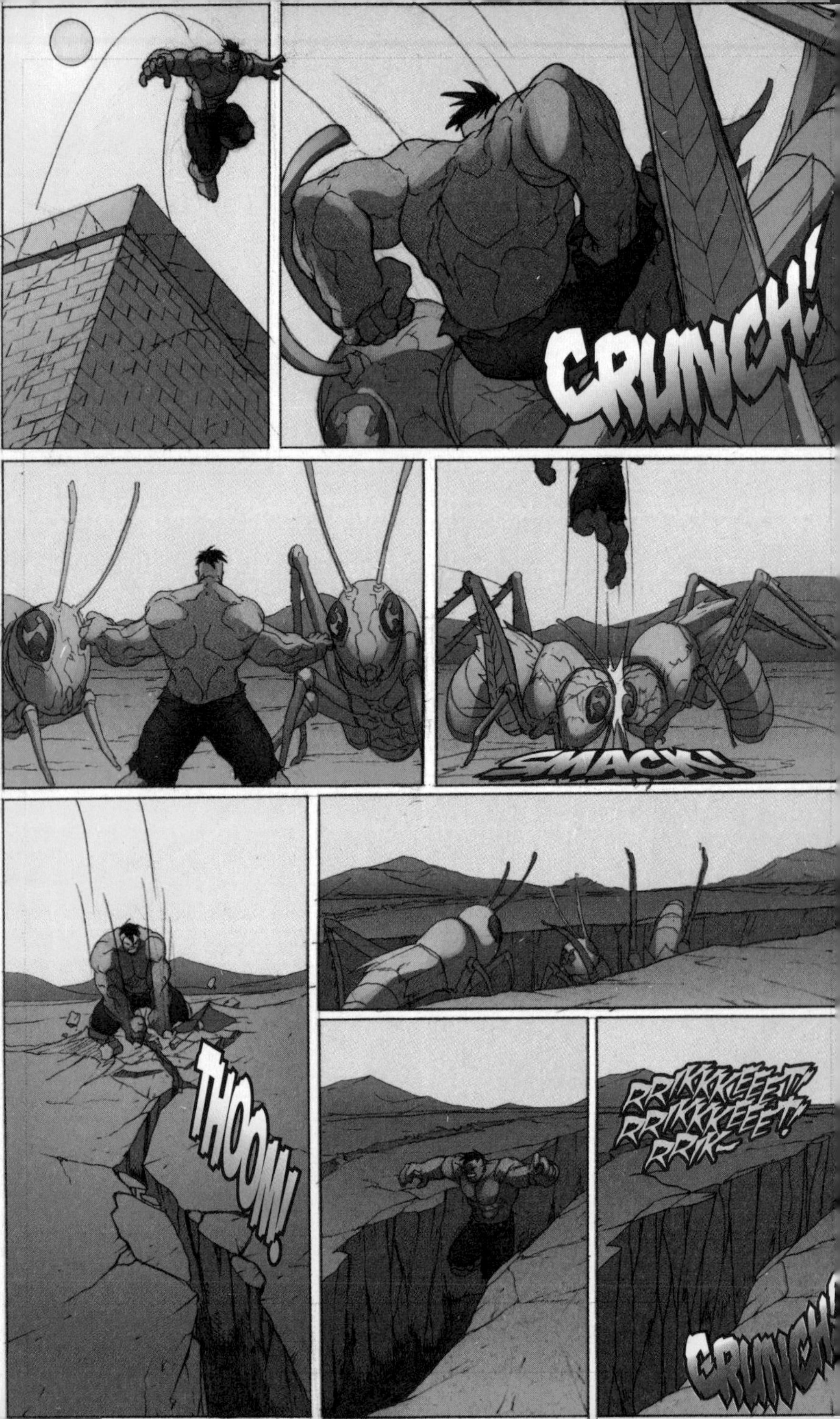
CRUNCH!
SMACK!
THOOM!
RRIKKKKEEET!
RRIKKKKEEET!
RRIK–
CRUNCH

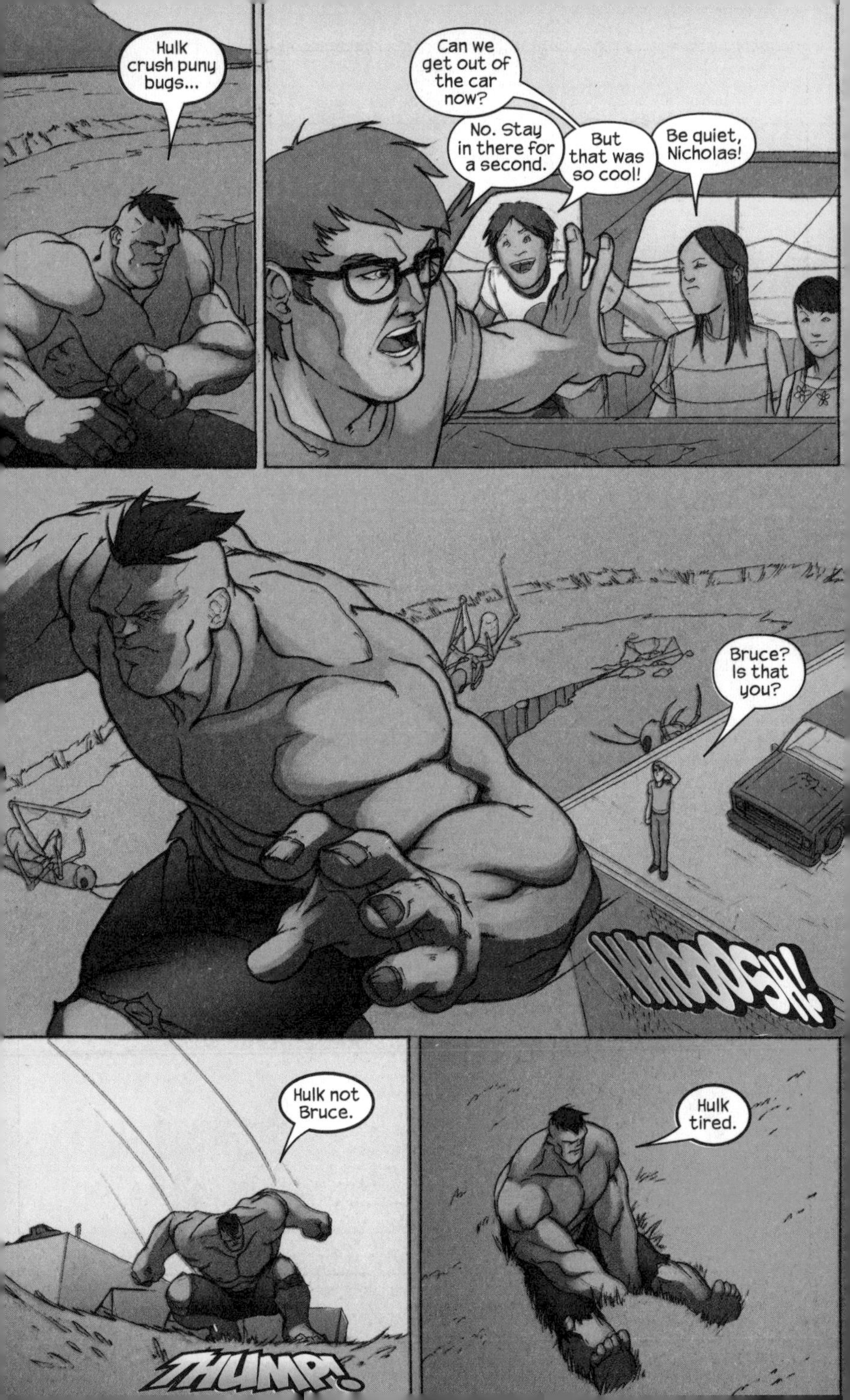
Hulk crush puny bugs...
Can we get out of the car now?
No. Stay in there for a second.
But that was so cool!
Be quiet, Nicholas!
Bruce? Is that you?
WHOOOSH!
Hulk not Bruce.
THUMP!
Hulk tired.

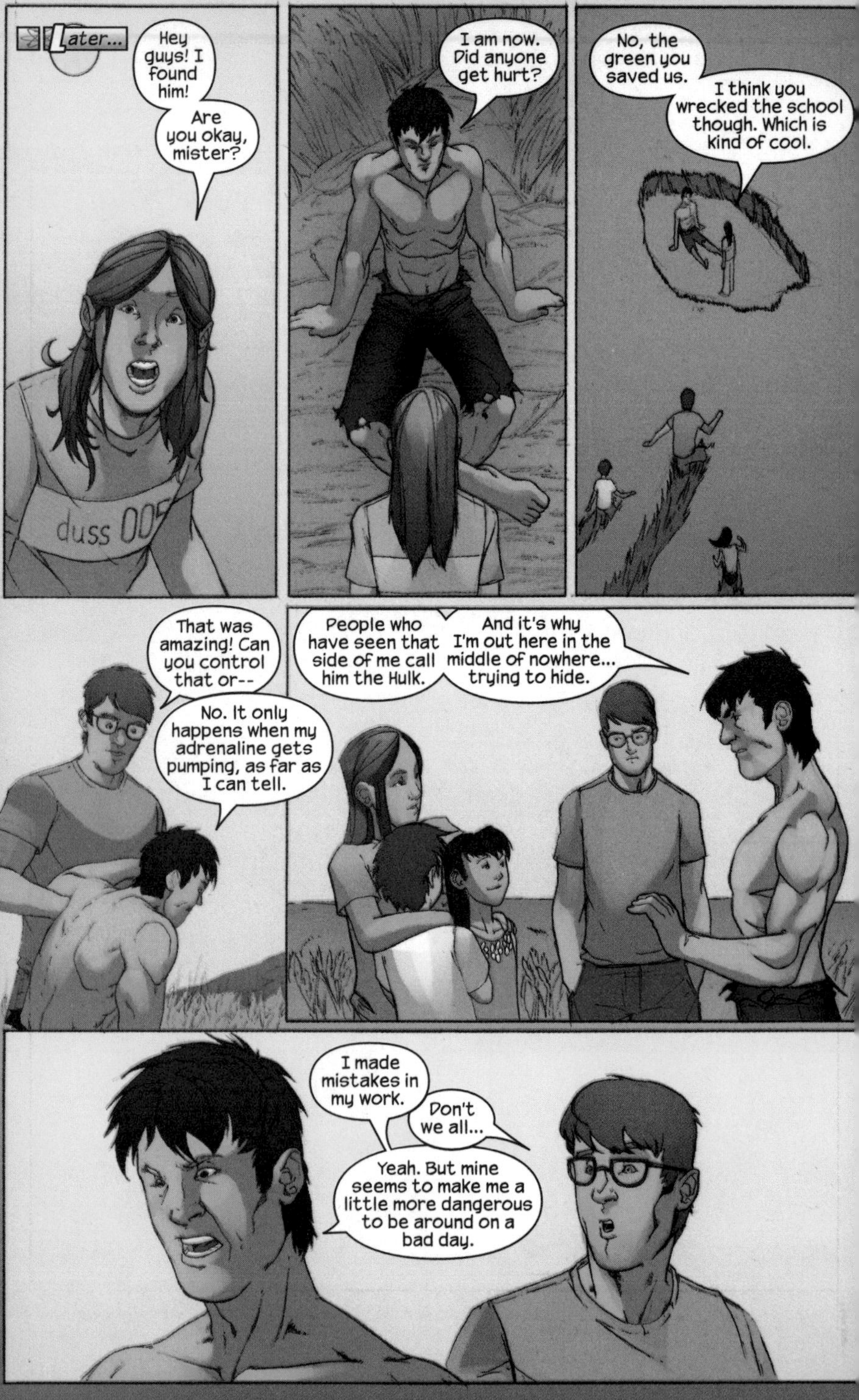
Later...
Hey guys! I found him!
Are you okay, mister?
duss 00
I am now. Did anyone get hurt?
No, the green you saved us.
I think you wrecked the school though. Which is kind of cool.
That was amazing! Can you control that or--
No. It only happens when my adrenaline gets pumping, as far as I can tell.
People who have seen that side of me call him the Hulk.
And it's why I'm out here in the middle of nowhere... trying to hide.
I made mistakes in my work.
Don't we all...
Yeah. But mine seems to make me a little more dangerous to be around on a bad day.

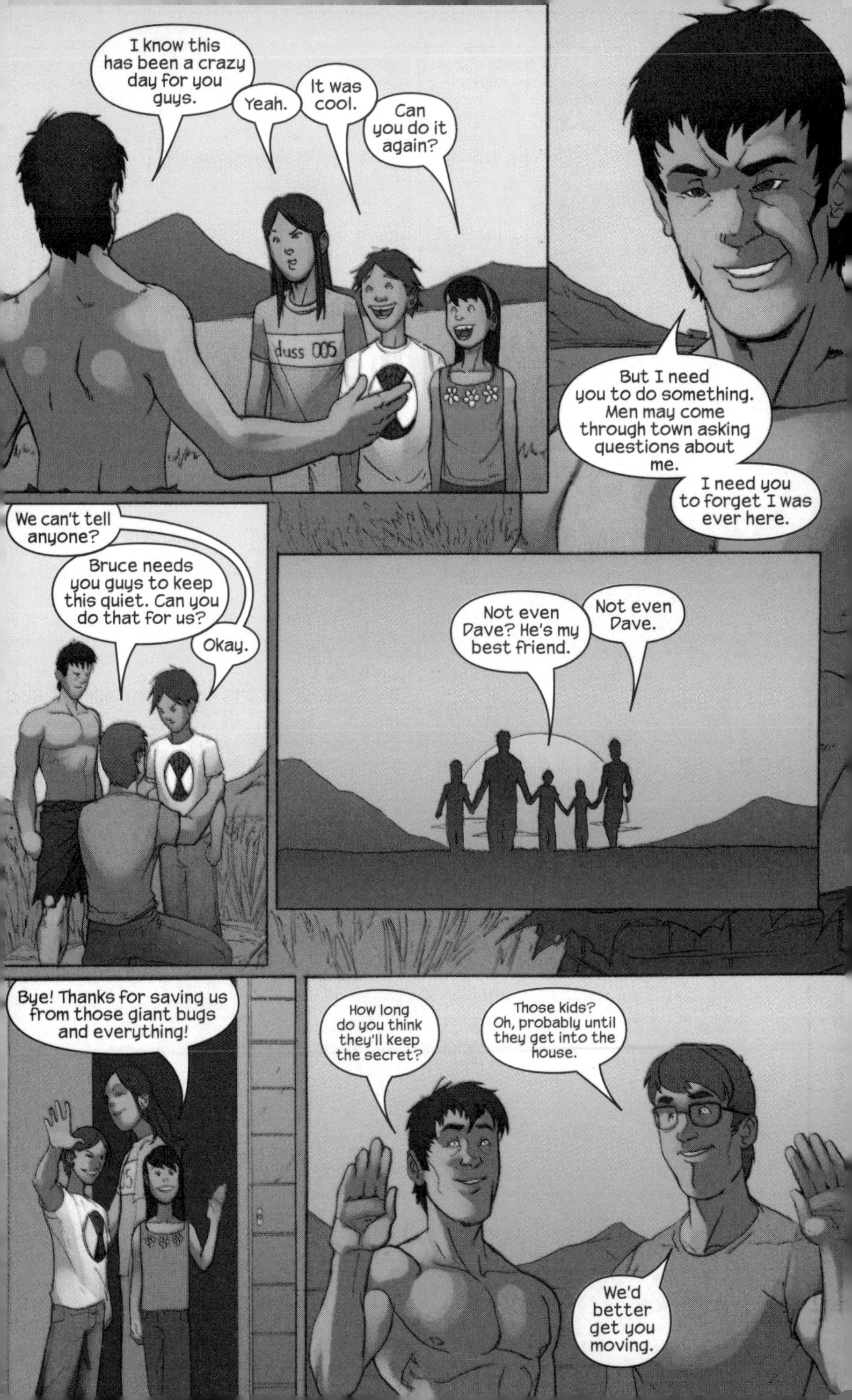

I know this has been a crazy day for you guys.
Yeah.
It was cool.
Can you do it again?
duss 005
But I need you to do something. Men may come through town asking questions about me.
I need you to forget I was ever here.
We can't tell anyone?
Bruce needs you guys to keep this quiet. Can you do that for us?
Okay.
Not even Dave? He's my best friend.
Not even Dave.
Bye! Thanks for saving us from those giant bugs and everything!
How long do you think they'll keep the secret?
Those kids? Oh, probably until they get into the house.
We'd better get you moving.

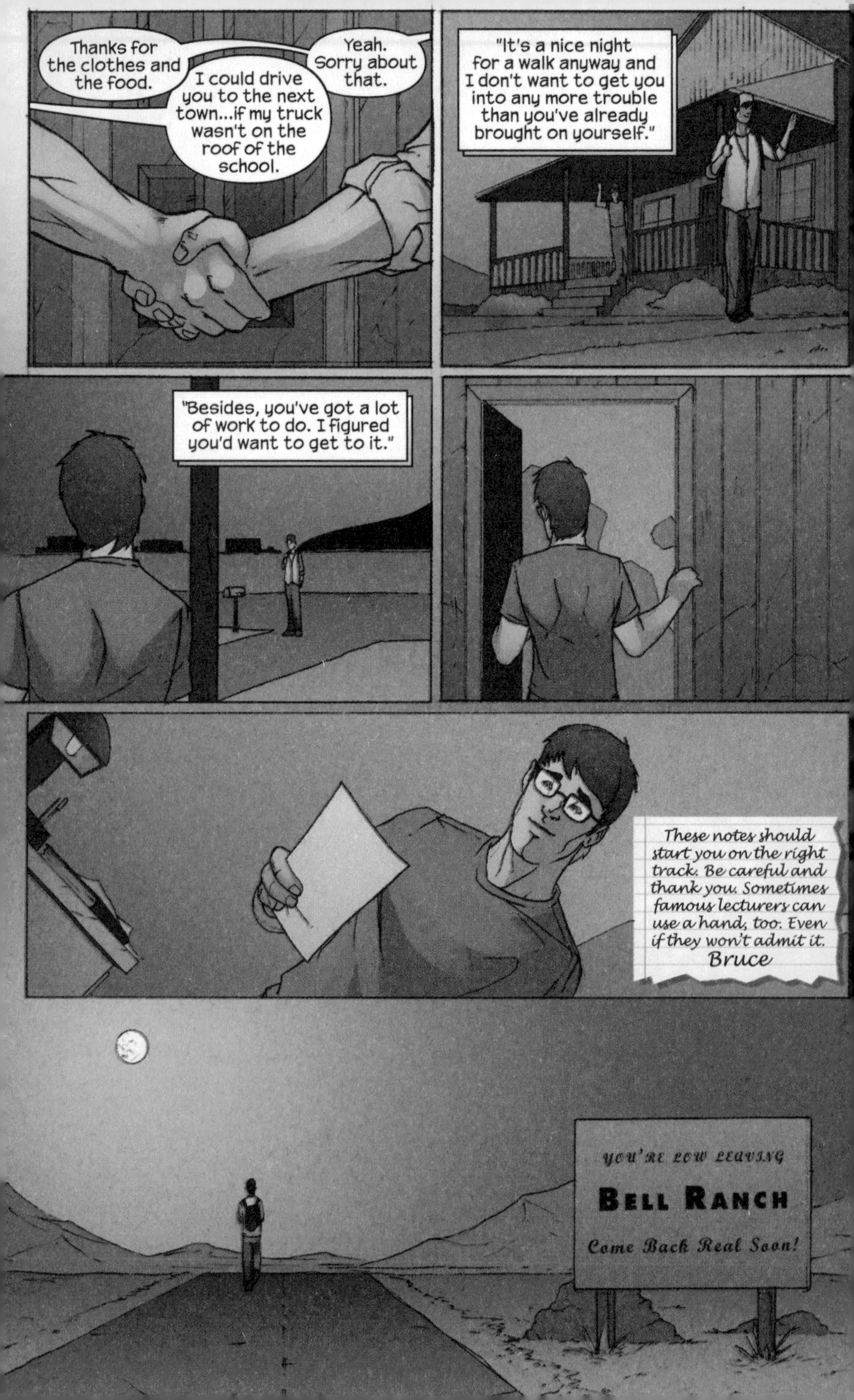
Thanks for the clothes and the food.
Yeah. Sorry about that.
I could drive you to the next town...if my truck wasn't on the roof of the school.
"It's a nice night for a walk anyway and I don't want to get you into any more trouble than you've already brought on yourself."
"Besides, you've got a lot of work to do. I figured you'd want to get to it."
These notes should start you on the right track. Be careful and thank you. Sometimes famous lecturers can use a hand, too. Even if they won't admit it.
Bruce
BELL RANCH
Come Back Real Soon!

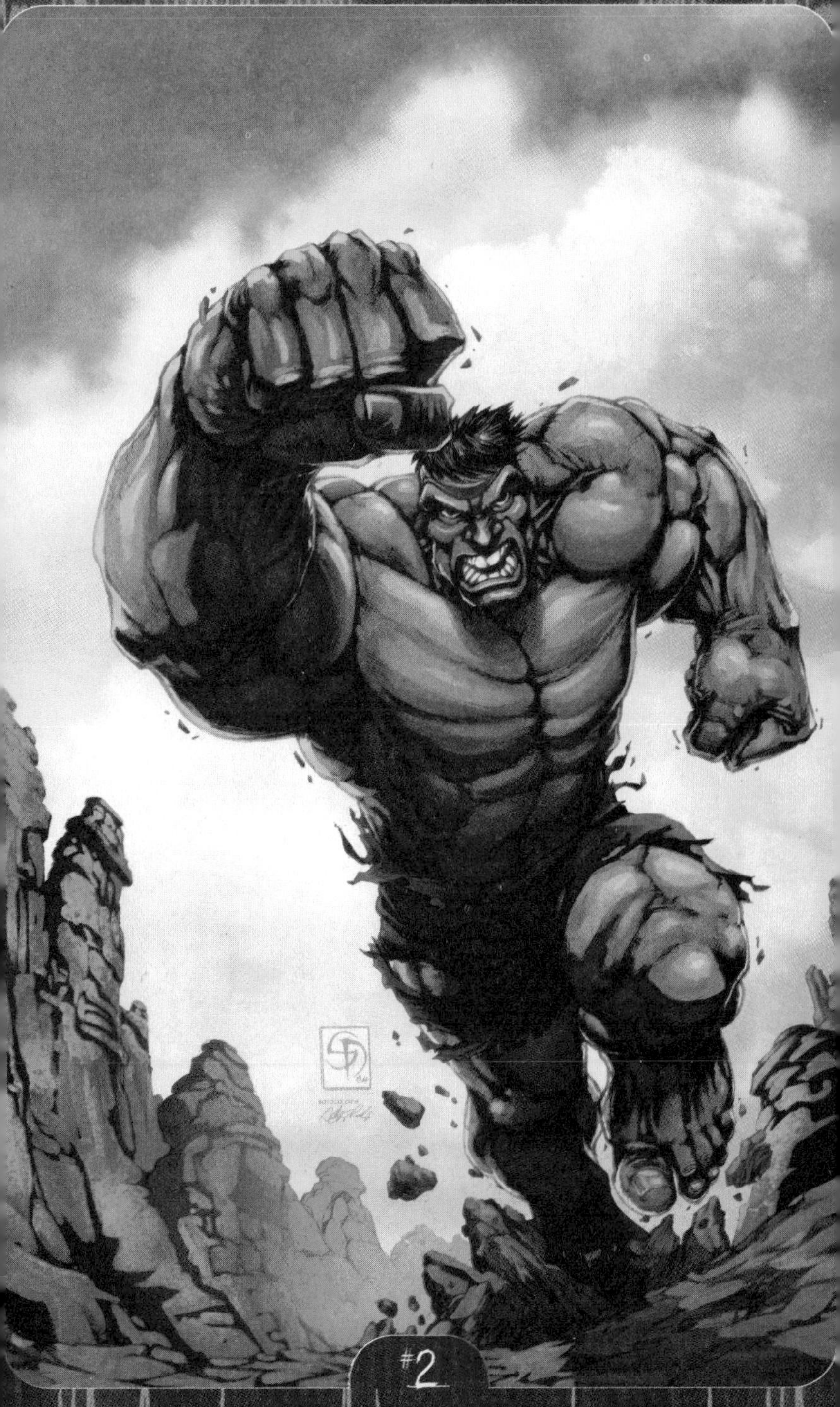

#2

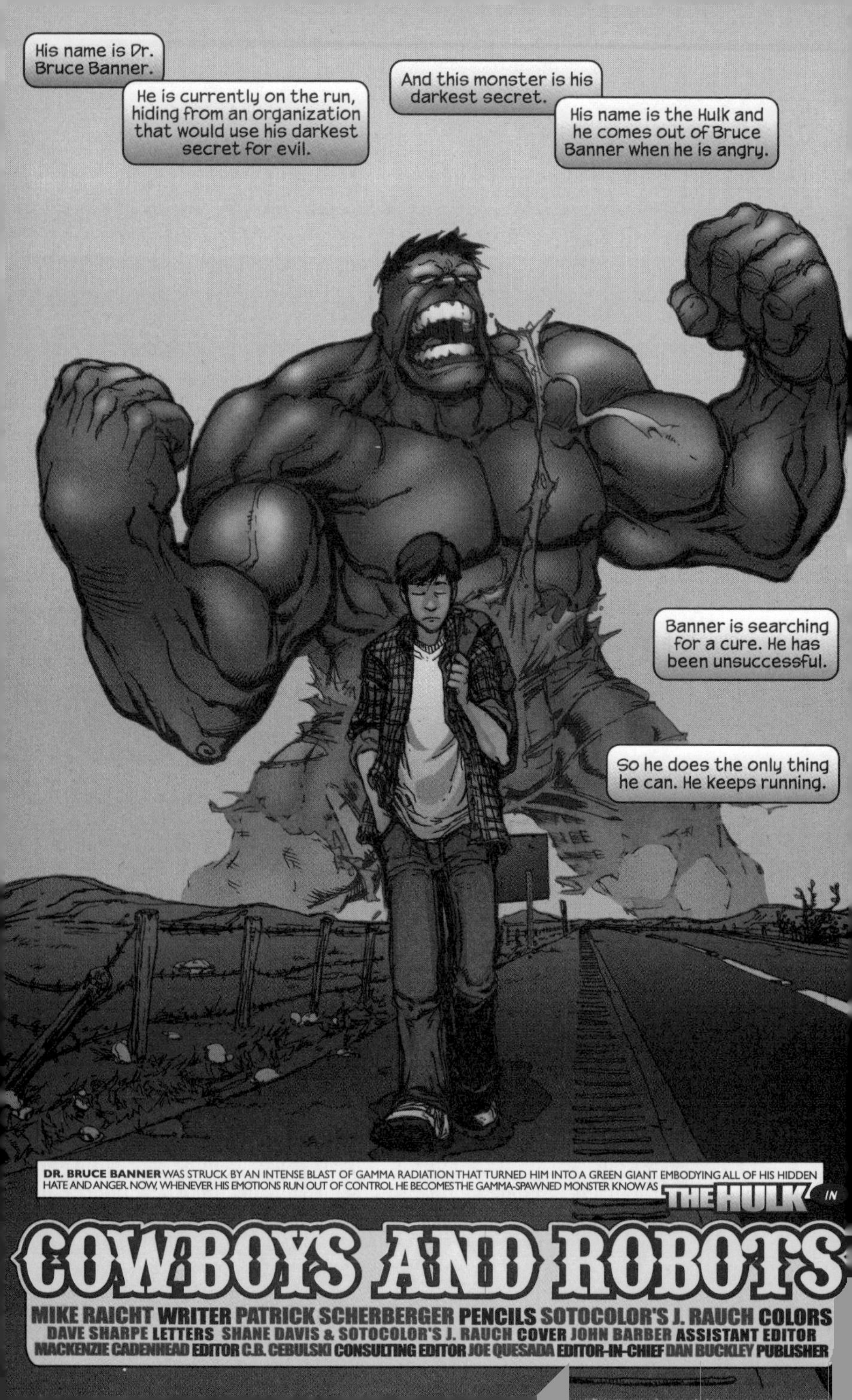
His name is Dr. Bruce Banner.
He is currently on the run, hiding from an organization that would use his darkest secret for evil.
And this monster is his darkest secret.
His name is the Hulk and he comes out of Bruce Banner when he is angry.
Banner is searching for a cure. He has been unsuccessful.
So he does the only thing he can. He keeps running.
DR. BRUCE BANNER WAS STRUCK BY AN INTENSE BLAST OF GAMMA RADIATION THAT TURNED HIM INTO A GREEN GIANT EMBODYING ALL OF HIS HIDDEN HATE AND ANGER. NOW, WHENEVER HIS EMOTIONS RUN OUT OF CONTROL HE BECOMES THE GAMMA-SPAWNED MONSTER KNOW AS THE HULK IN
COWBOYS AND ROBOTS
MIKE RAICHT WRITER PATRICK SCHERBERGER PENCILS SOTOCOLOR'S J. RAUCH COLORS
DAVE SHARPE LETTERS SHANE DAVIS & SOTOCOLOR'S J. RAUCH COVER JOHN BARBER ASSISTANT EDITOR
MACKENZIE CADENHEAD EDITOR C.B. CEBULSKI CONSULTING EDITOR JOE QUESADA EDITOR-IN-CHIEF DAN BUCKLEY PUBLISHER

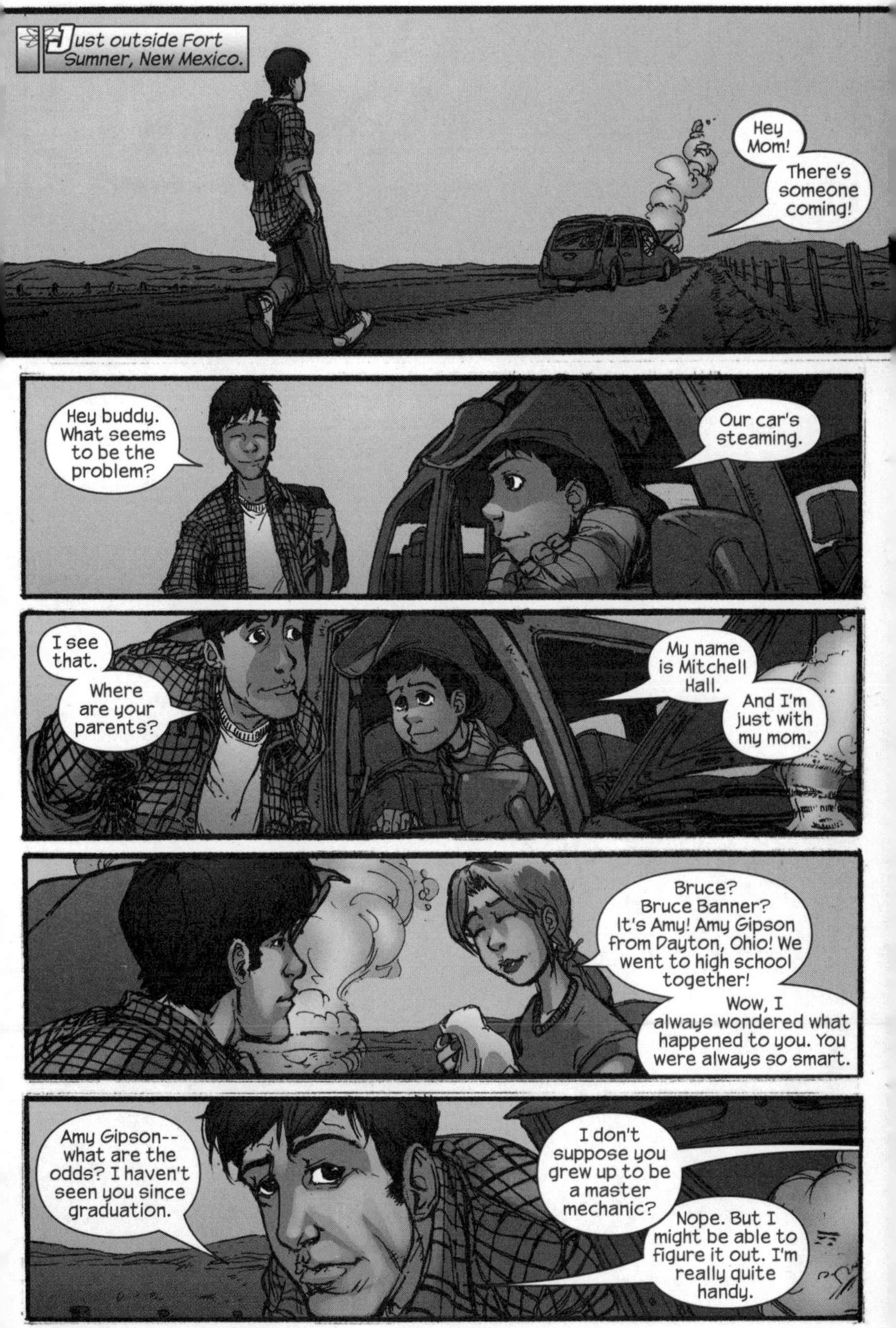
Just outside Fort Sumner, New Mexico.
Hey Mom!
There's someone coming!
Hey buddy. What seems to be the problem?
Our car's steaming.
I see that.
Where are your parents?
My name is Mitchell Hall.
And I'm just with my mom.
Bruce? Bruce Banner? It's Amy! Amy Gipson from Dayton, Ohio! We went to high school together!
Wow, I always wondered what happened to you. You were always so smart.
Amy Gipson--what are the odds? I haven't seen you since graduation.
I don't suppose you grew up to be a master mechanic?
Nope. But I might be able to figure it out. I'm really quite handy.

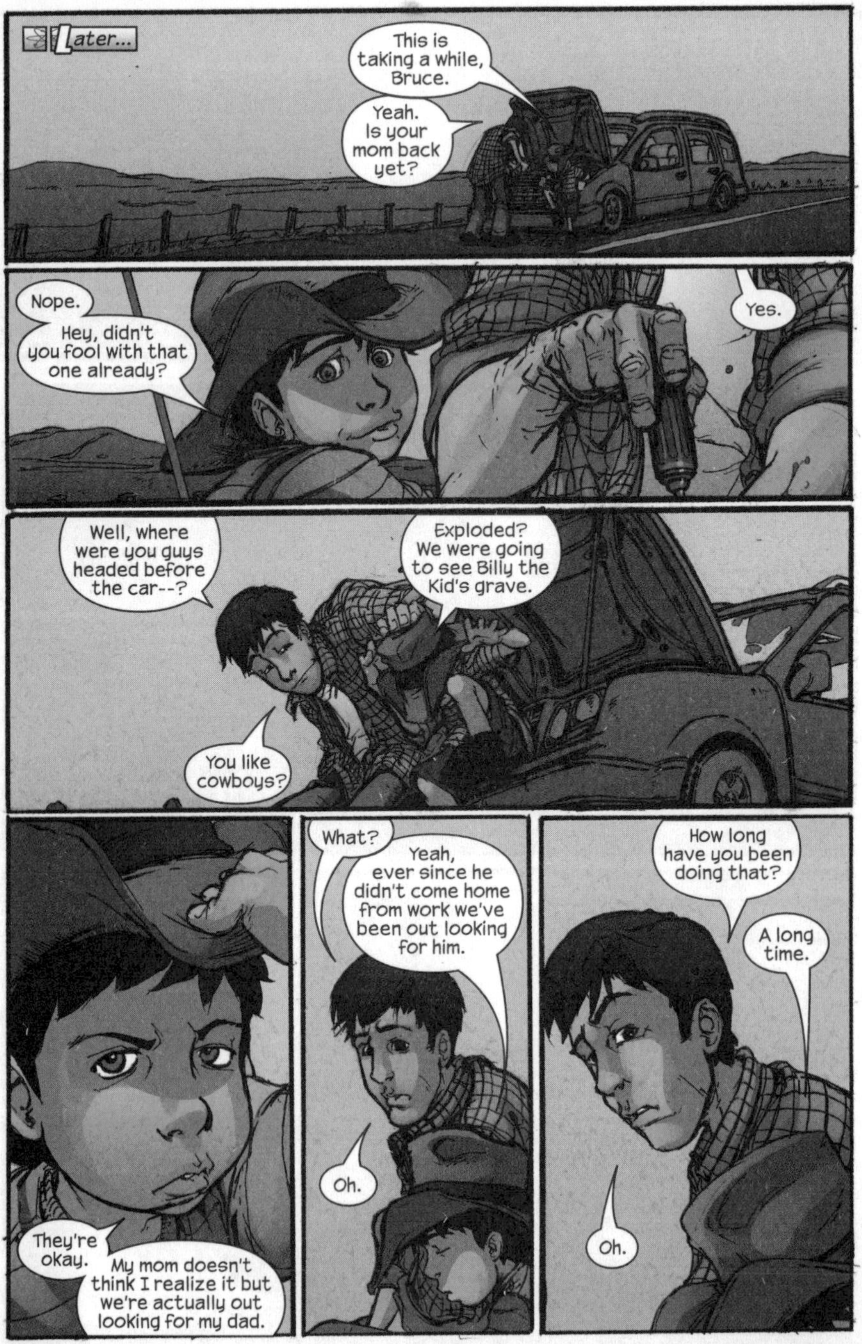
Later...
This is taking a while, Bruce.
Yeah. Is your mom back yet?
Nope.
Hey, didn't you fool with that one already?
Yes.
Well, where were you guys headed before the car--?
Exploded? We were going to see Billy the Kid's grave.
You like cowboys?
They're okay.
My mom doesn't think I realize it but we're actually out looking for my dad.
What?
Yeah, ever since he didn't come home from work we've been out looking for him.
Oh.
How long have you been doing that?
A long time.
Oh.

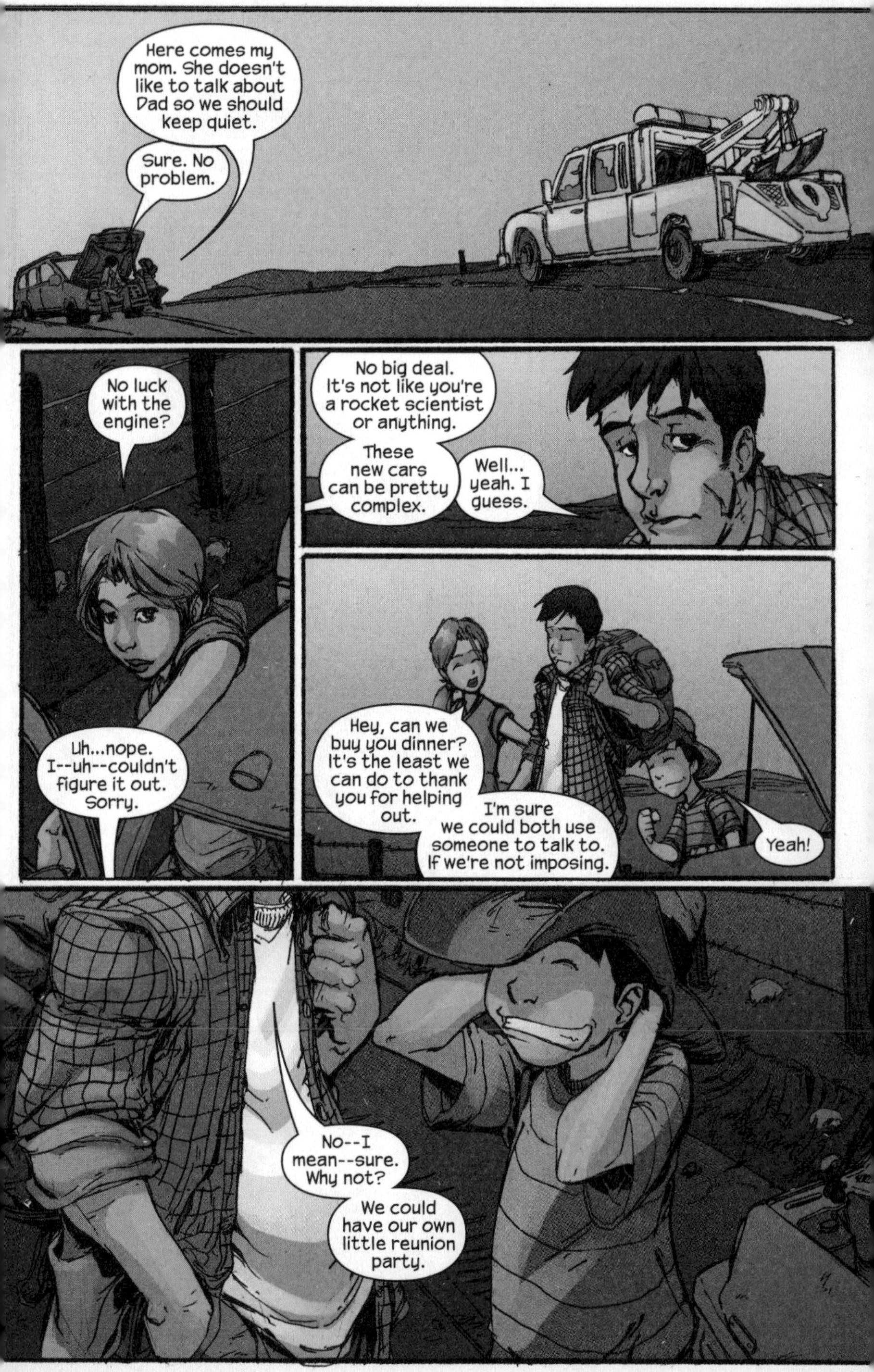
Here comes my mom. She doesn't like to talk about Dad so we should keep quiet.
Sure. No problem.
No luck with the engine?
Uh...nope. I--uh--couldn't figure it out. Sorry.
No big deal. It's not like you're a rocket scientist or anything.
These new cars can be pretty complex.
Well... yeah. I guess.
Hey, can we buy you dinner? It's the least we can do to thank you for helping out.
I'm sure we could both use someone to talk to. If we're not imposing.
Yeah!
No--I mean--sure. Why not?
We could have our own little reunion party.

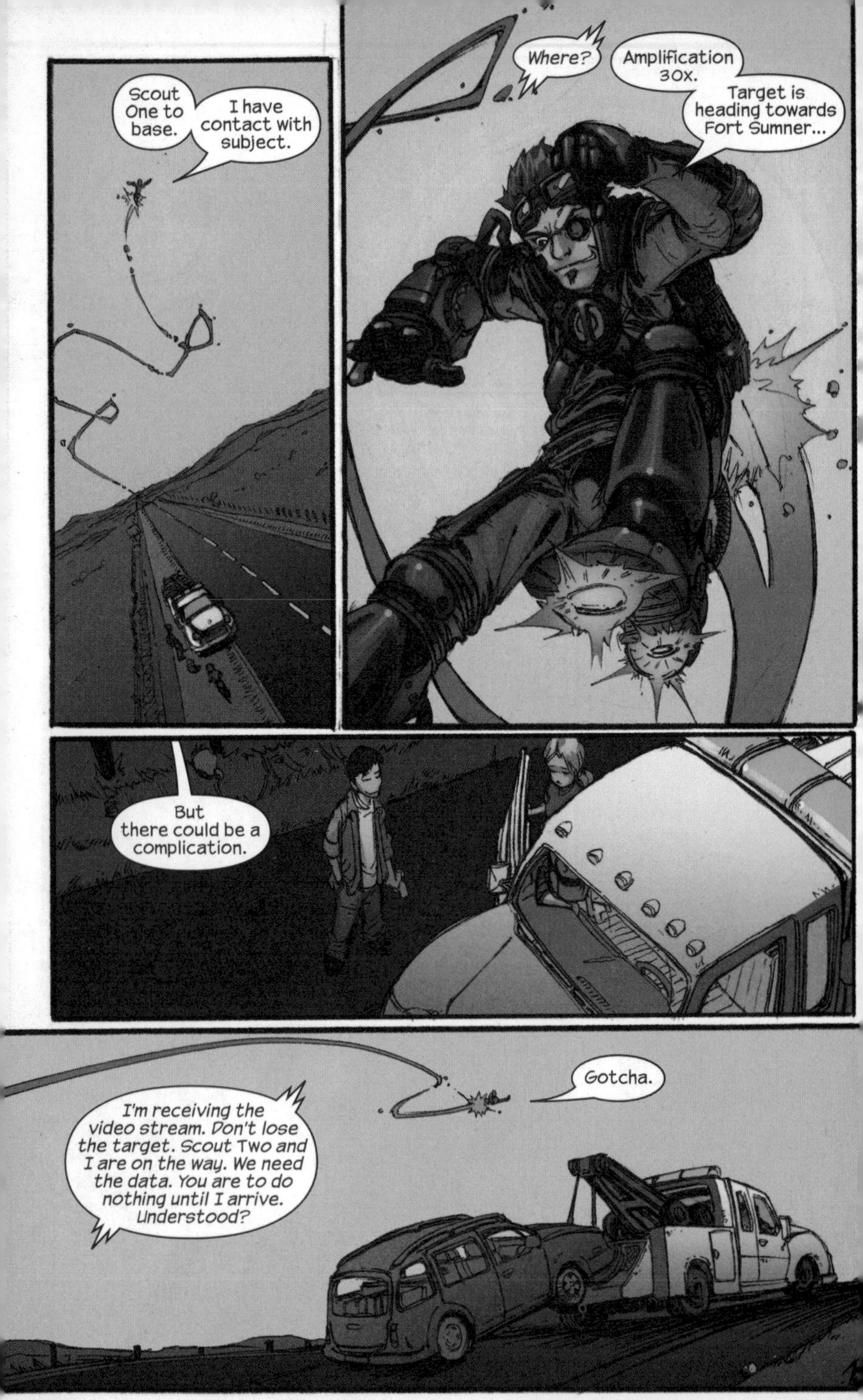
Scout One to base.
I have contact with subject.
Where?
Amplification 30X.
Target is heading towards Fort Sumner...
But there could be a complication.
Gotcha.
I'm receiving the video stream. Don't lose the target. Scout Two and I are on the way. We need the data. You are to do nothing until I arrive. Understood?

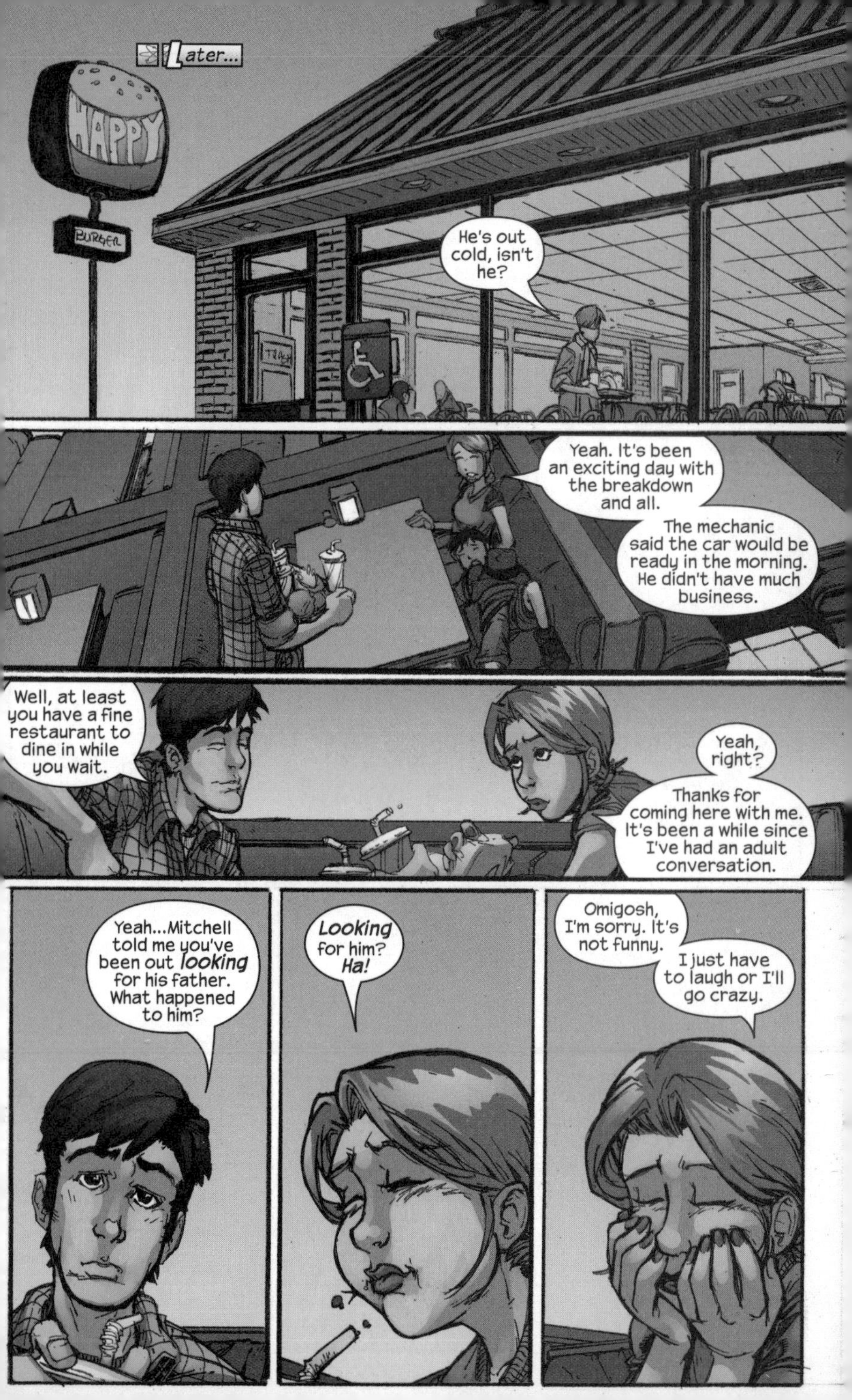
Later...
HAPPY
BURGER
He's out cold, isn't he?
Yeah. It's been an exciting day with the breakdown and all.
The mechanic said the car would be ready in the morning. He didn't have much business.
Well, at least you have a fine restaurant to dine in while you wait.
Yeah, right?
Thanks for coming here with me. It's been a while since I've had an adult conversation.
Yeah...Mitchell told me you've been out *looking* for his father. What happened to him?
Looking for him? *Ha!*
Omigosh, I'm sorry. It's not funny.
I just have to laugh or I'll go crazy.

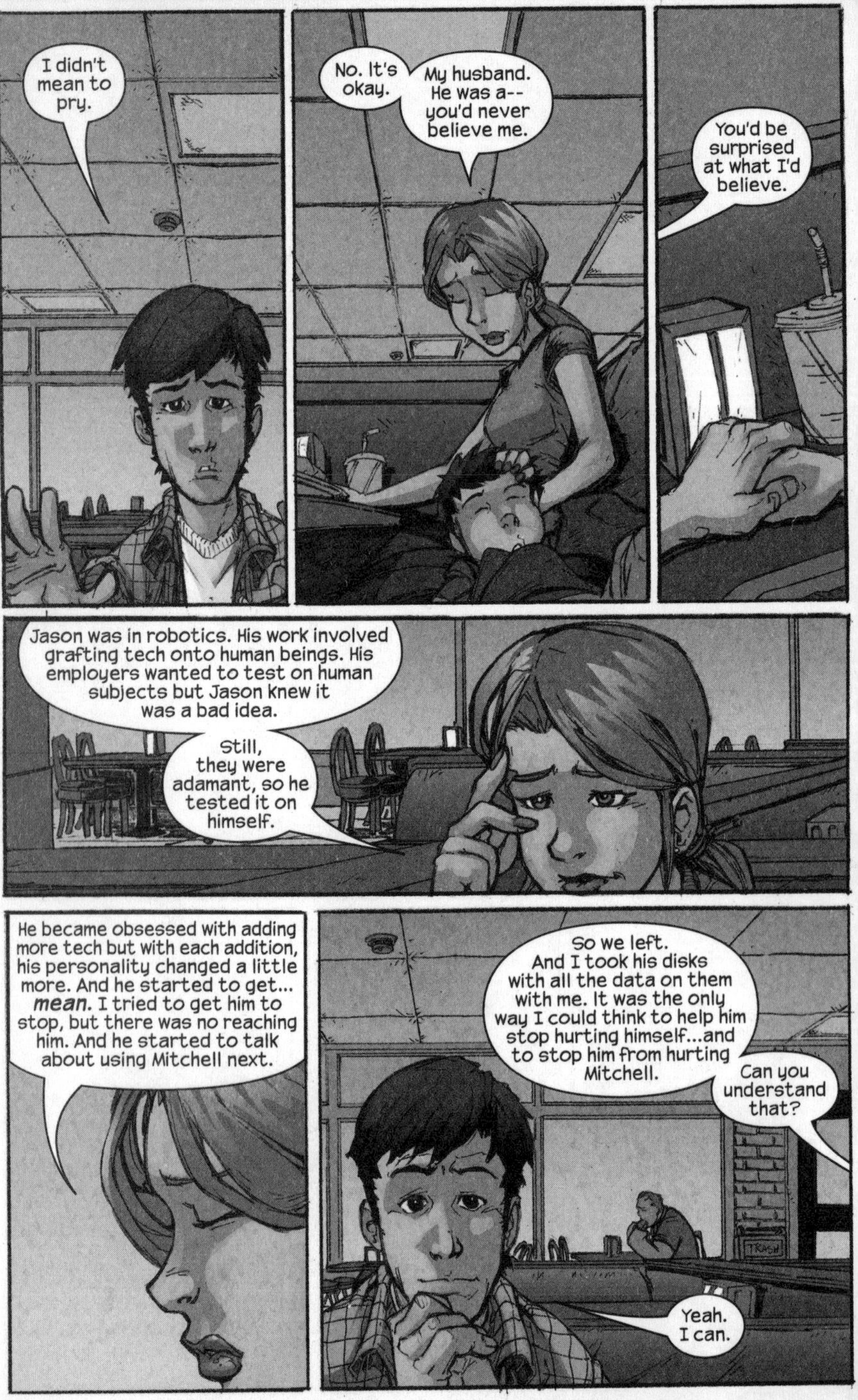
I didn't mean to pry.
No. It's okay.
My husband. He was a-- you'd never believe me.
You'd be surprised at what I'd believe.
Jason was in robotics. His work involved grafting tech onto human beings. His employers wanted to test on human subjects but Jason knew it was a bad idea.
Still, they were adamant, so he tested it on himself.
He became obsessed with adding more tech but with each addition, his personality changed a little more. And he started to get... *mean*. I tried to get him to stop, but there was no reaching him. And he started to talk about using Mitchell next.
So we left. And I took his disks with all the data on them with me. It was the only way I could think to help him stop hurting himself...and to stop him from hurting Mitchell.
Can you understand that?
Yeah. I can.
TRASH

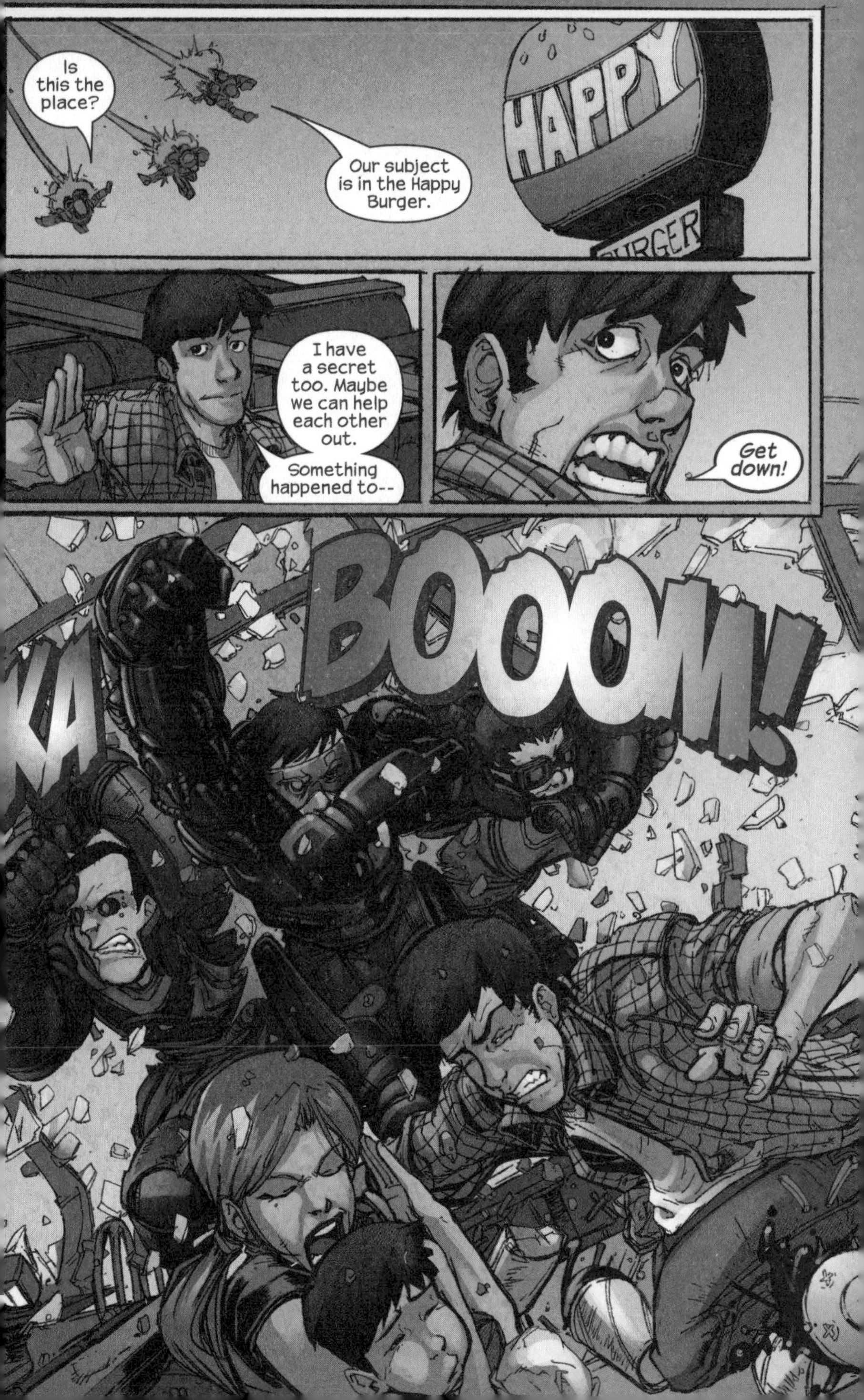
Is this the place?
Our subject is in the Happy Burger.
HAPPY
BURGER
I have a secret too. Maybe we can help each other out.
Something happened to--
Get down!
KA
BOOOM!

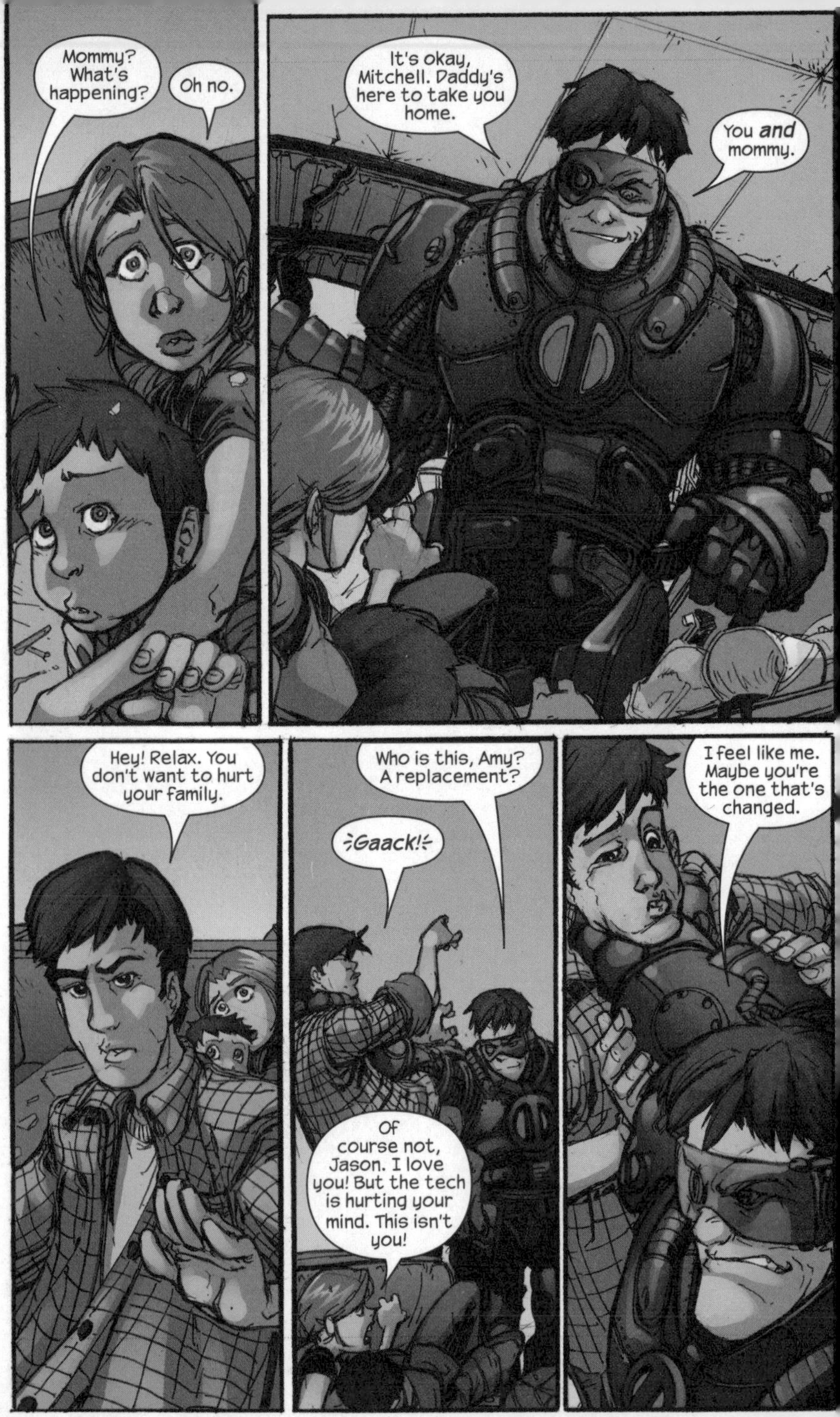
Mommy? What's happening?
Oh no.
It's okay, Mitchell. Daddy's here to take you home.
You **and** mommy.
Hey! Relax. You don't want to hurt your family.
Who is this, Amy? A replacement?
Gaack!
Of course not, Jason. I love you! But the tech is hurting your mind. This isn't you!
I feel like me. Maybe you're the one that's changed.

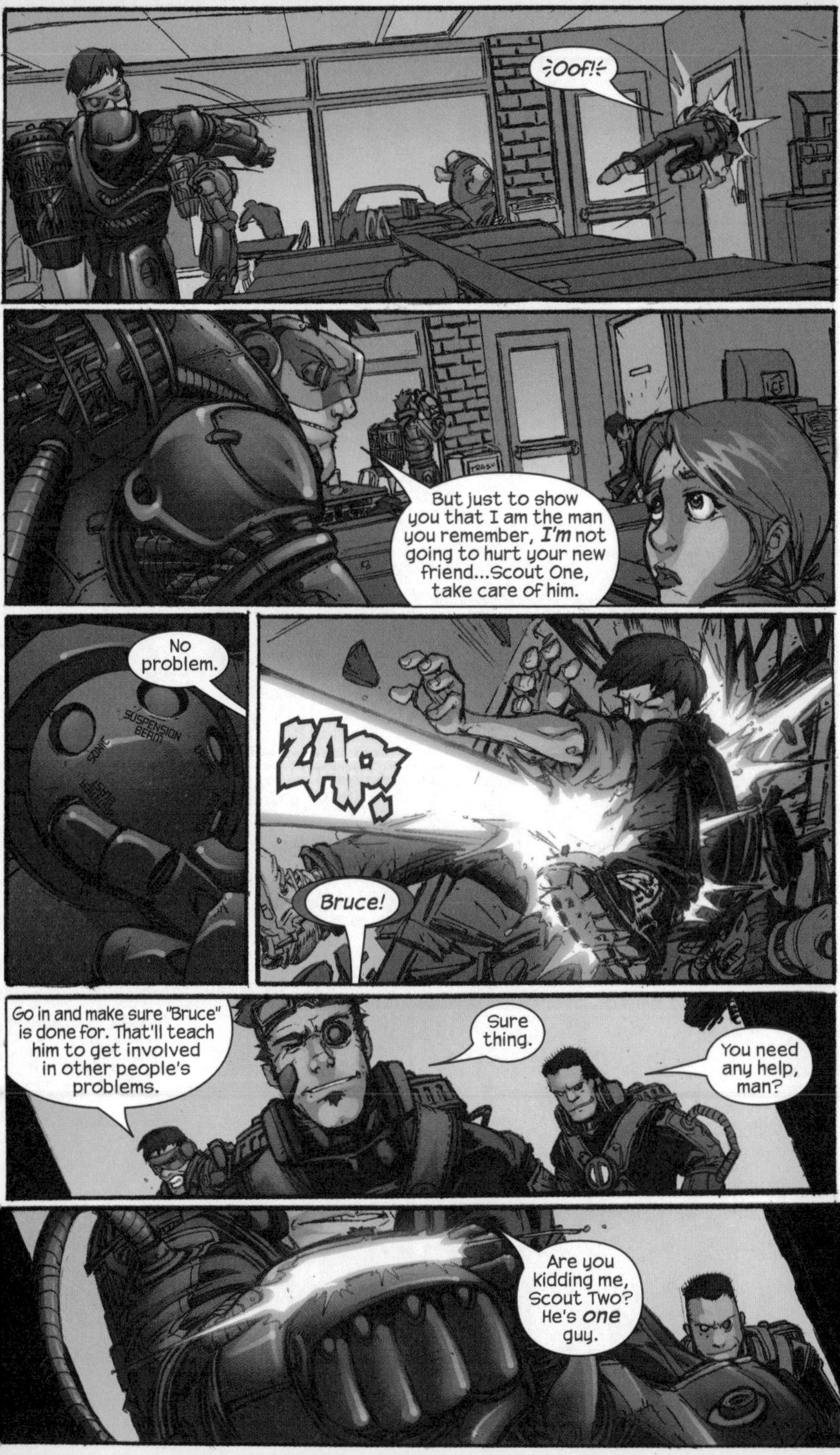
Oof!
But just to show you that I am the man you remember, *I'm* not going to hurt your new friend...Scout One, take care of him.
No problem.
SUSPENSION BEAM
SONIC
ZAP!
Bruce!
Go in and make sure "Bruce" is done for. That'll teach him to get involved in other people's problems.
Sure thing.
You need any help, man?
Are you kidding me, Scout Two? He's *one* guy.

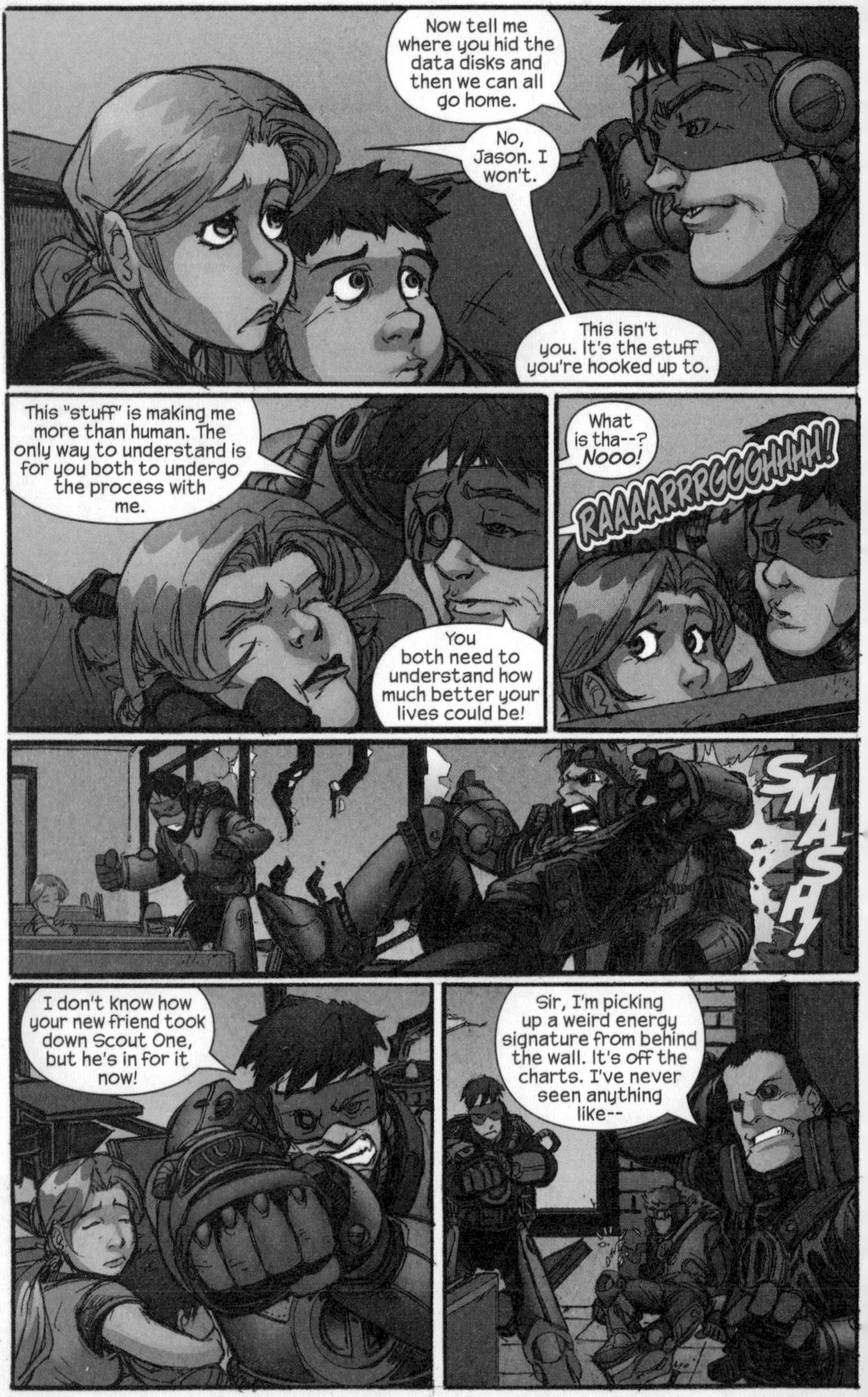

Now tell me where you hid the data disks and then we can all go home.
No, Jason. I won't.
This isn't you. It's the stuff you're hooked up to.
This "stuff" is making me more than human. The only way to understand is for you both to undergo the process with me.
You both need to understand how much better your lives could be!
What is tha--? Nooo!
RAAAARRRGGGHHHH!
SMASH!
I don't know how your new friend took down Scout One, but he's in for it now!
Sir, I'm picking up a weird energy signature from behind the wall. It's off the charts. I've never seen anything like--

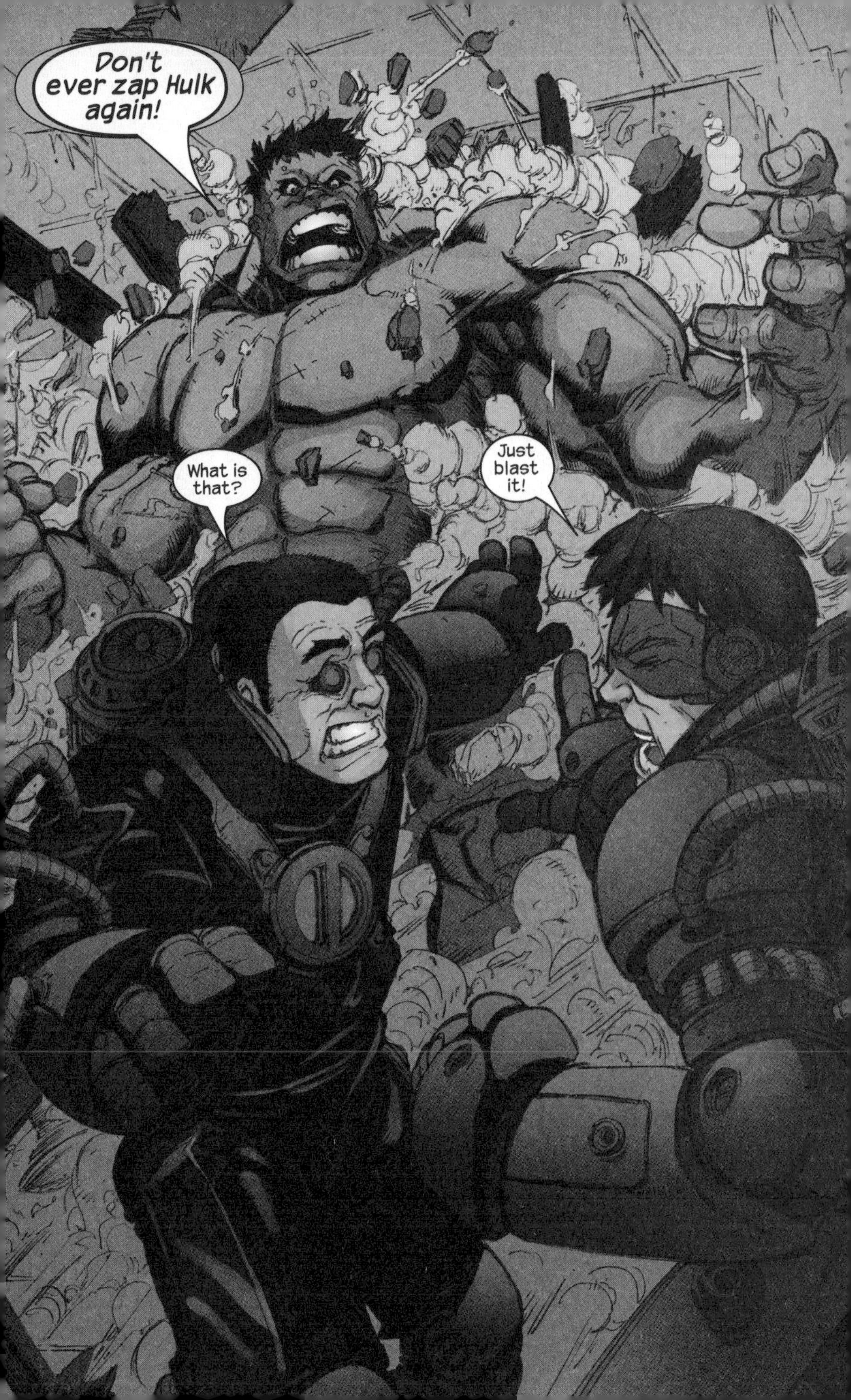
Don't ever zap Hulk again!
What is that?
Just blast it!

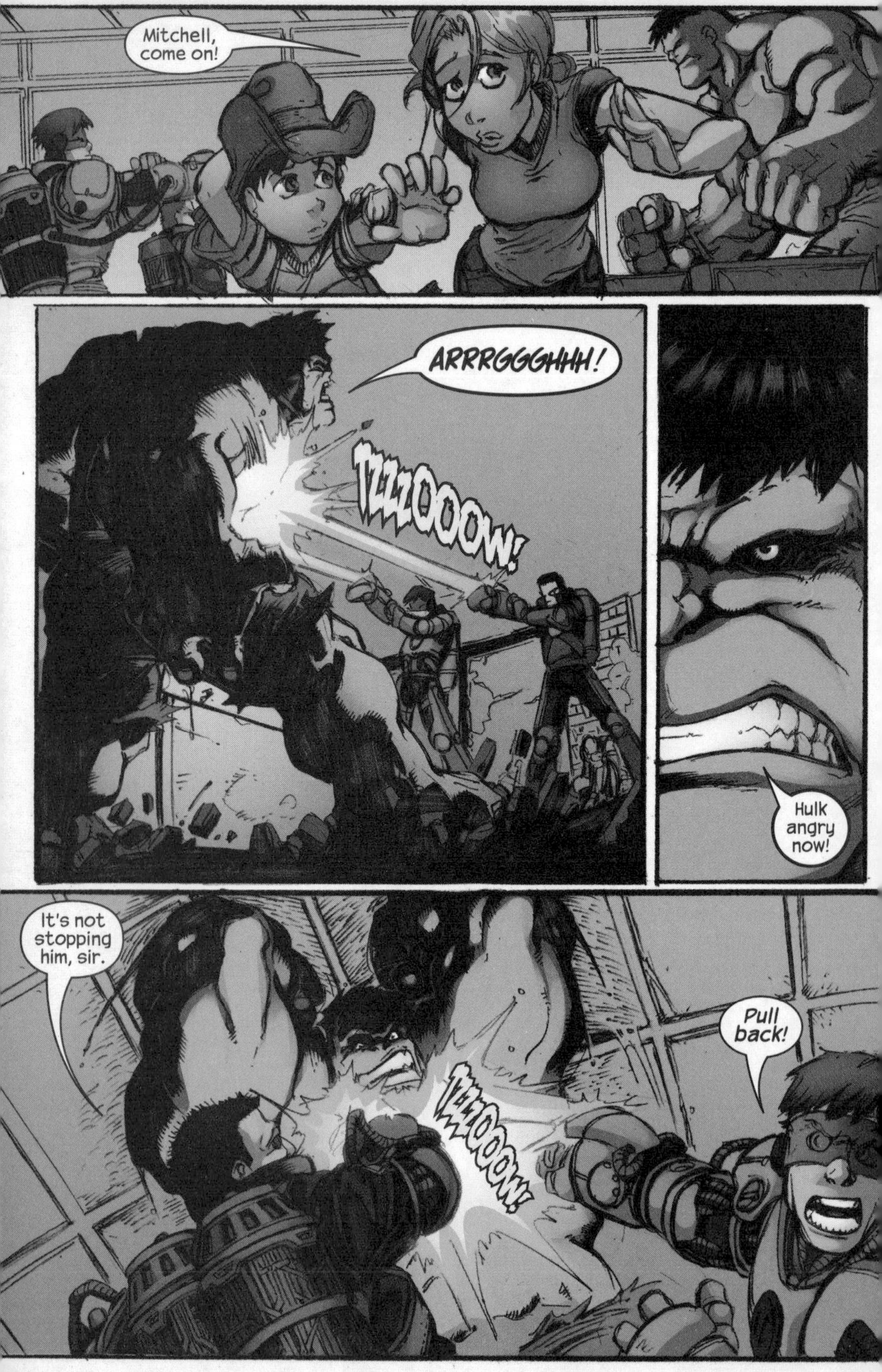
Mitchell, come on!
ARRRGGGHHH!
TZZZOOOW!
Hulk angry now!
It's not stopping him, sir.
Pull back!
TZZOOOW!

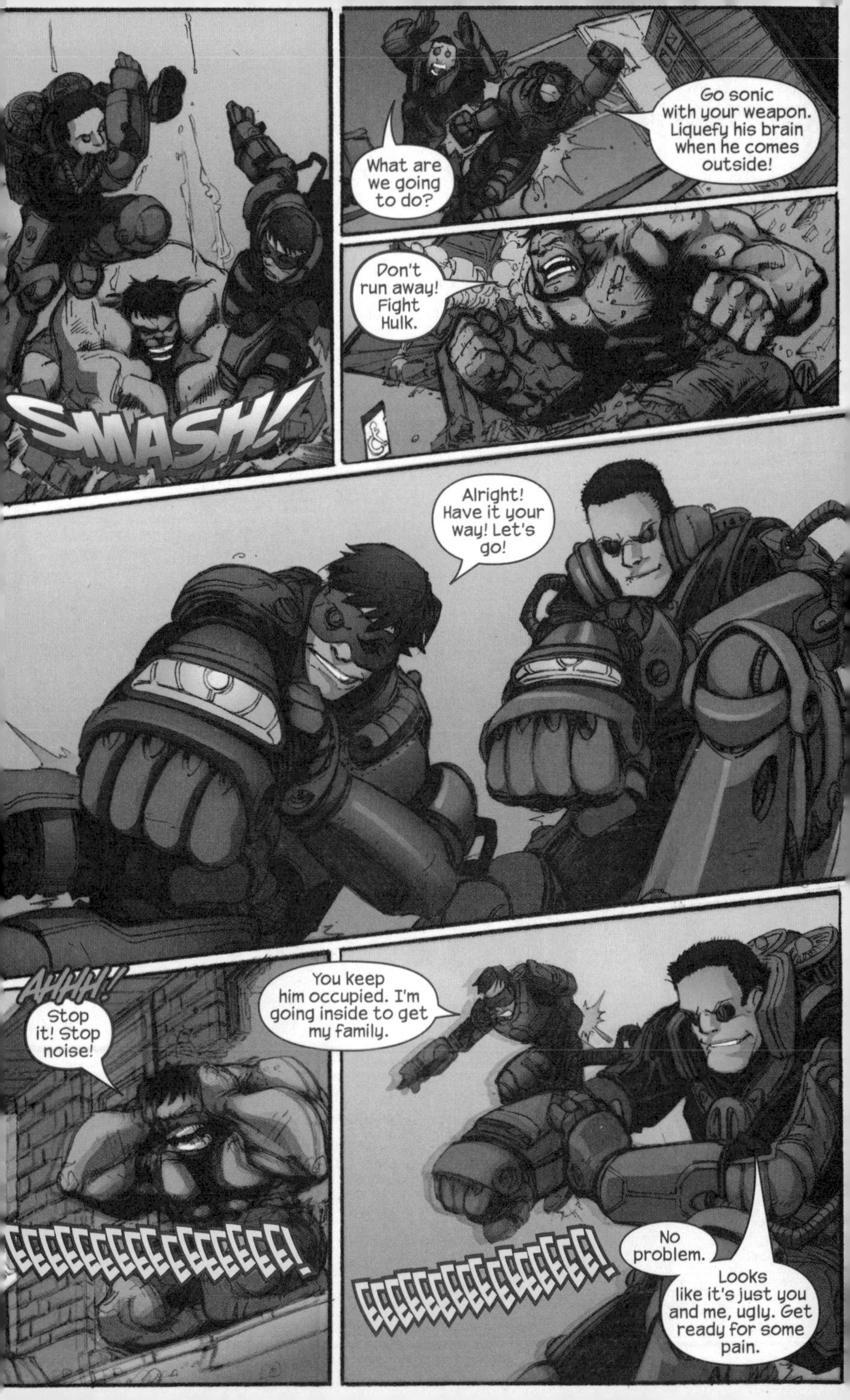
SMASH!
What are we going to do?
Go sonic with your weapon. Liquefy his brain when he comes outside!
Don't run away! Fight Hulk.
Alright! Have it your way! Let's go!
AHHH!
Stop it! Stop noise!
EEEEEEEEEEEEEEEEEE!
You keep him occupied. I'm going inside to get my family.
No problem.
Looks like it's just you and me, ugly. Get ready for some pain.
EEEEEEEEEEEEEEEEEE!

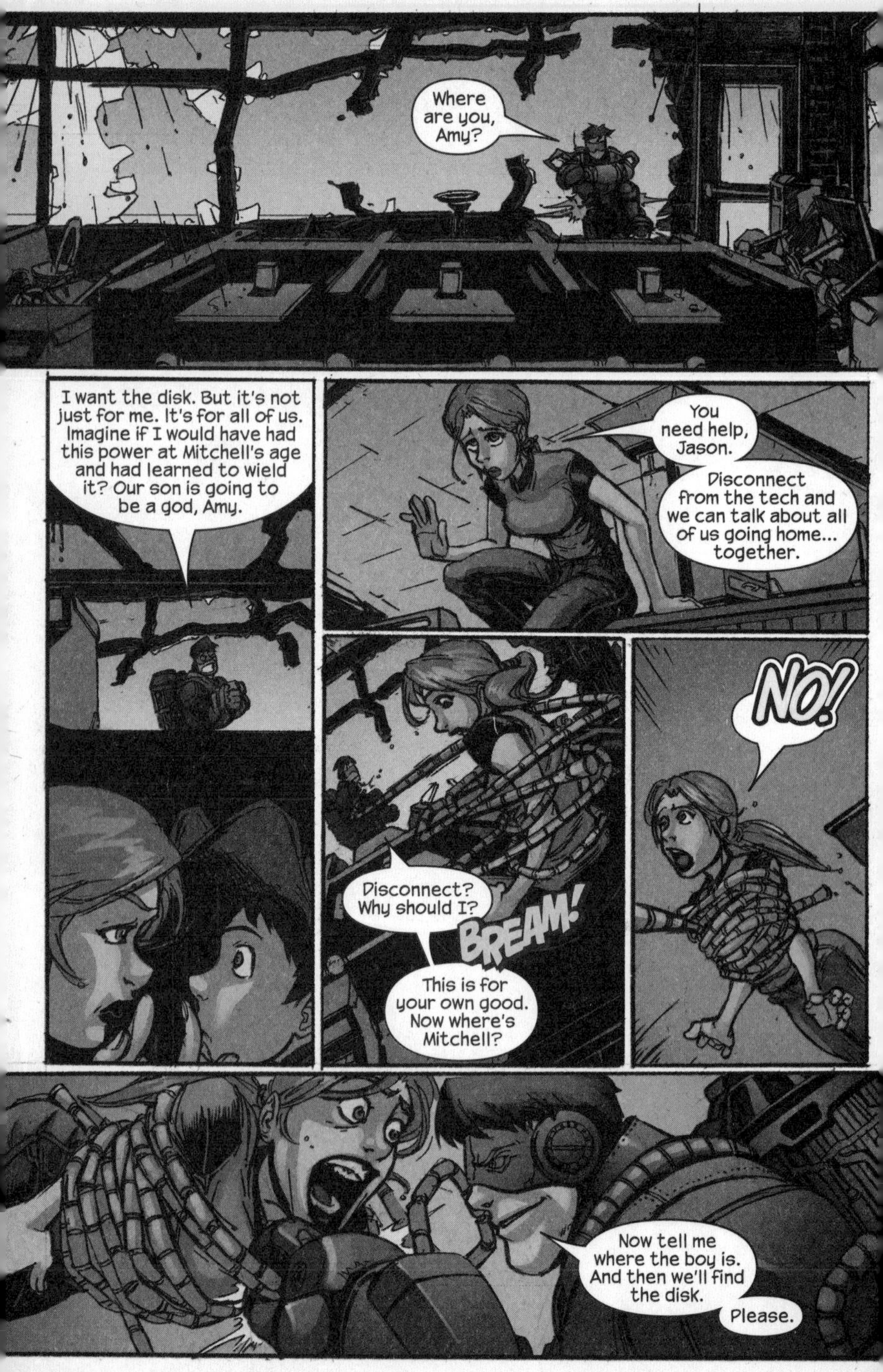

Where are you, Amy?
I want the disk. But it's not just for me. It's for all of us. Imagine if I would have had this power at Mitchell's age and had learned to wield it? Our son is going to be a god, Amy.
You need help, Jason.
Disconnect from the tech and we can talk about all of us going home... together.
Disconnect? Why should I?
BREAM!
This is for your own good. Now where's Mitchell?
NO!
Now tell me where the boy is. And then we'll find the disk.
Please.

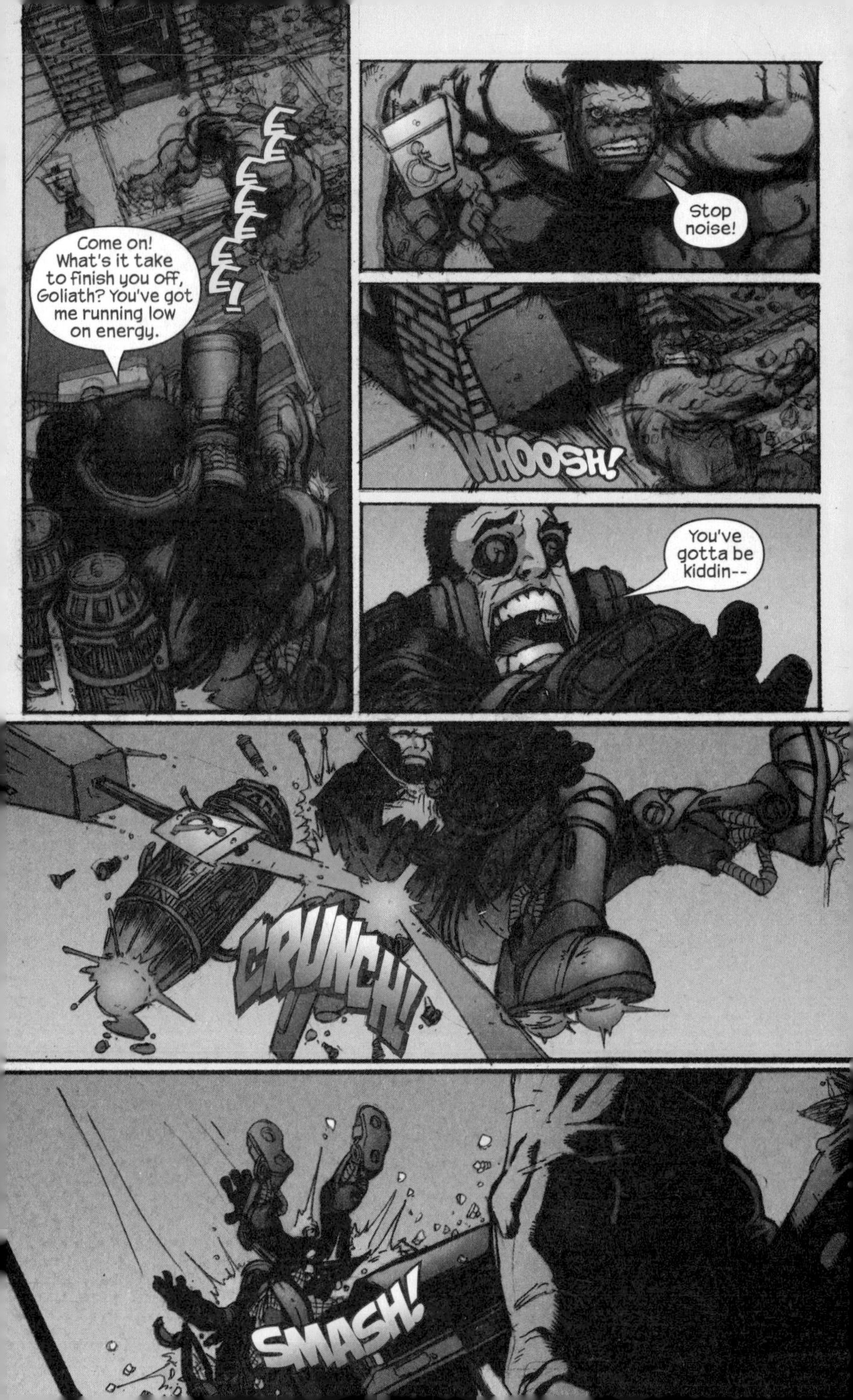
EEEEEEEEEE!
Come on! What's it take to finish you off, Goliath? You've got me running low on energy.
Stop noise!
WHOOSH!
You've gotta be kiddin--
CRUNCH!
SMASH!

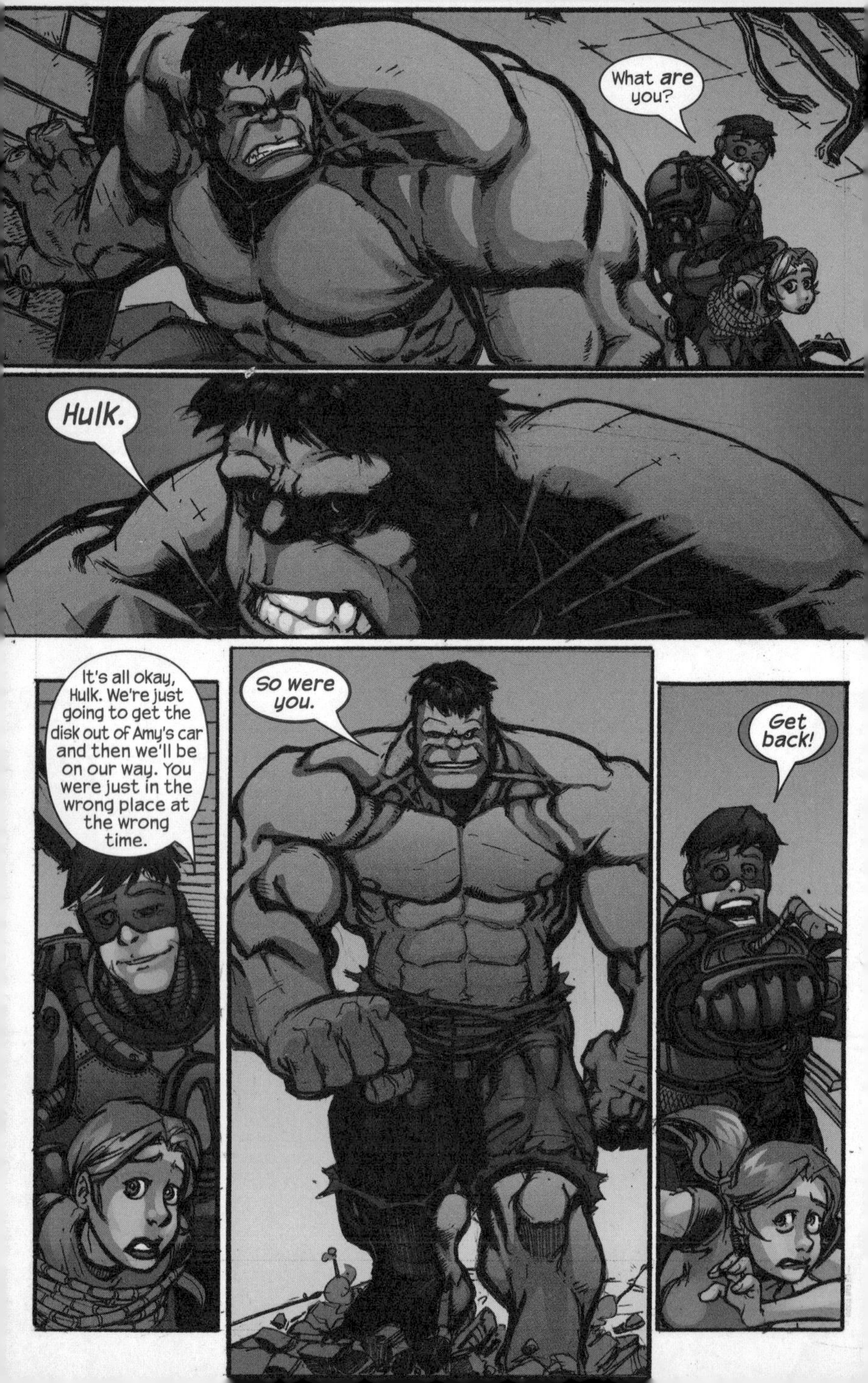
What are you?
Hulk.
It's all okay, Hulk. We're just going to get the disk out of Amy's car and then we'll be on our way. You were just in the wrong place at the wrong time.
So were you.
Get back!

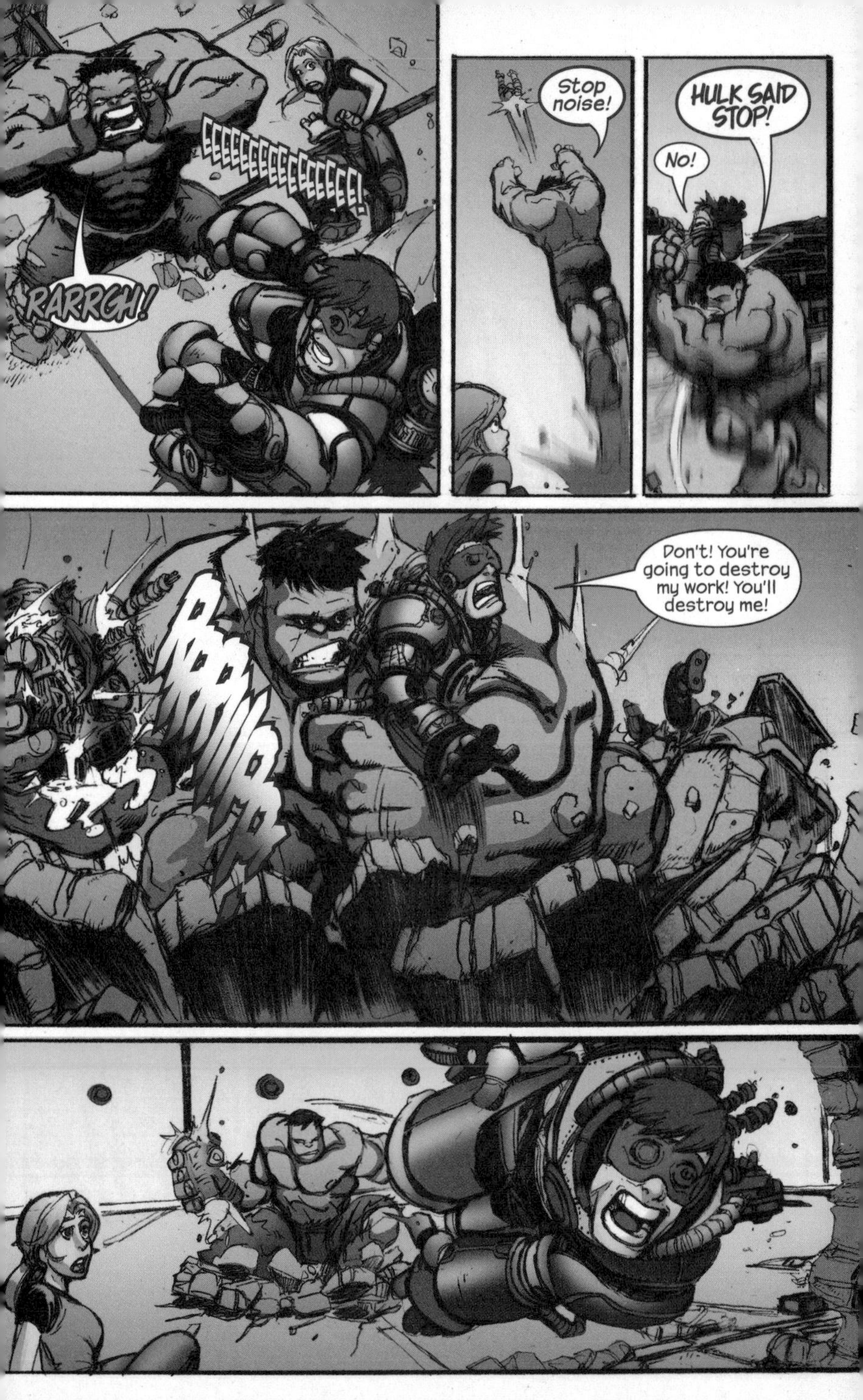
EEEEEEEEEEEEEEEEE!
RARRGH!
Stop noise!
HULK SAID STOP!
No!
Don't! You're going to destroy my work! You'll destroy me!

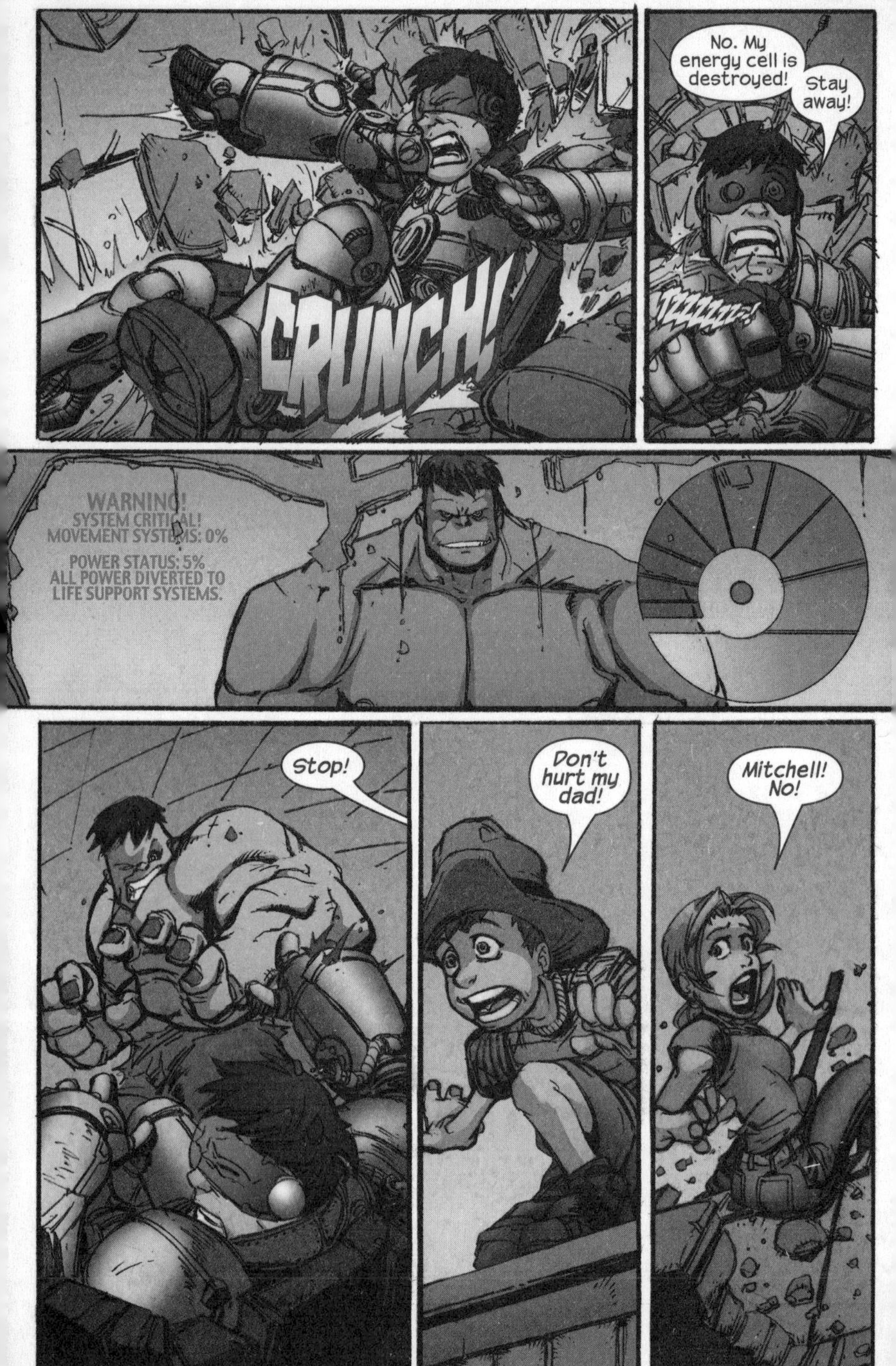
CRUNCH!
No. My energy cell is destroyed!
Stay away!
ZZZZZZZT
WARNING!
SYSTEM CRITICAL!
MOVEMENT SYSTEMS: 0%
POWER STATUS: 5%
ALL POWER DIVERTED TO LIFE SUPPORT SYSTEMS.
Stop!
Don't hurt my dad!
Mitchell! No!

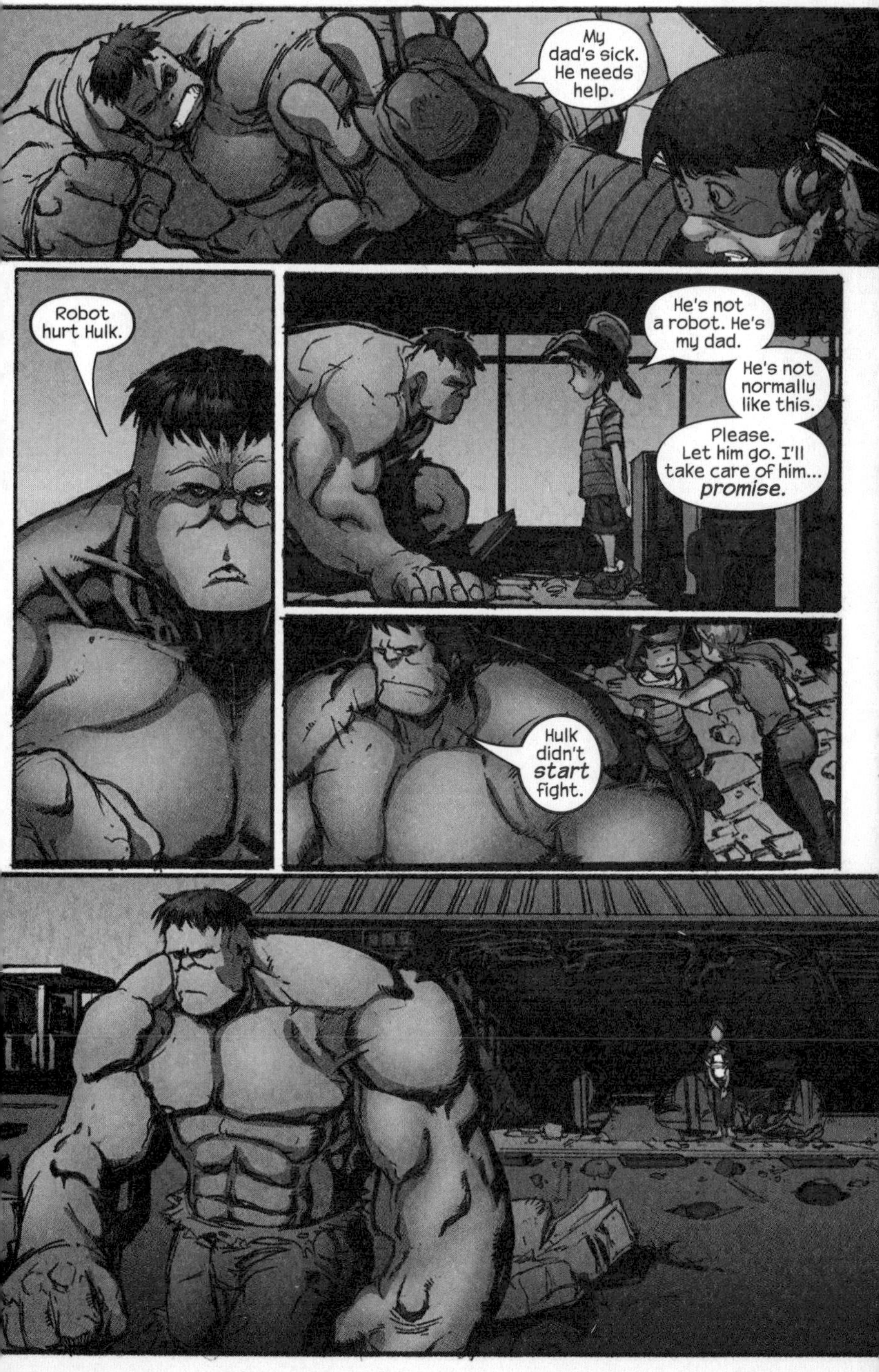

My dad's sick. He needs help.
Robot hurt Hulk.
He's not a robot. He's my dad.
He's not normally like this.
Please. Let him go. I'll take care of him... *promise.*
Hulk didn't *start* fight.

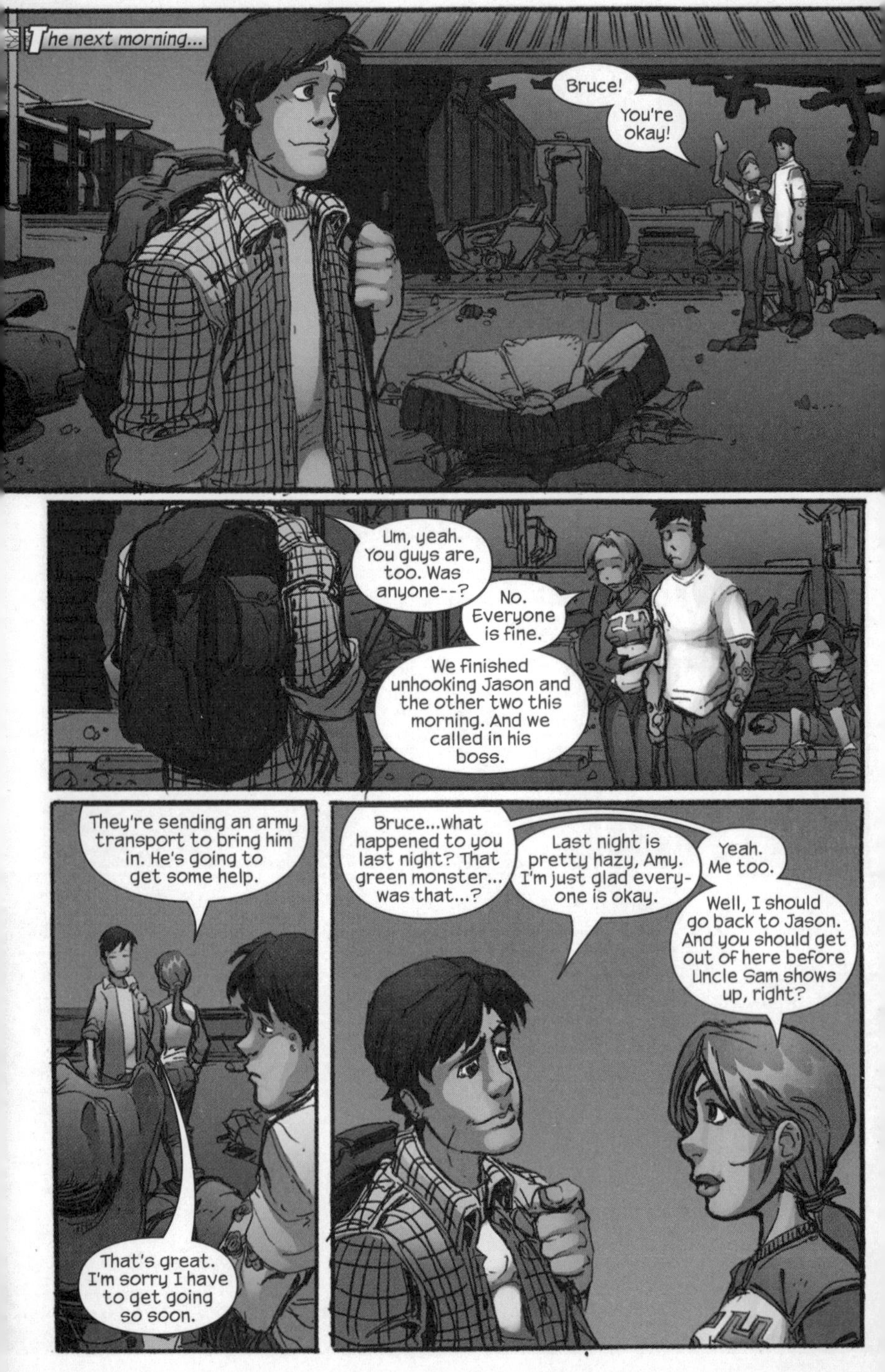
The next morning...
Bruce!
You're okay!
Um, yeah. You guys are, too. Was anyone--?
No. Everyone is fine.
We finished unhooking Jason and the other two this morning. And we called in his boss.
They're sending an army transport to bring him in. He's going to get some help.
That's great. I'm sorry I have to get going so soon.
Bruce...what happened to you last night? That green monster... was that...?
Last night is pretty hazy, Amy. I'm just glad every-one is okay.
Yeah. Me too.
Well, I should go back to Jason. And you should get out of here before Uncle Sam shows up, right?

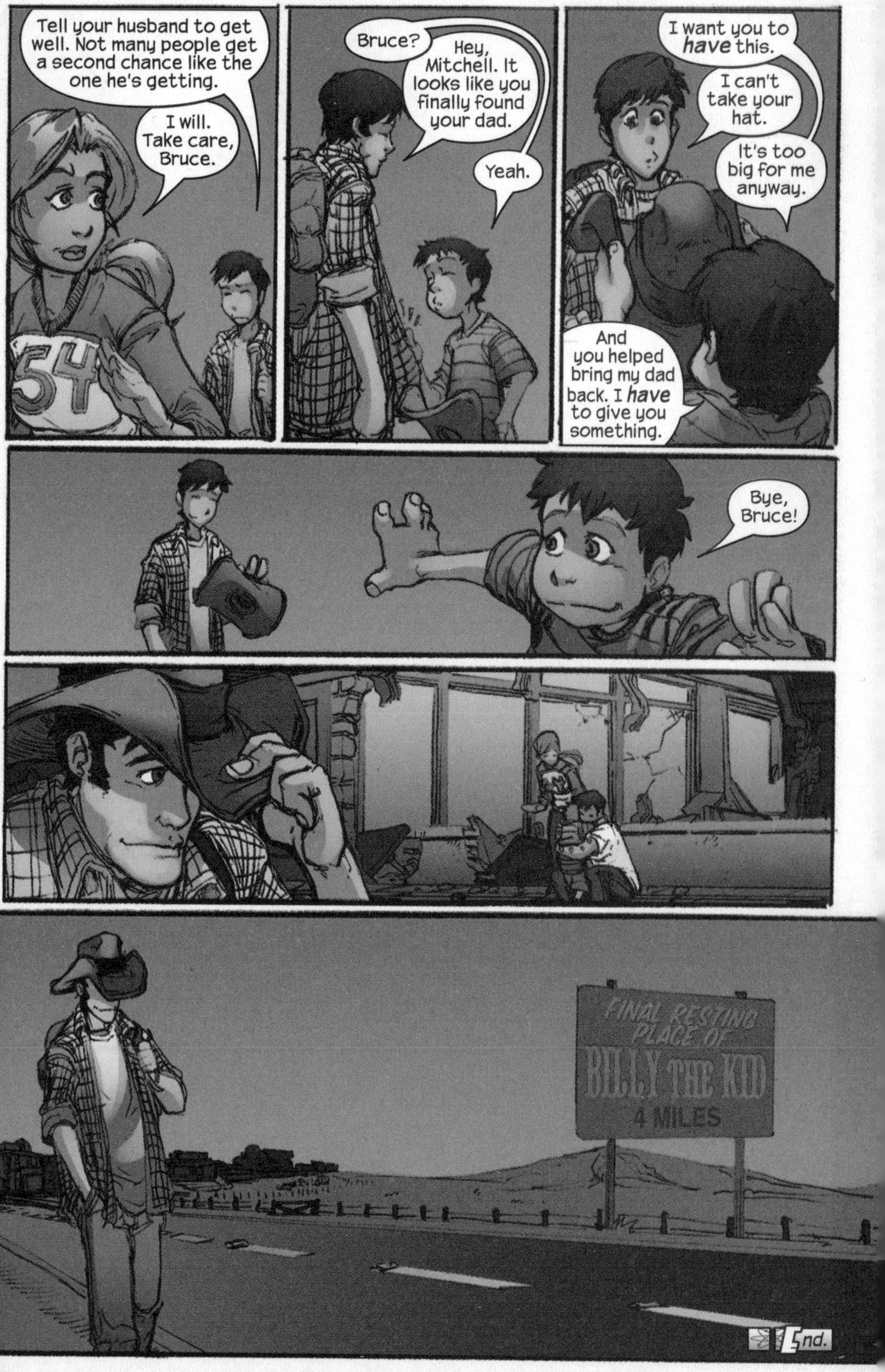
Tell your husband to get well. Not many people get a second chance like the one he's getting.
I will. Take care, Bruce.
Bruce?
Hey, Mitchell. It looks like you finally found your dad.
Yeah.
I want you to *have* this.
I can't take your hat.
It's too big for me anyway.
And you helped bring my dad back. I *have* to give you something.
Bye, Bruce!
FINAL RESTING PLACE OF
BILLY THE KID
4 MILES
End.

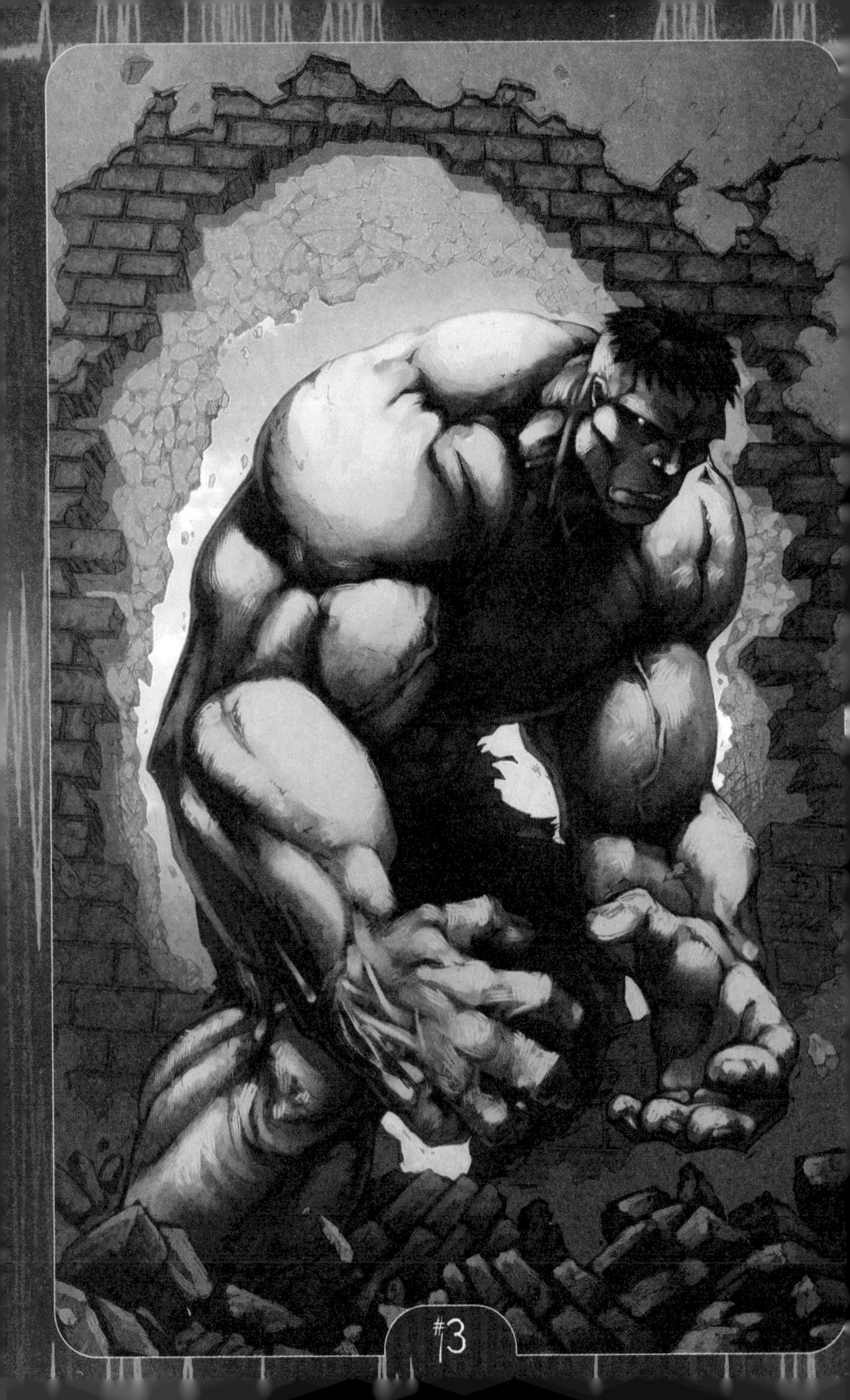
#13

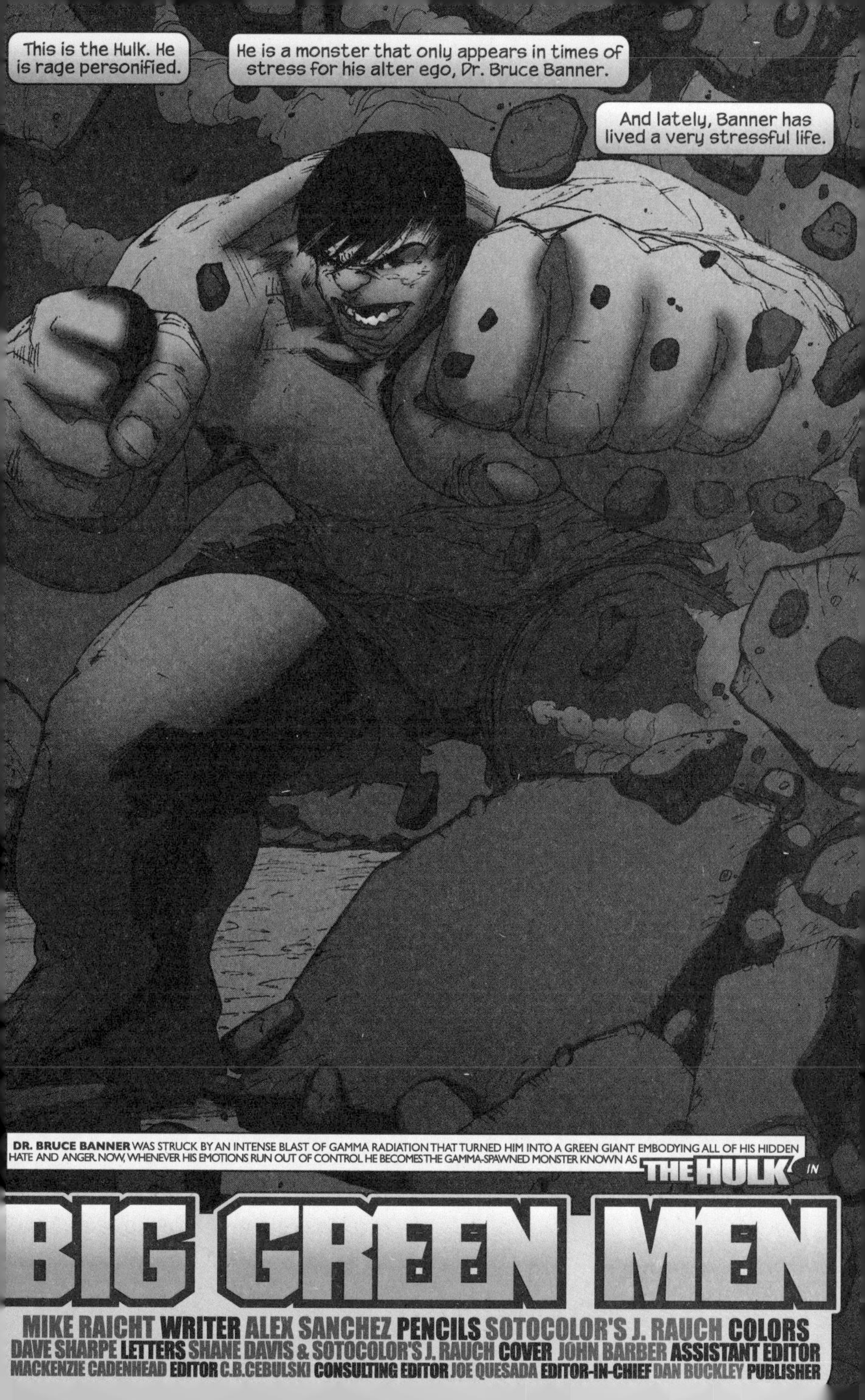
This is the Hulk. He is rage personified.
He is a monster that only appears in times of stress for his alter ego, Dr. Bruce Banner.
And lately, Banner has lived a very stressful life.
DR. BRUCE BANNER WAS STRUCK BY AN INTENSE BLAST OF GAMMA RADIATION THAT TURNED HIM INTO A GREEN GIANT EMBODYING ALL OF HIS HIDDEN HATE AND ANGER. NOW, WHENEVER HIS EMOTIONS RUN OUT OF CONTROL HE BECOMES THE GAMMA-SPAWNED MONSTER KNOWN AS THE HULK IN
BIG GREEN MEN
MIKE RAICHT WRITER ALEX SANCHEZ PENCILS SOTOCOLOR'S J. RAUCH COLORS
DAVE SHARPE LETTERS SHANE DAVIS & SOTOCOLOR'S J. RAUCH COVER JOHN BARBER ASSISTANT EDITOR
MACKENZIE CADENHEAD EDITOR C.B.CEBULSKI CONSULTING EDITOR JOE QUESADA EDITOR-IN-CHIEF DAN BUCKLEY PUBLISHER

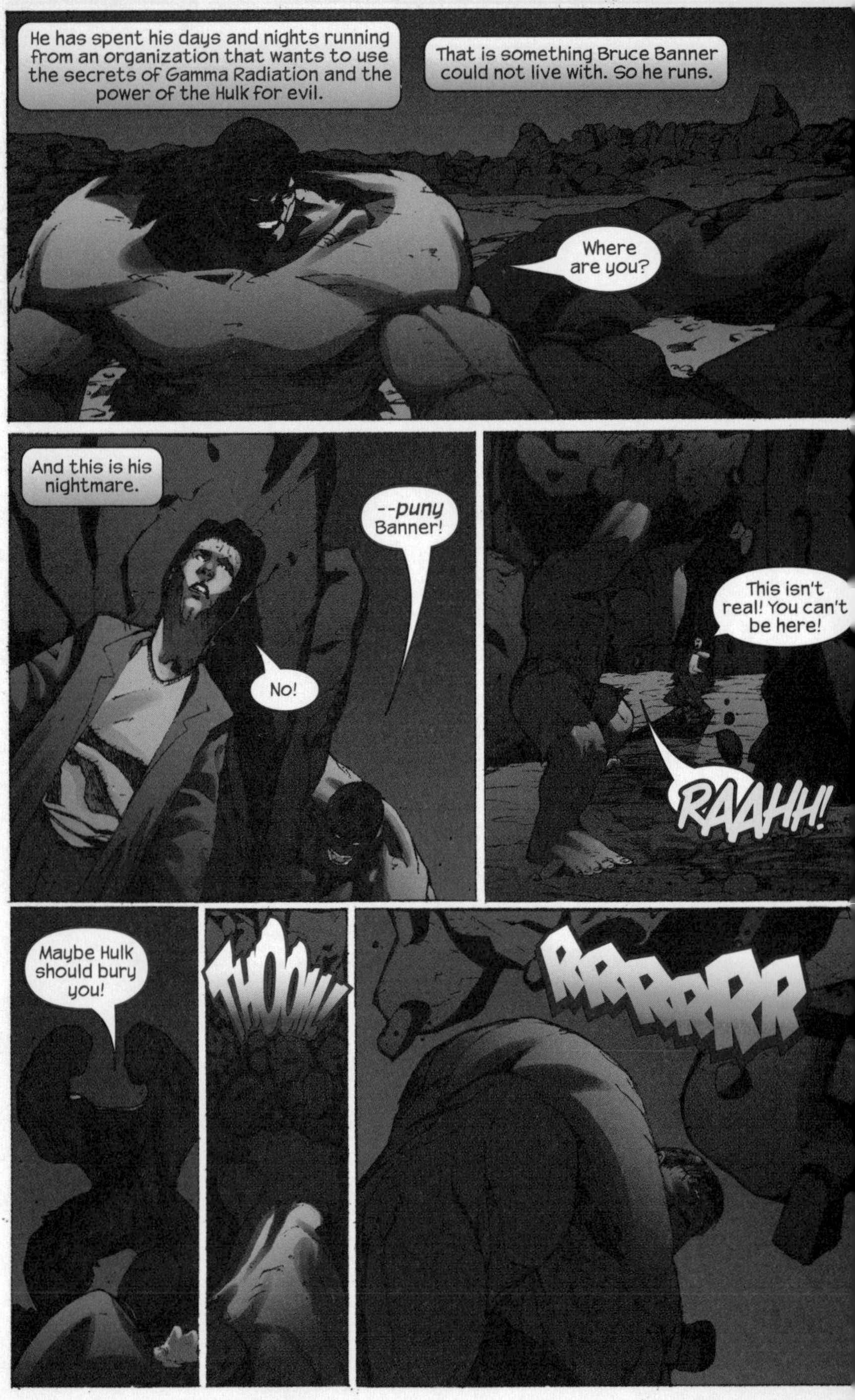
He has spent his days and nights running from an organization that wants to use the secrets of Gamma Radiation and the power of the Hulk for evil.
That is something Bruce Banner could not live with. So he runs.
Where are you?
And this is his nightmare.
--puny Banner!
No!
This isn't real! You can't be here!
RAAHH!
Maybe Hulk should bury you!
THOOM!
RRRRRRRR

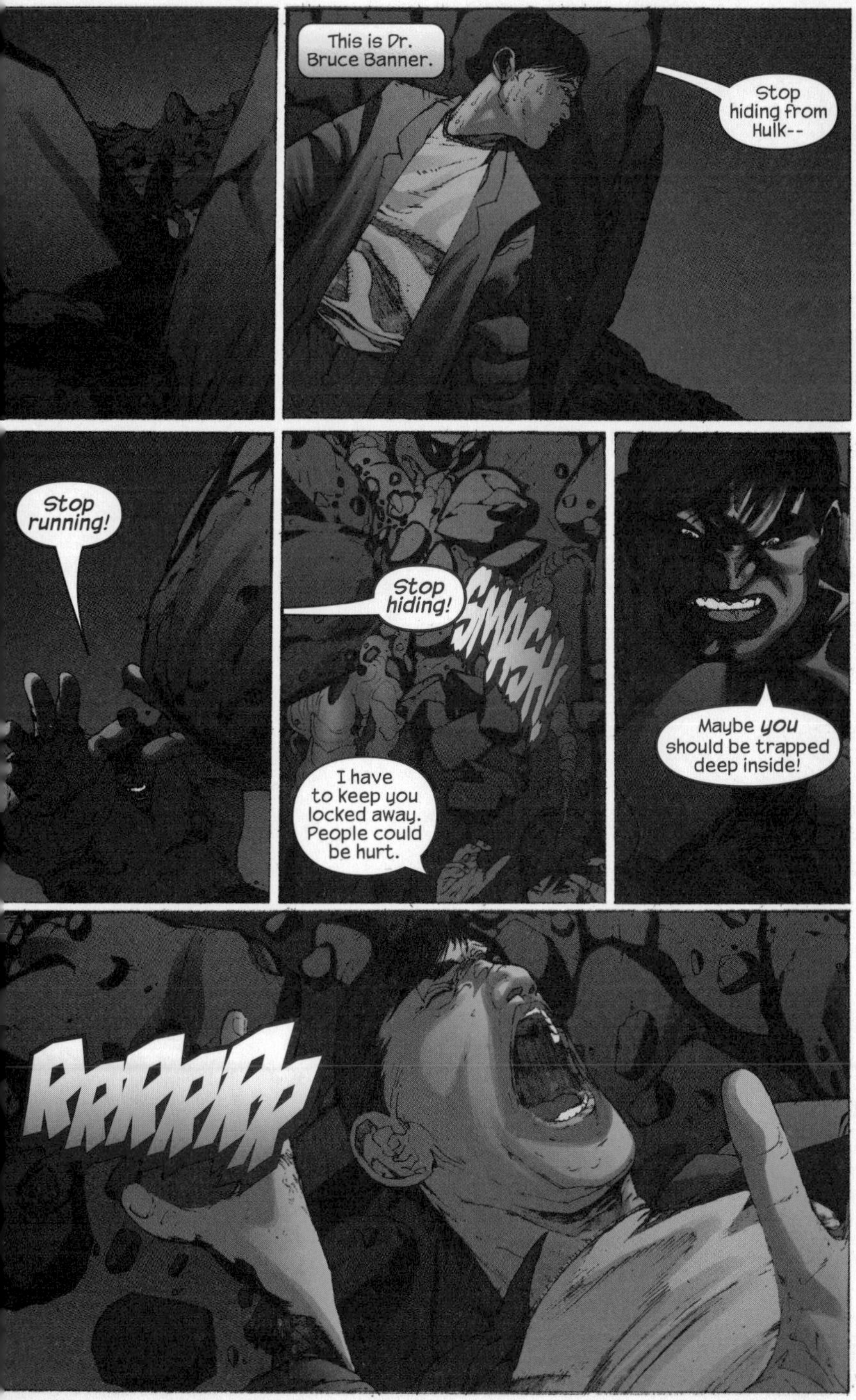
This is Dr. Bruce Banner.
Stop hiding from Hulk--
Stop running!
Stop hiding!
SMASH!
I have to keep you locked away. People could be hurt.
Maybe you should be trapped deep inside!
RRRRRR

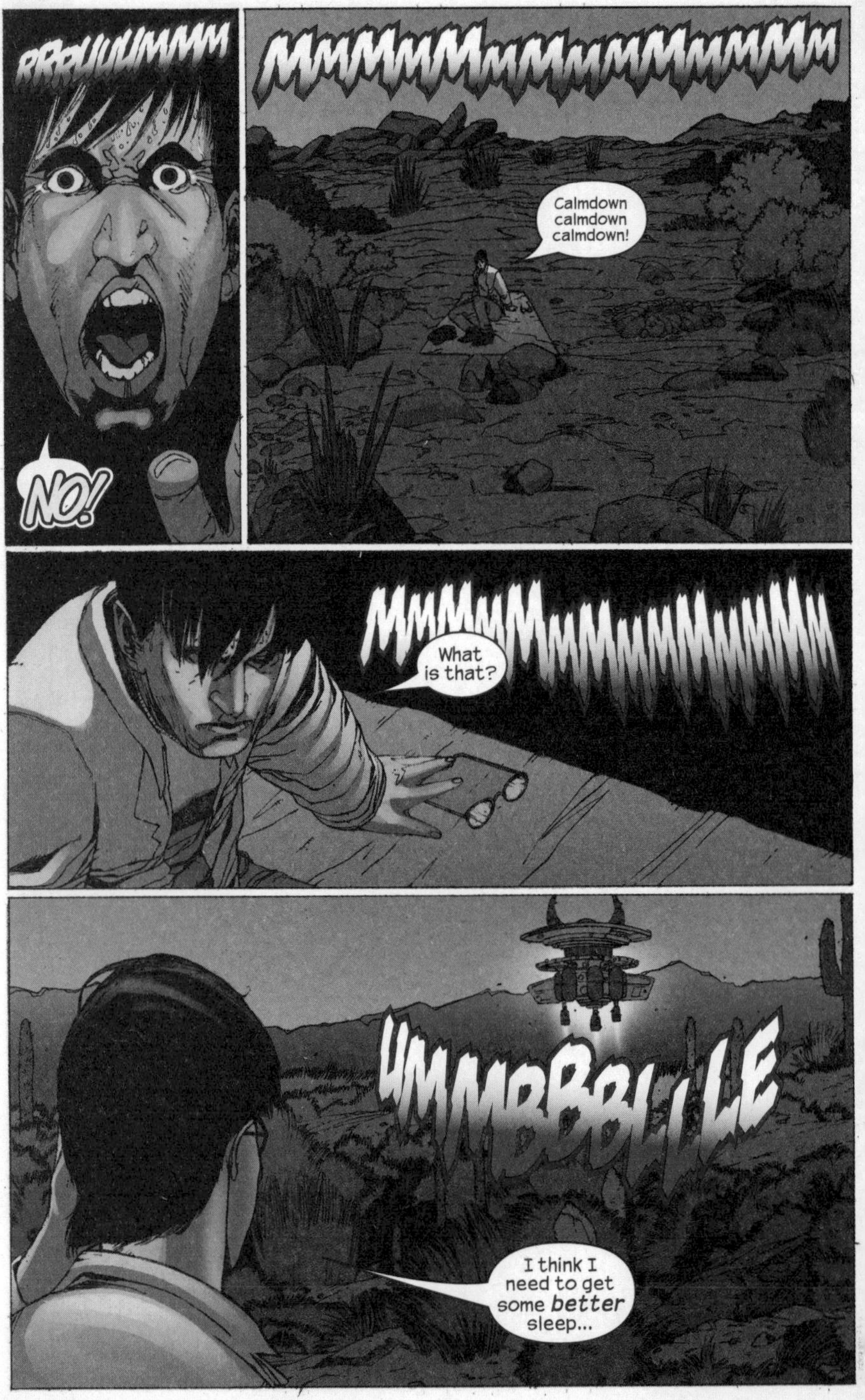
RRRUUMMM
NO!
MMMMMMMMMMMMMMMMM
Calmdown
calmdown
calmdown!
MMMMMMMMMMMMMMMMM
What is that?
UMMBBLLLE
I think I need to get some *better* sleep...

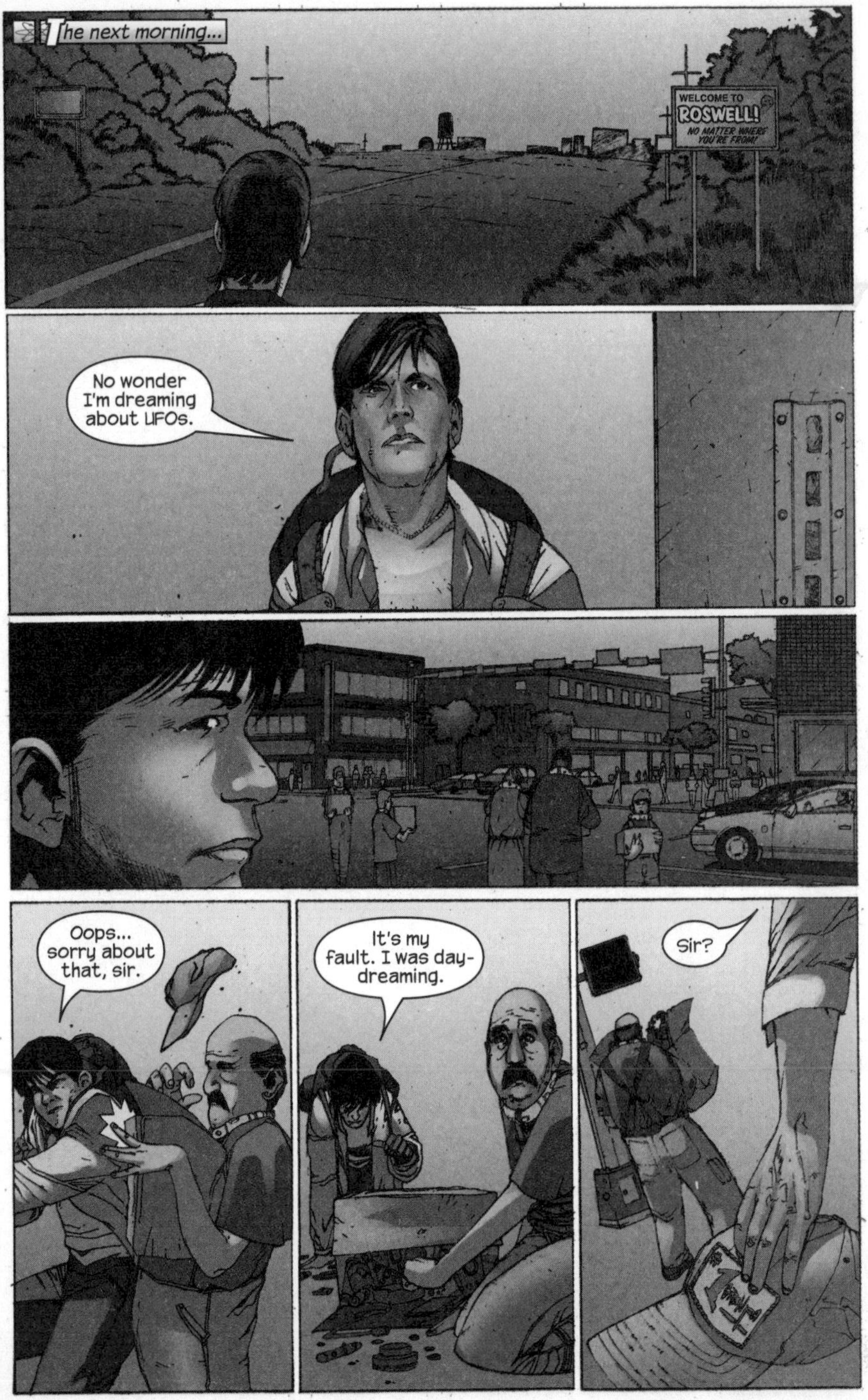
The next morning...
WELCOME TO
ROSWELL!
NO MATTER WHERE YOU'RE FROM!
No wonder I'm dreaming about UFOs.
Oops... sorry about that, sir.
It's my fault. I was day-dreaming.
Sir?

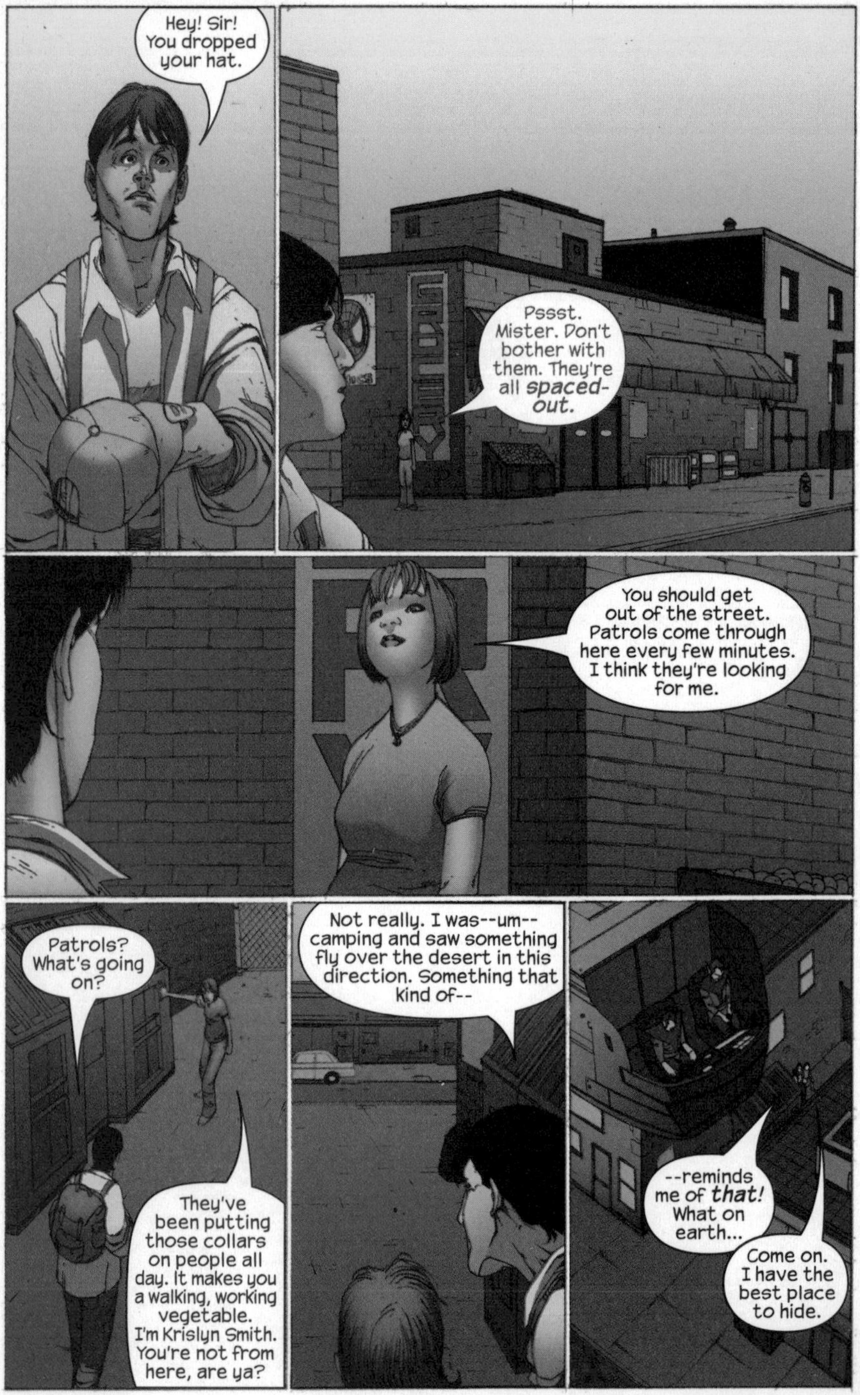
Hey! Sir! You dropped your hat.
Pssst. Mister. Don't bother with them. They're all *spaced-out.*
You should get out of the street. Patrols come through here every few minutes. I think they're looking for me.
Patrols? What's going on?
They've been putting those collars on people all day. It makes you a walking, working vegetable. I'm Krislyn Smith. You're not from here, are ya?
Not really. I was--um--camping and saw something fly over the desert in this direction. Something that kind of--
--reminds me of *that!* What on earth...
Come on. I have the best place to hide.

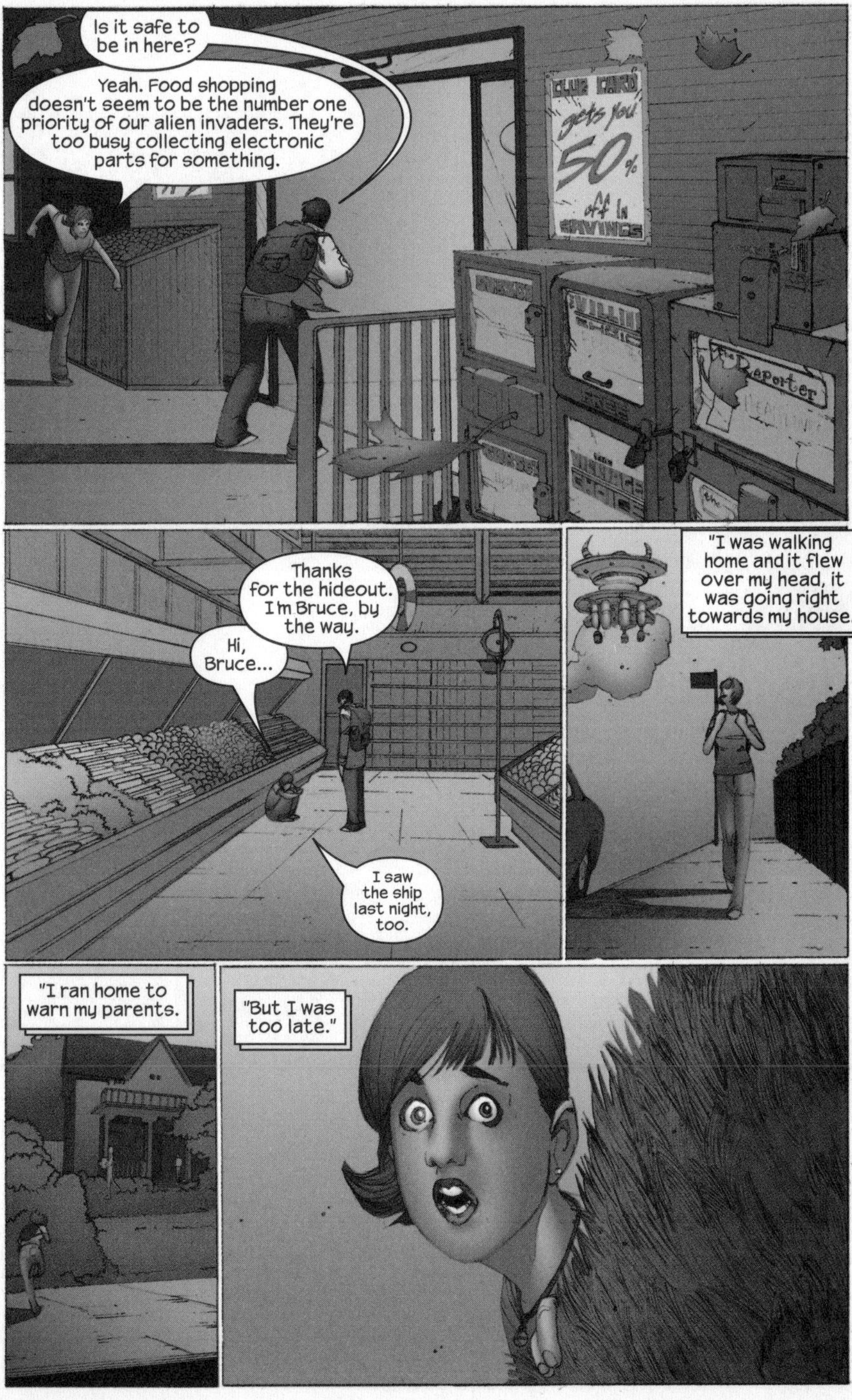
Is it safe to be in here?
Yeah. Food shopping doesn't seem to be the number one priority of our alien invaders. They're too busy collecting electronic parts for something.
CLUB CARD gets you 50% off in SAVINGS
Reporter
Thanks for the hideout. I'm Bruce, by the way.
Hi, Bruce...
I saw the ship last night, too.
"I was walking home and it flew over my head, it was going right towards my house.
"I ran home to warn my parents.
"But I was too late."

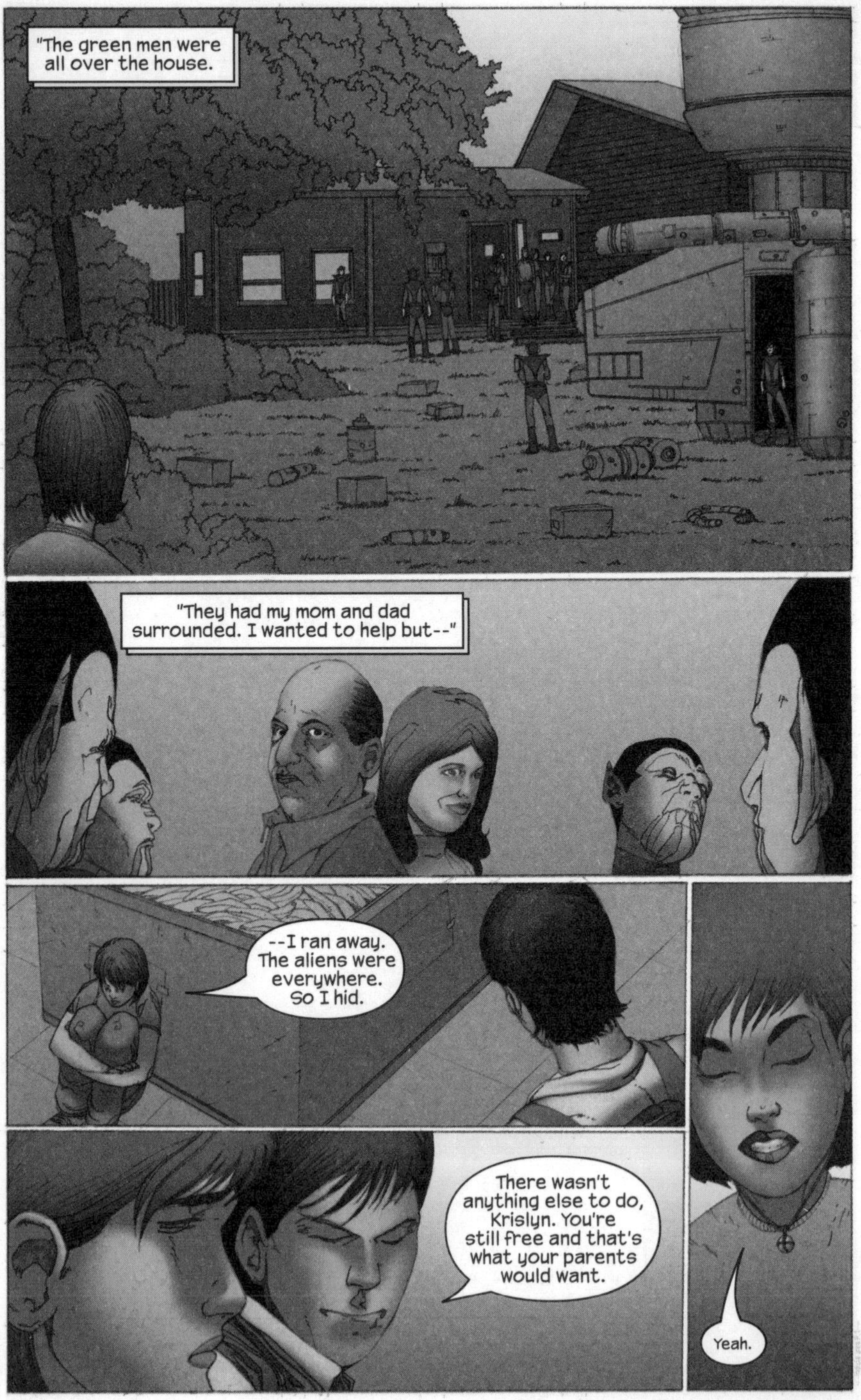
"The green men were all over the house.
"They had my mom and dad surrounded. I wanted to help but--"
--I ran away. The aliens were everywhere. So I hid.
There wasn't anything else to do, Krislyn. You're still free and that's what your parents would want.
Yeah.

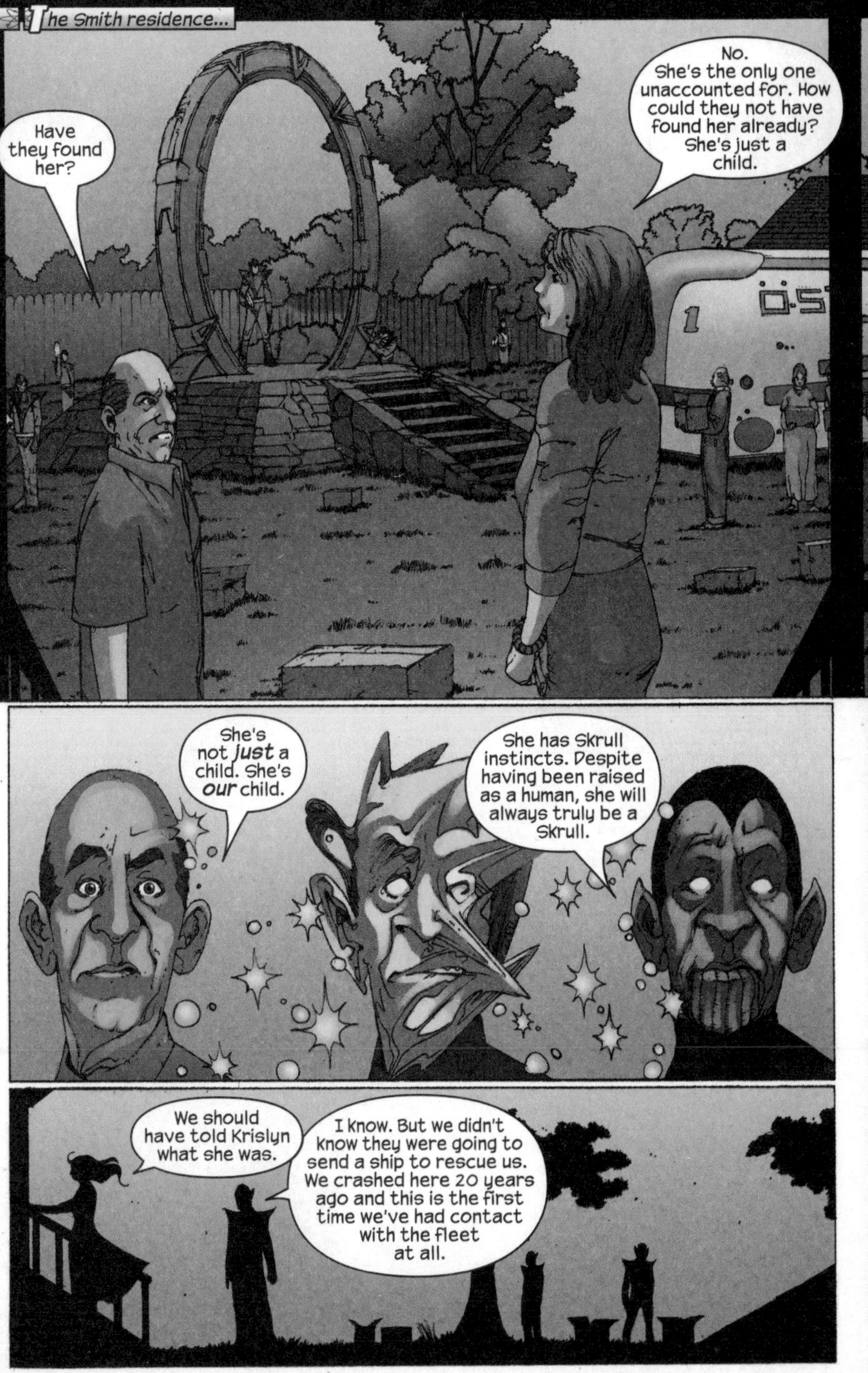
The Smith residence...
Have they found her?
No. She's the only one unaccounted for. How could they not have found her already? She's just a child.
She's not *just* a child. She's *our* child.
She has Skrull instincts. Despite having been raised as a human, she will always truly be a Skrull.
We should have told Krislyn what she was.
I know. But we didn't know they were going to send a ship to rescue us. We crashed here 20 years ago and this is the first time we've had contact with the fleet at all.

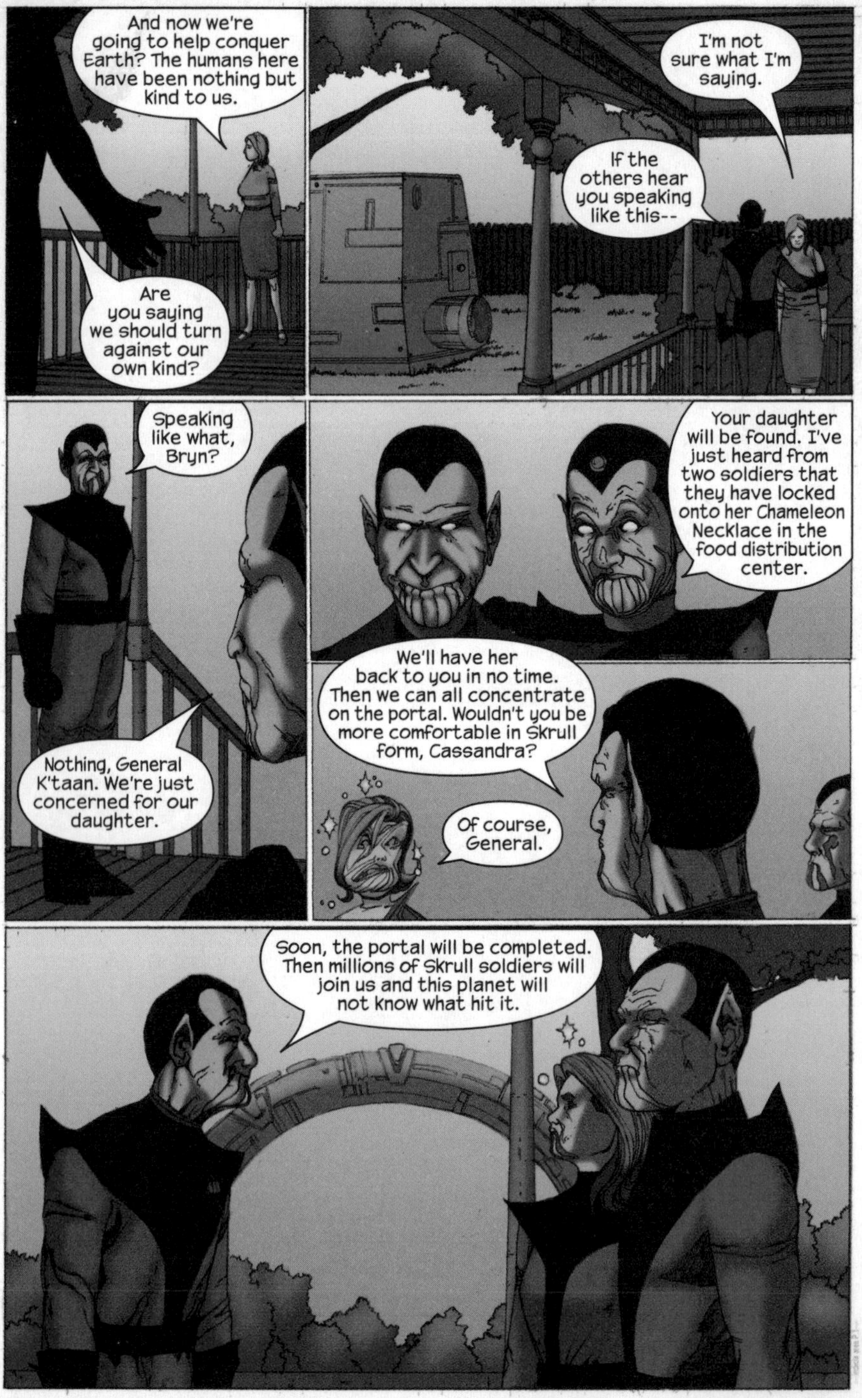
And now we're going to help conquer Earth? The humans here have been nothing but kind to us.
Are you saying we should turn against our own kind?
I'm not sure what I'm saying.
If the others hear you speaking like this--
Speaking like what, Bryn?
Nothing, General K'taan. We're just concerned for our daughter.
Your daughter will be found. I've just heard from two soldiers that they have locked onto her Chameleon Necklace in the food distribution center.
We'll have her back to you in no time. Then we can all concentrate on the portal. Wouldn't you be more comfortable in Skrull form, Cassandra?
Of course, General.
Soon, the portal will be completed. Then millions of Skrull soldiers will join us and this planet will not know what hit it.

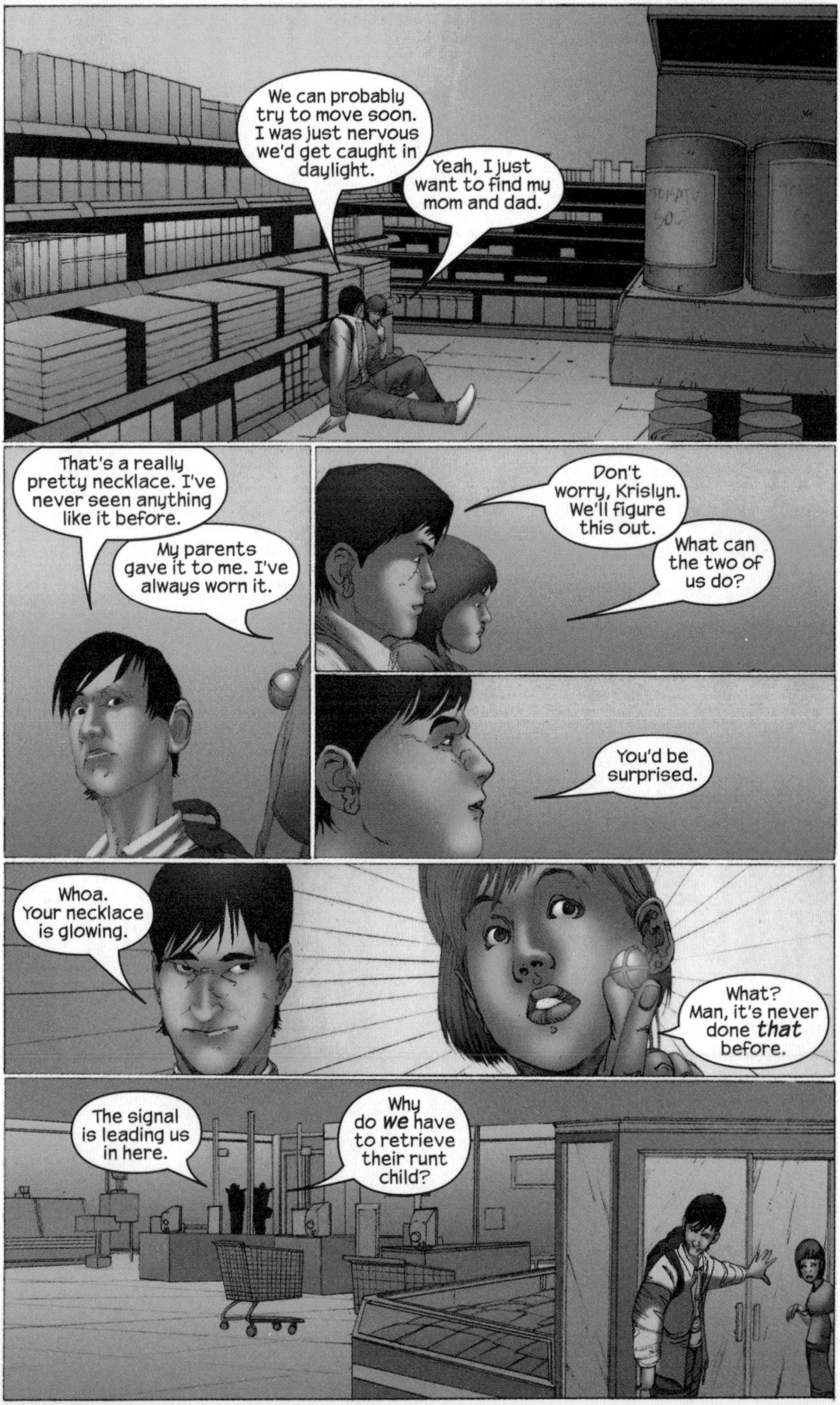
We can probably try to move soon. I was just nervous we'd get caught in daylight.
Yeah, I just want to find my mom and dad.
That's a really pretty necklace. I've never seen anything like it before.
My parents gave it to me. I've always worn it.
Don't worry, Krislyn. We'll figure this out.
What can the two of us do?
You'd be surprised.
Whoa. Your necklace is glowing.
What? Man, it's never done *that* before.
The signal is leading us in here.
Why do *we* have to retrieve their runt child?

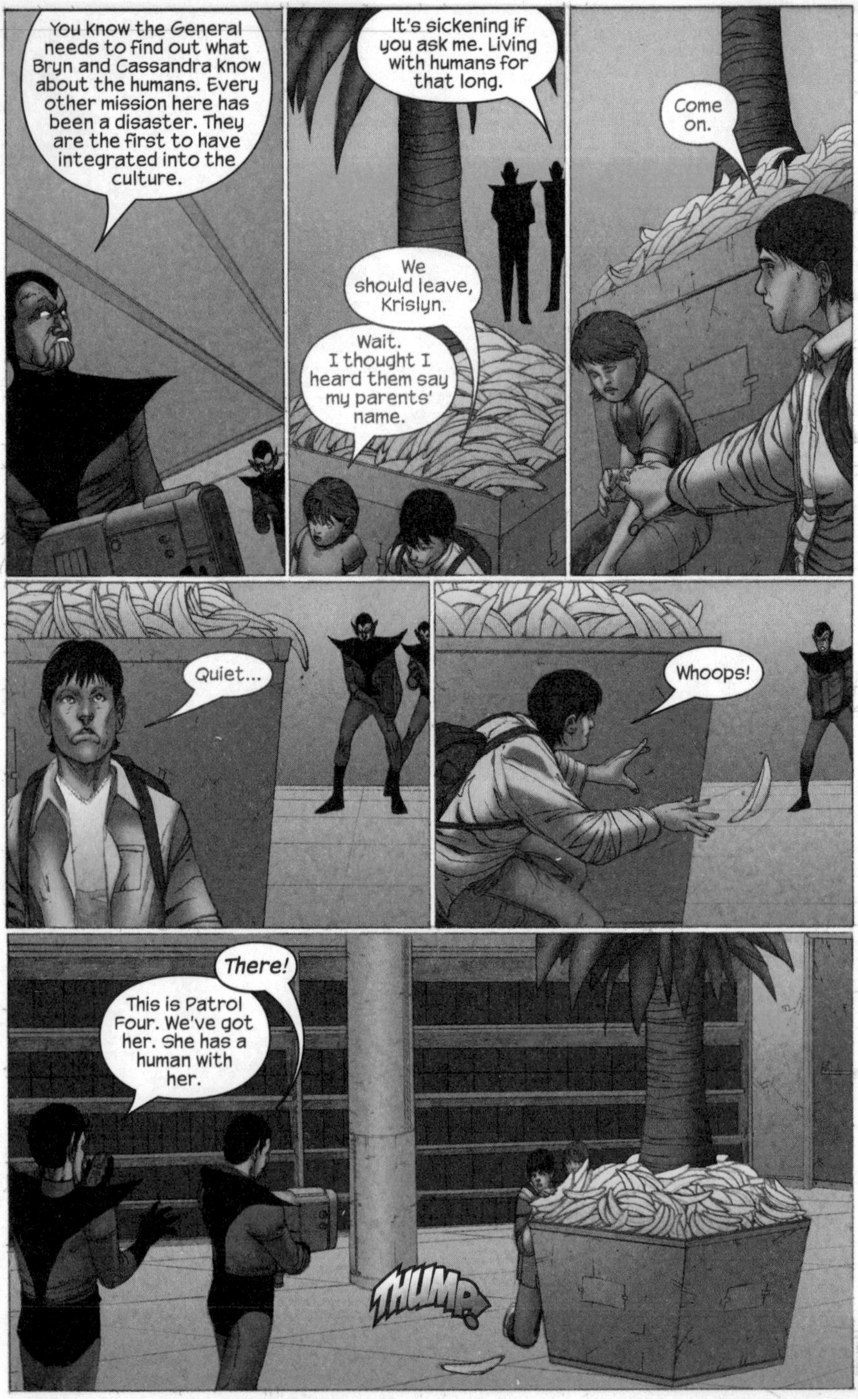
You know the General needs to find out what Bryn and Cassandra know about the humans. Every other mission here has been a disaster. They are the first to have integrated into the culture.
It's sickening if you ask me. Living with humans for that long.
We should leave, Krislyn.
Wait. I thought I heard them say my parents' name.
Come on.
Quiet...
Whoops!
There!
This is Patrol Four. We've got her. She has a human with her.
THUMP

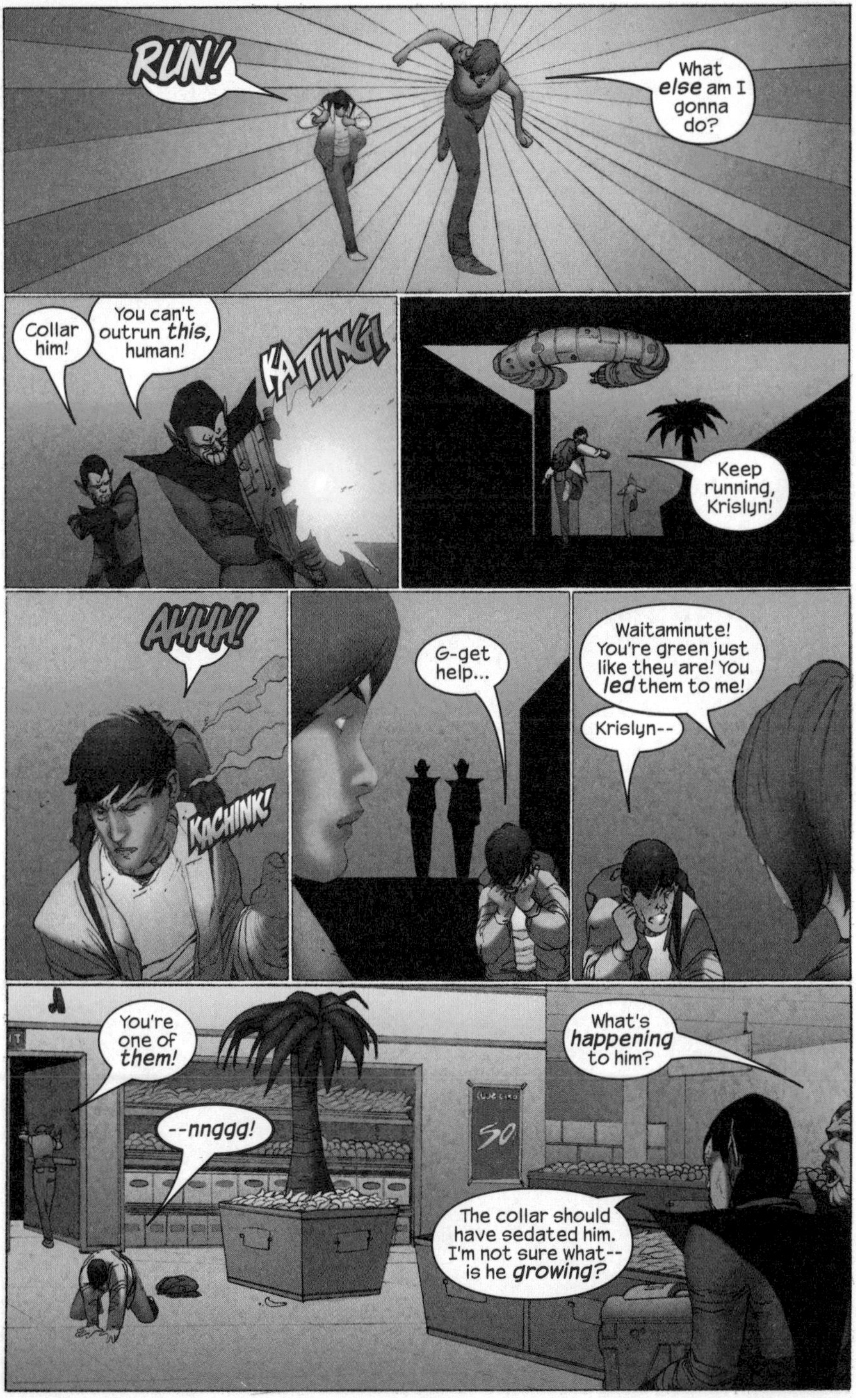
RUN!
What else am I gonna do?
Collar him!
You can't outrun this, human!
KATING!
Keep running, Krislyn!
AHHH!
KACHINK!
G-get help...
Waitaminute! You're green just like they are! You led them to me!
Krislyn--
You're one of them!
--nnggg!
What's happening to him?
The collar should have sedated him. I'm not sure what-- is he growing?

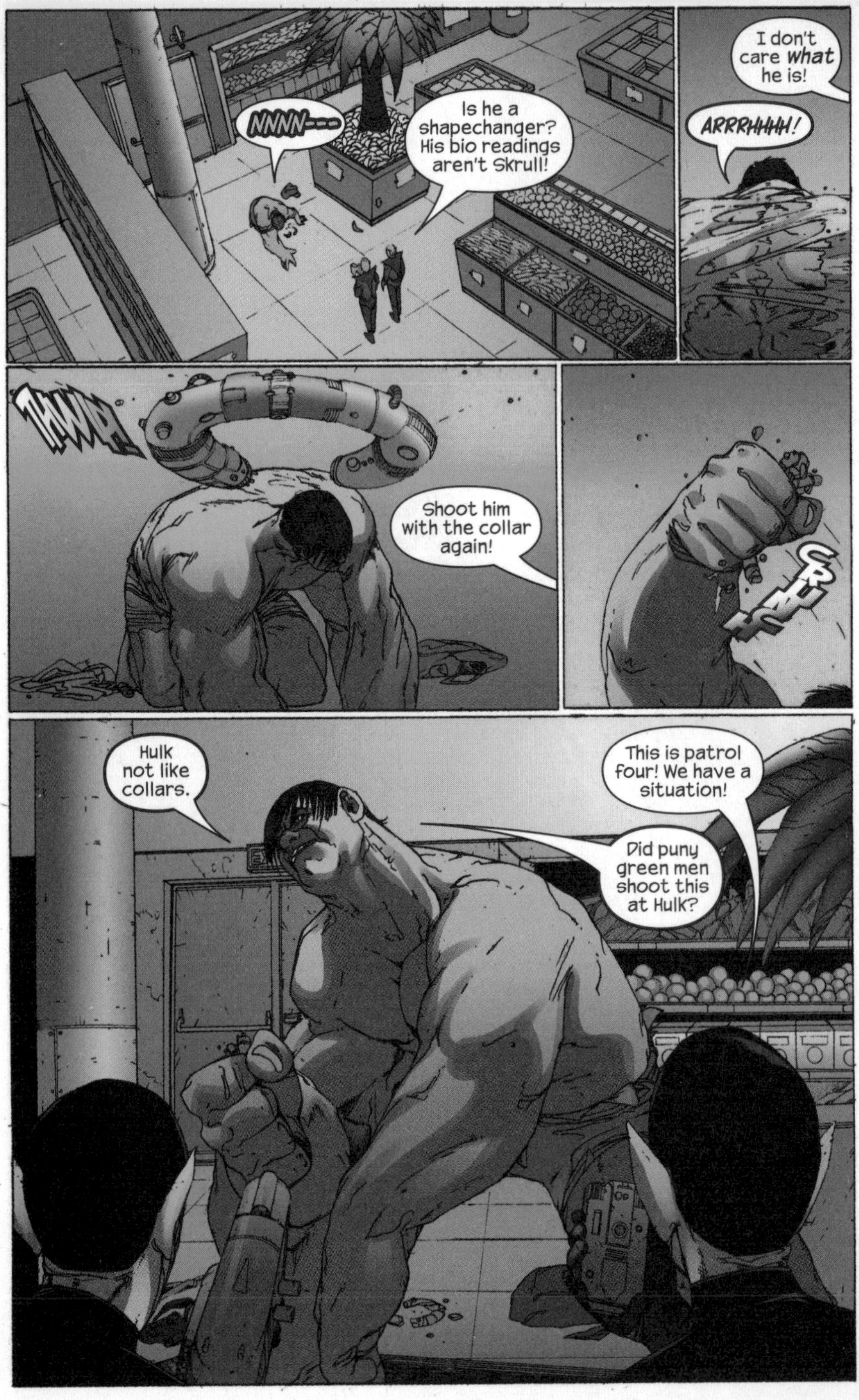
NNNN---
Is he a shapechanger? His bio readings aren't Skrull!
I don't care what he is!
ARRRHHHH!
THWIP!
Shoot him with the collar again!
CRNCH
Hulk not like collars.
This is patrol four! We have a situation!
Did puny green men shoot this at Hulk?

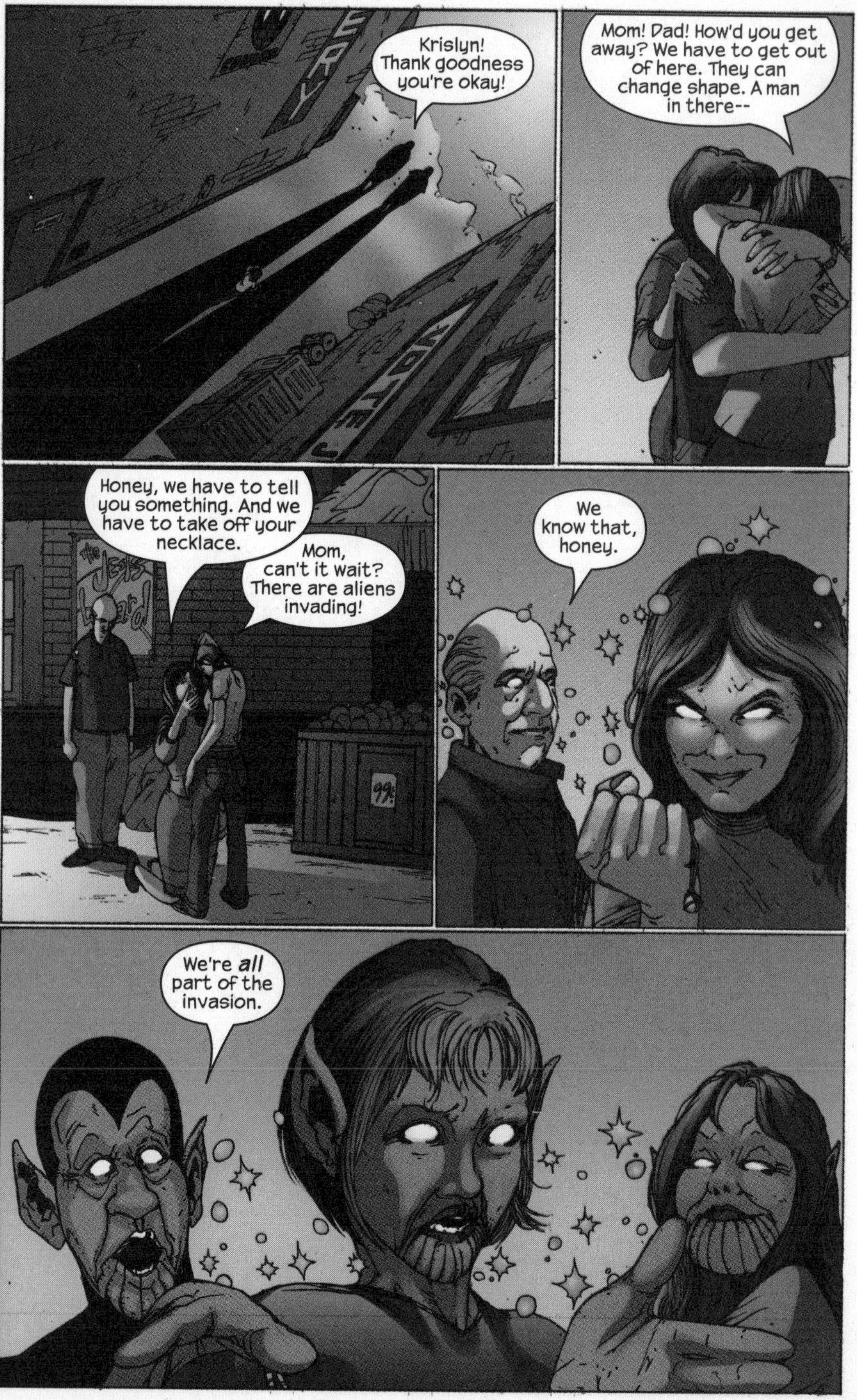
Krislyn! Thank goodness you're okay!
Mom! Dad! How'd you get away? We have to get out of here. They can change shape. A man in there--
Honey, we have to tell you something. And we have to take off your necklace.
Mom, can't it wait? There are aliens invading!
We know that, honey.
We're *all* part of the invasion.

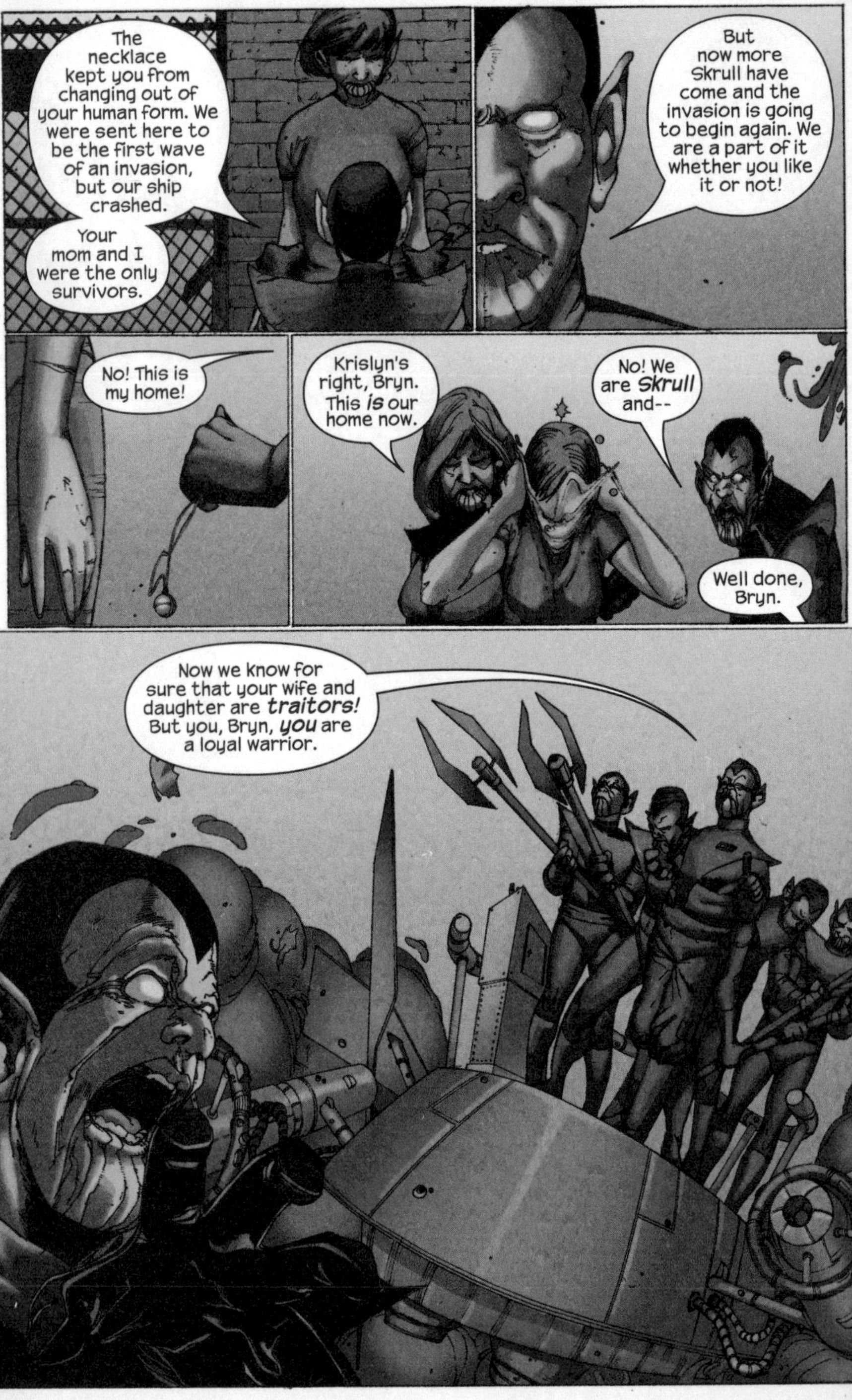
The necklace kept you from changing out of your human form. We were sent here to be the first wave of an invasion, but our ship crashed.
Your mom and I were the only survivors.
But now more Skrull have come and the invasion is going to begin again. We are a part of it whether you like it or not!
No! This is my home!
Krislyn's right, Bryn. This *is* our home now.
No! We are *Skrull* and--
Well done, Bryn.
Now we know for sure that your wife and daughter are *traitors!* But you, Bryn, *you* are a loyal warrior.

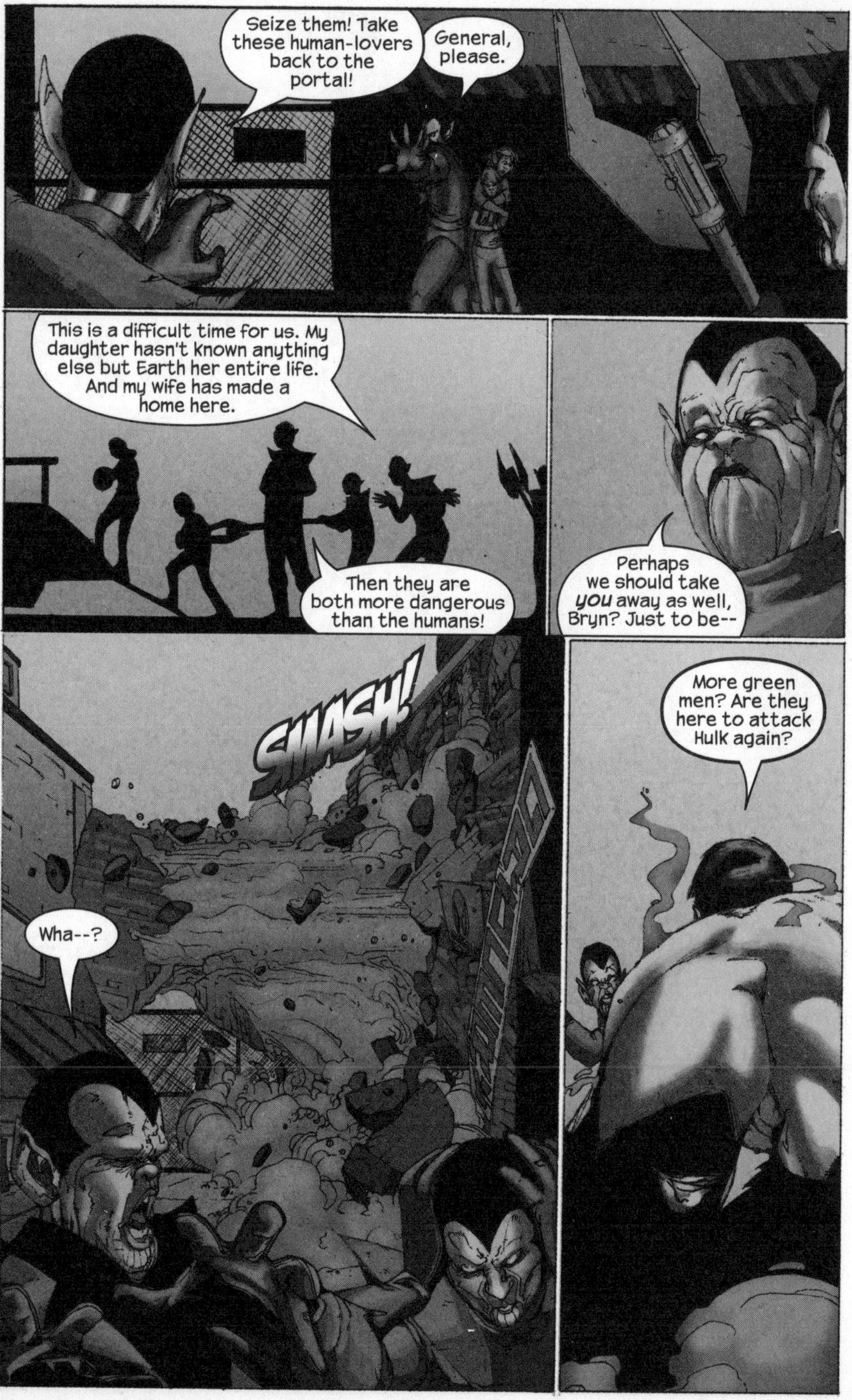
Seize them! Take these human-lovers back to the portal!
General, please.
This is a difficult time for us. My daughter hasn't known anything else but Earth her entire life. And my wife has made a home here.
Then they are both more dangerous than the humans!
Perhaps we should take *YOU* away as well, Bryn? Just to be--
SMASH!
Wha--?
More green men? Are they here to attack Hulk again?

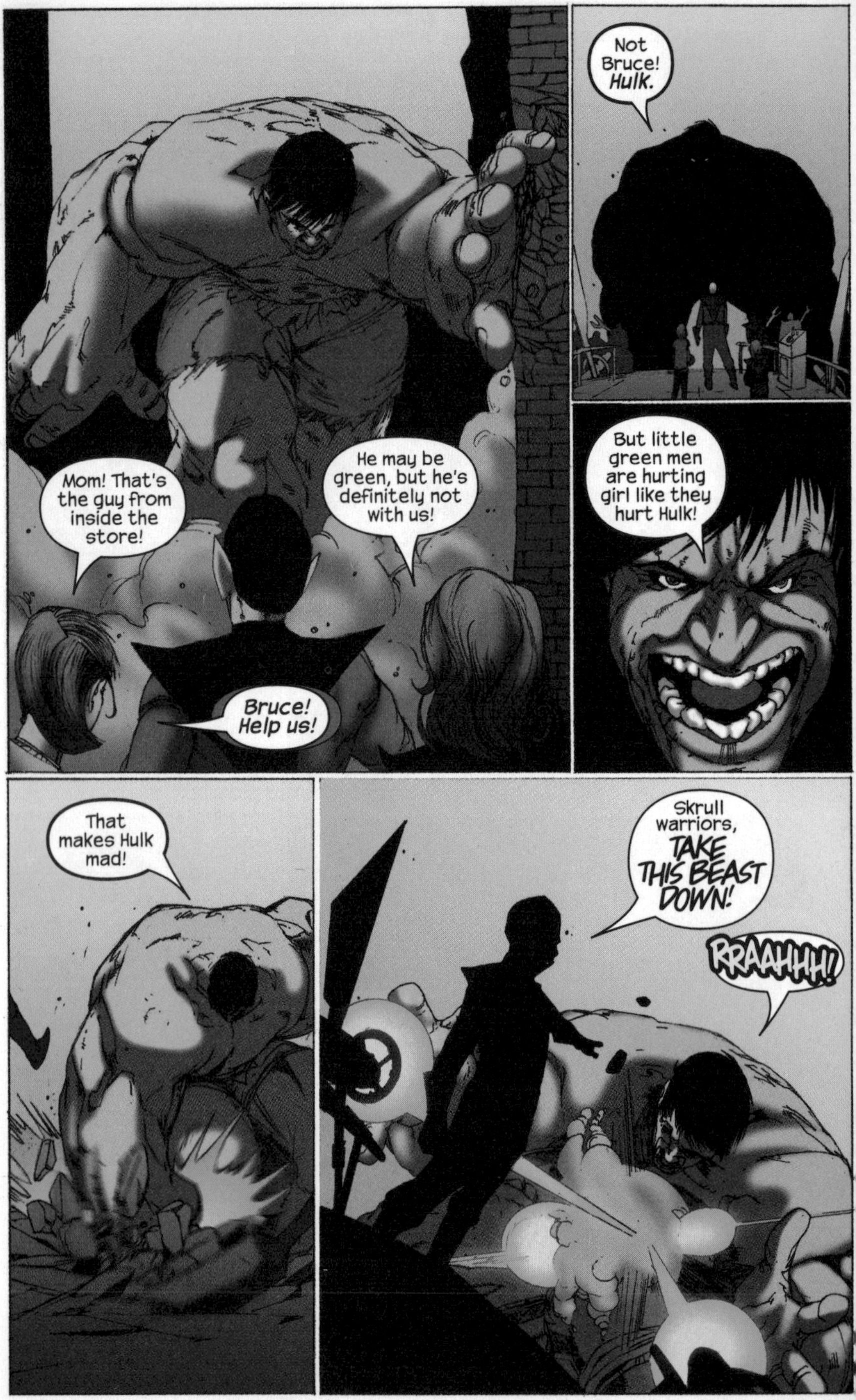
Not Bruce! Hulk.
Mom! That's the guy from inside the store!
He may be green, but he's definitely not with us!
Bruce! Help us!
But little green men are hurting girl like they hurt Hulk!
That makes Hulk mad!
Skrull warriors, TAKE THIS BEAST DOWN!
RRAAHHH!!

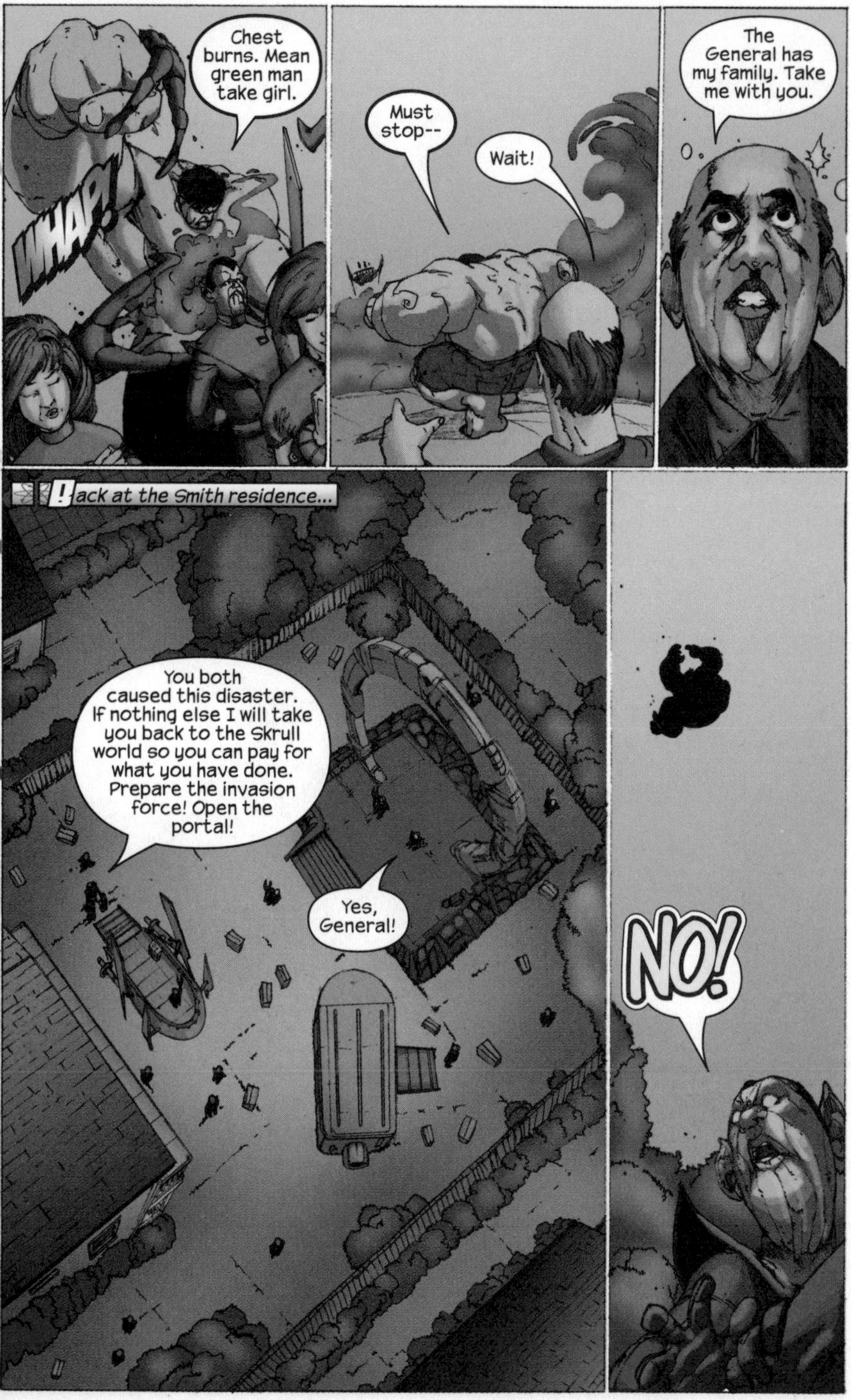
Chest burns. Mean green man take girl.
WHAP!
Must stop--
Wait!
The General has my family. Take me with you.
Back at the Smith residence...
You both caused this disaster. If nothing else I will take you back to the Skrull world so you can pay for what you have done. Prepare the invasion force! Open the portal!
Yes, General!
NO!

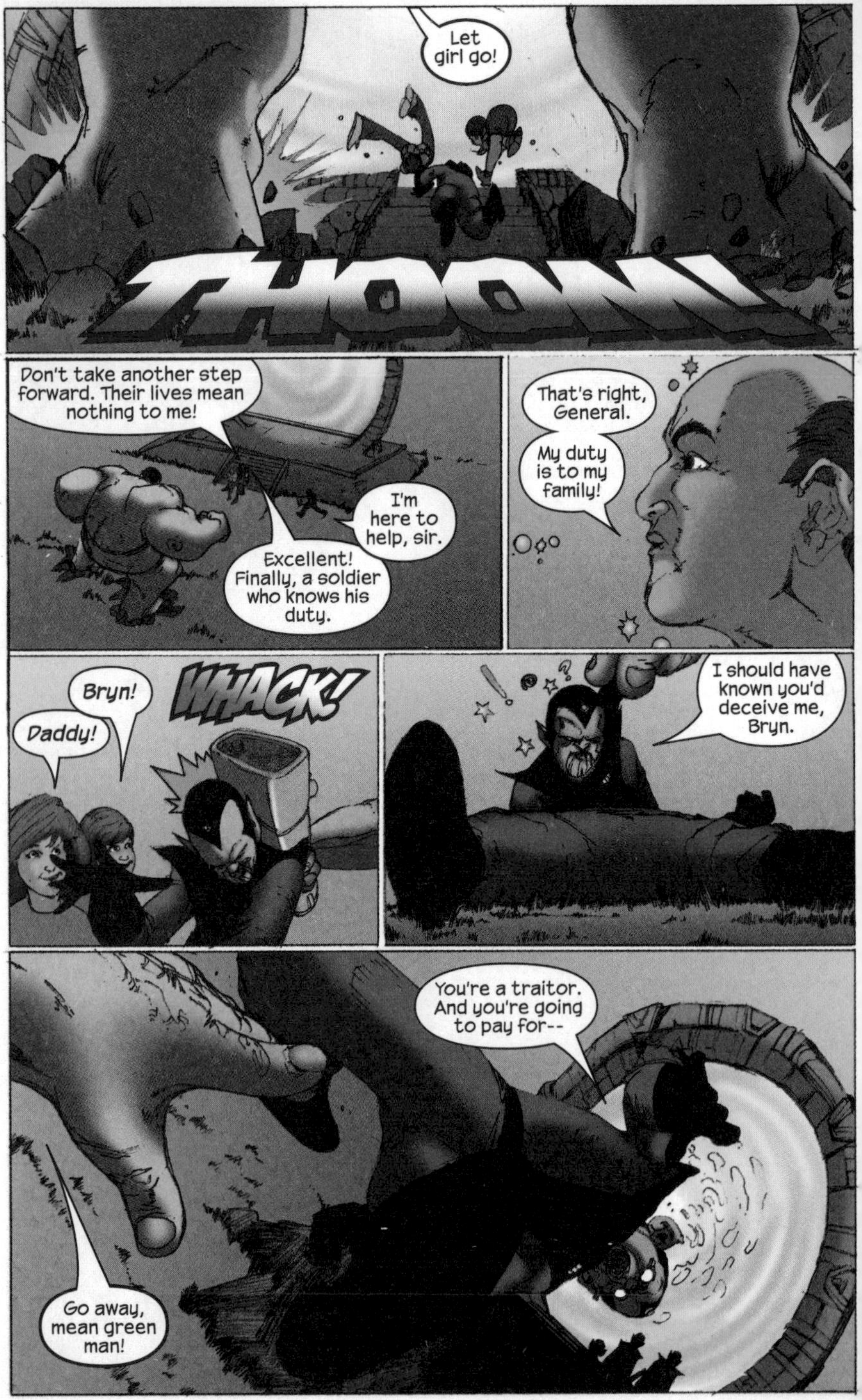
Let girl go!
THOOM!
Don't take another step forward. Their lives mean nothing to me!
I'm here to help, sir.
Excellent! Finally, a soldier who knows his duty.
That's right, General.
My duty is to my family!
Bryn!
Daddy!
WHACK!
I should have known you'd deceive me, Bryn.
You're a traitor. And you're going to pay for--
Go away, mean green man!

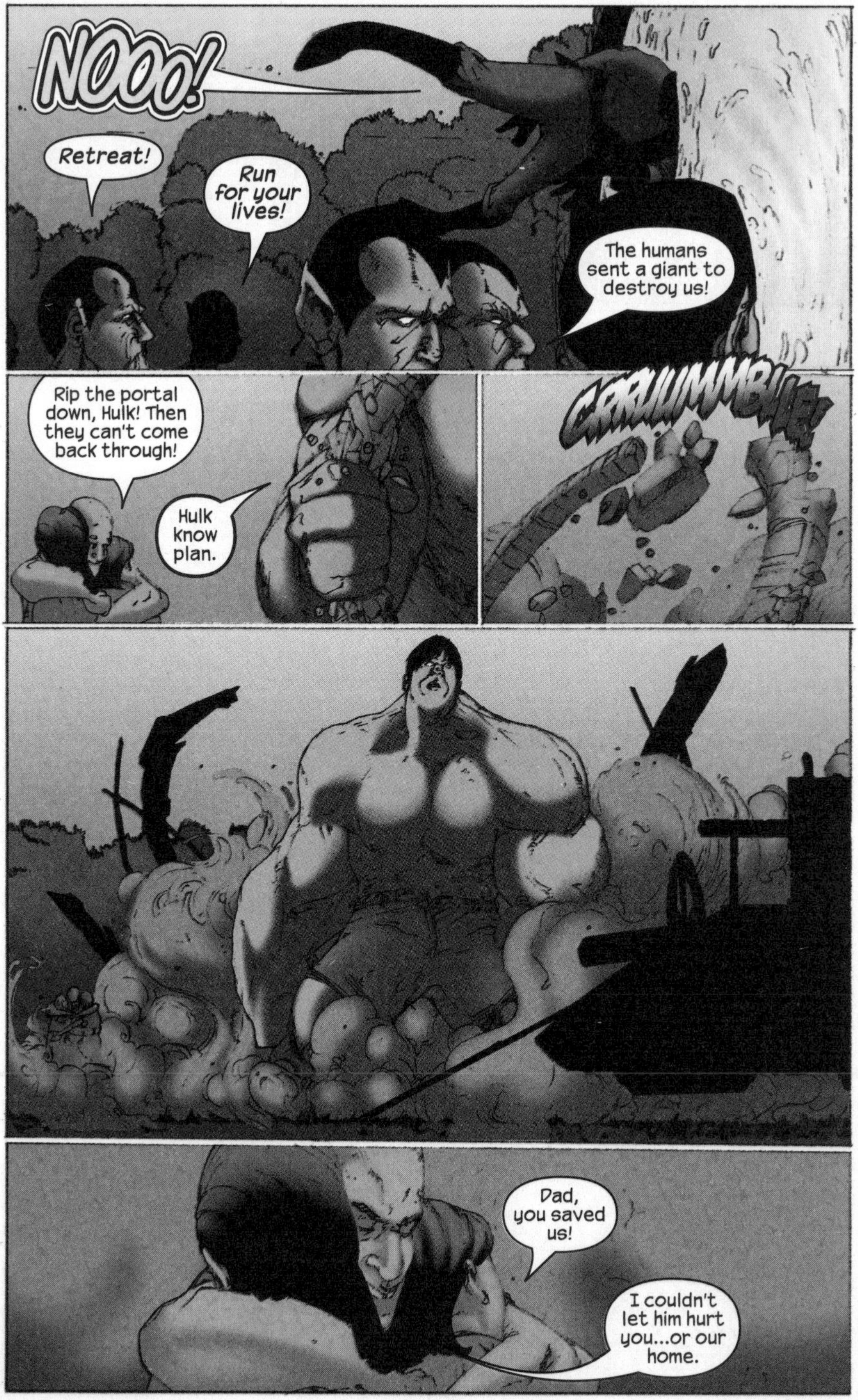
NOOO!
Retreat!
Run for your lives!
The humans sent a giant to destroy us!
Rip the portal down, Hulk! Then they can't come back through!
Hulk know plan.
CRRUUMMBLE!
Dad, you saved us!
I couldn't let him hurt you...or our home.

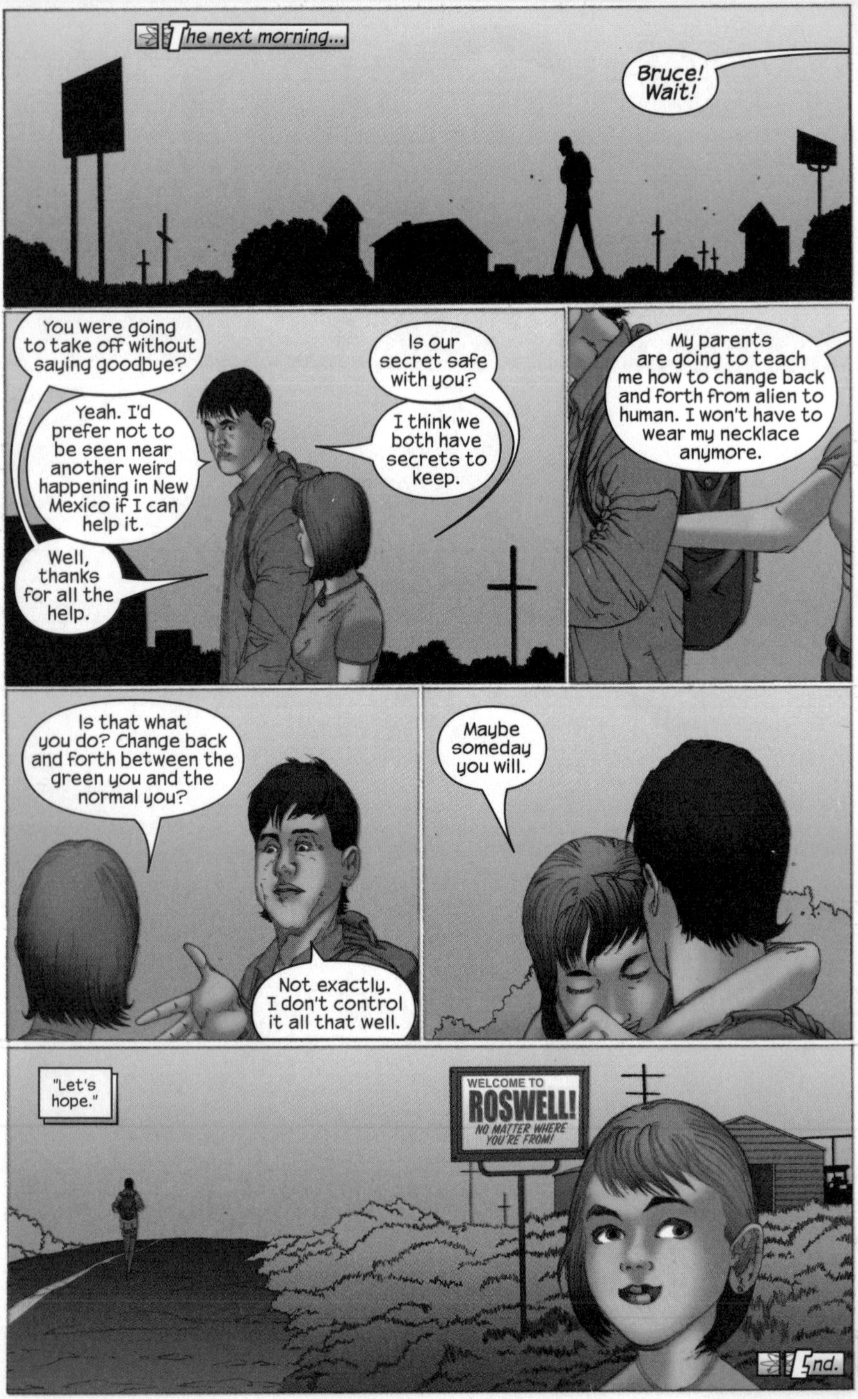
The next morning...
Bruce! Wait!
You were going to take off without saying goodbye?
Yeah. I'd prefer not to be seen near another weird happening in New Mexico if I can help it.
Well, thanks for all the help.
Is our secret safe with you?
I think we both have secrets to keep.
My parents are going to teach me how to change back and forth from alien to human. I won't have to wear my necklace anymore.
Is that what you do? Change back and forth between the green you and the normal you?
Not exactly. I don't control it all that well.
Maybe someday you will.
"Let's hope."
WELCOME TO ROSWELL! NO MATTER WHERE YOU'RE FROM!
End.

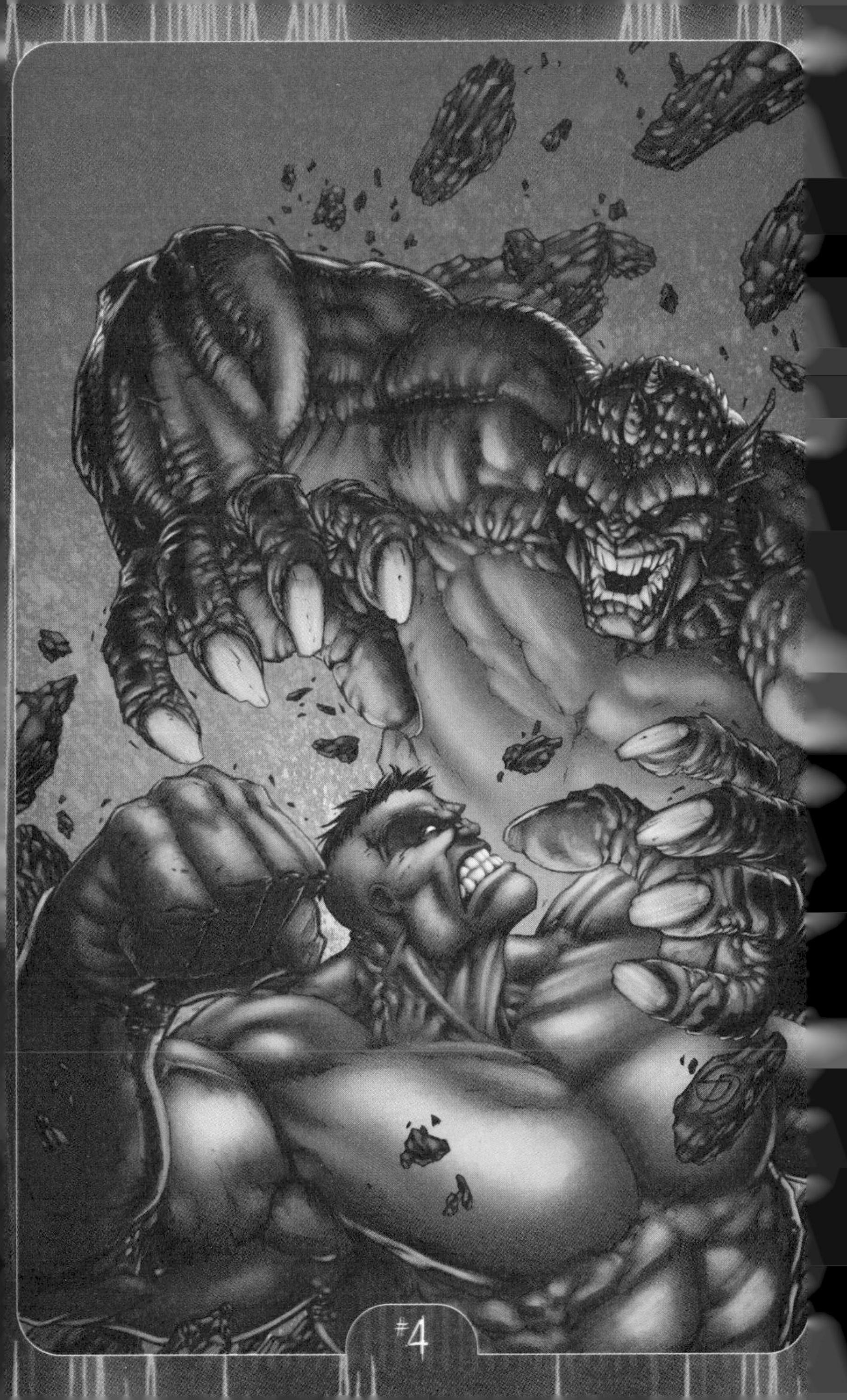
#4

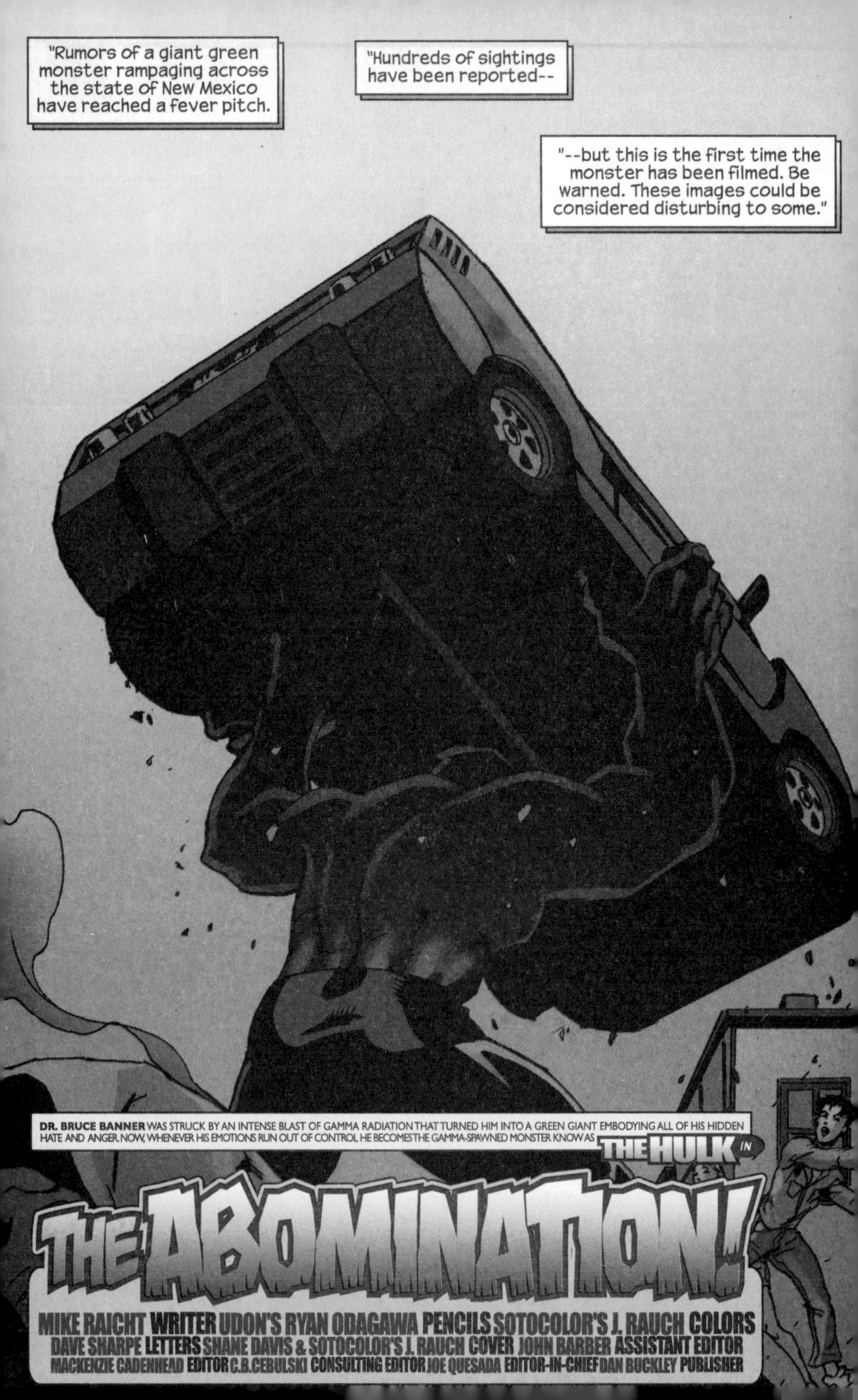

"Rumors of a giant green monster rampaging across the state of New Mexico have reached a fever pitch.
"Hundreds of sightings have been reported--
"--but this is the first time the monster has been filmed. Be warned. These images could be considered disturbing to some."
DR. BRUCE BANNER WAS STRUCK BY AN INTENSE BLAST OF GAMMA RADIATION THAT TURNED HIM INTO A GREEN GIANT EMBODYING ALL OF HIS HIDDEN HATE AND ANGER. NOW, WHENEVER HIS EMOTIONS RUN OUT OF CONTROL HE BECOMES THE GAMMA-SPAWNED MONSTER KNOWN AS THE HULK IN
THE ABOMINATION!
MIKE RAICHT WRITER UDON'S RYAN ODAGAWA PENCILS SOTOCOLOR'S J. RAUCH COLORS
DAVE SHARPE LETTERS SHANE DAVIS & SOTOCOLOR'S J. RAUCH COVER JOHN BARBER ASSISTANT EDITOR
MACKENZIE CADENHEAD EDITOR C.B.CEBULSKI CONSULTING EDITOR JOE QUESADA EDITOR-IN-CHIEF DAN BUCKLEY PUBLISHER

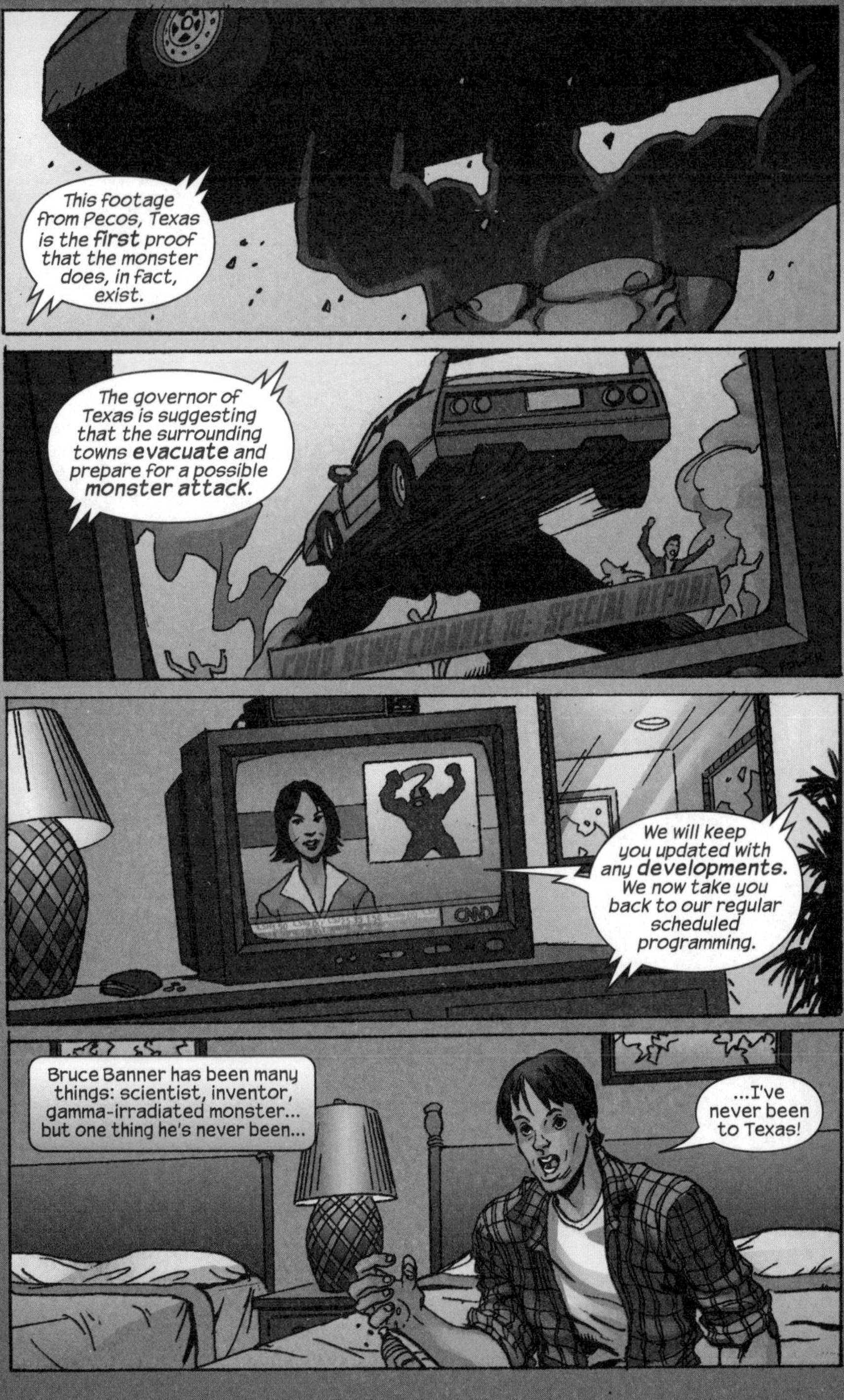
This footage from Pecos, Texas is the first proof that the monster does, in fact, exist.
The governor of Texas is suggesting that the surrounding towns evacuate and prepare for a possible monster attack.
CNND NEWS CHANNEL 10: SPECIAL REPORT
CNND
We will keep you updated with any developments. We now take you back to our regular scheduled programming.
Bruce Banner has been many things: scientist, inventor, gamma-irradiated monster... but one thing he's never been...
...I've never been to Texas!

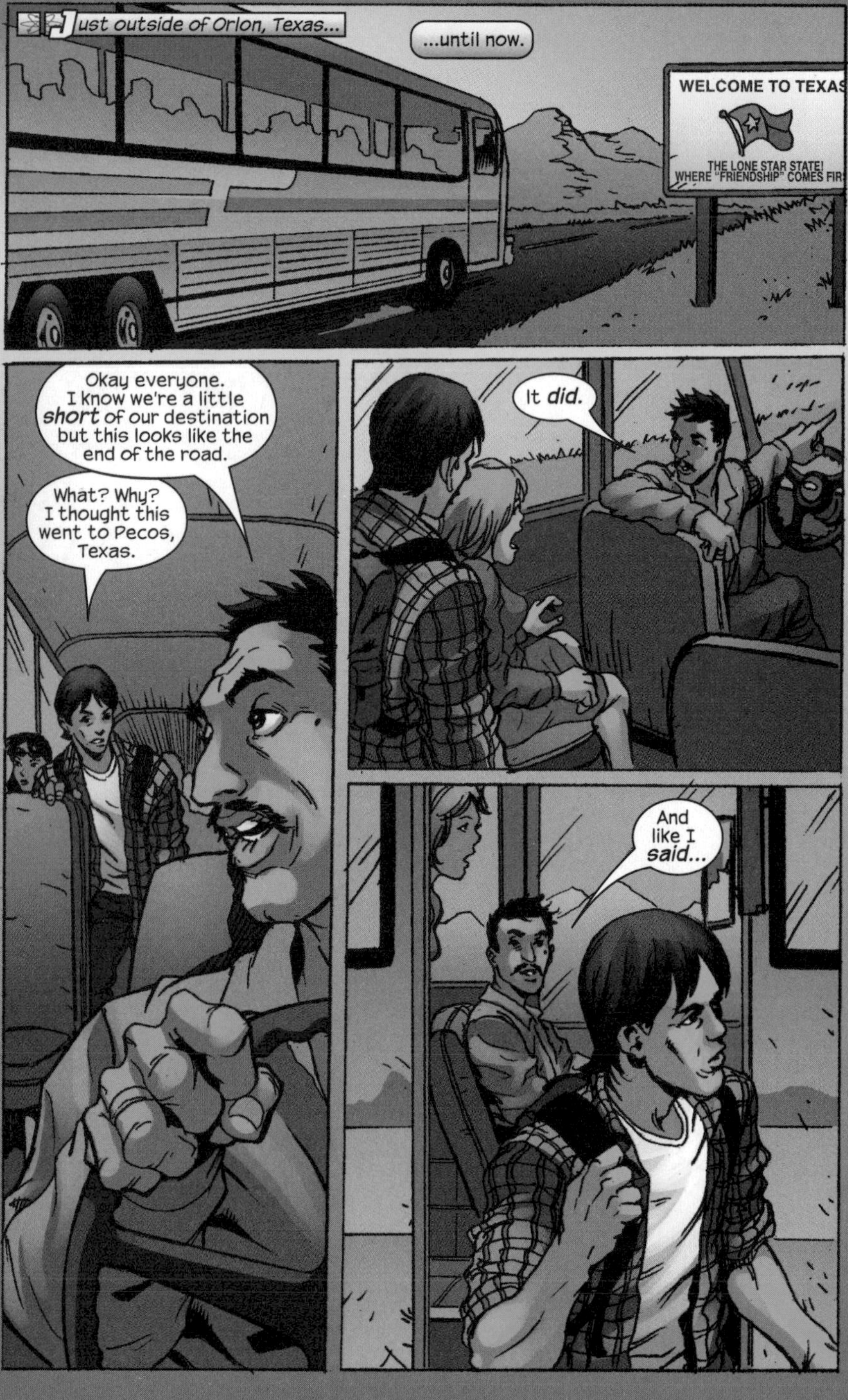

Just outside of Orlon, Texas...
...until now.
WELCOME TO TEXAS
THE LONE STAR STATE!
WHERE "FRIENDSHIP" COMES FIRS
Okay everyone. I know we're a little short of our destination but this looks like the end of the road.
What? Why? I thought this went to Pecos, Texas.
It did.
And like I said...

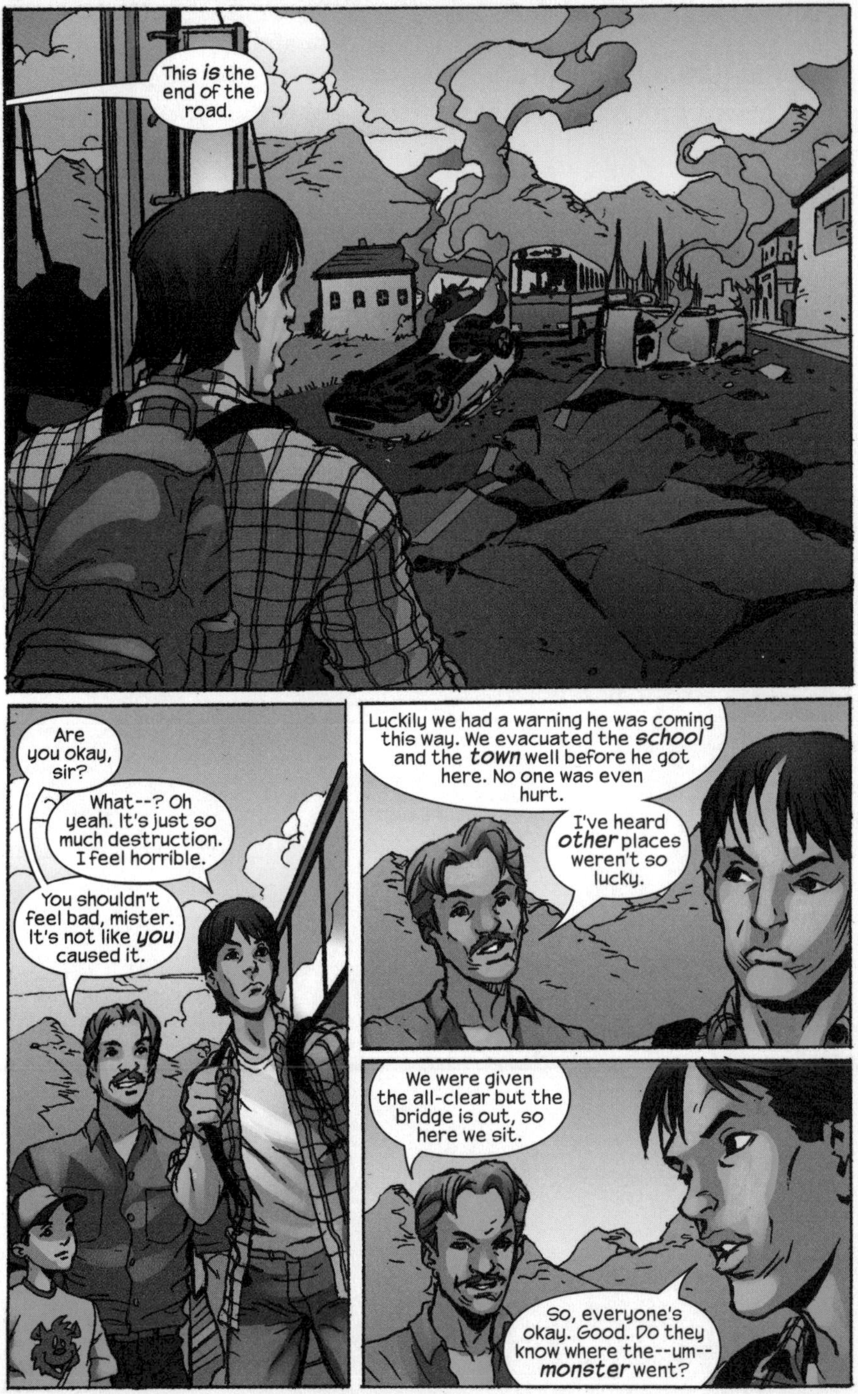
This *is* the end of the road.
Are you okay, sir?
What--? Oh yeah. It's just so much destruction. I feel horrible.
You shouldn't feel bad, mister. It's not like *you* caused it.
Luckily we had a warning he was coming this way. We evacuated the *school* and the *town* well before he got here. No one was even hurt.
I've heard *other* places weren't so lucky.
We were given the all-clear but the bridge is out, so here we sit.
So, everyone's okay. Good. Do they know where the--um--*monster* went?

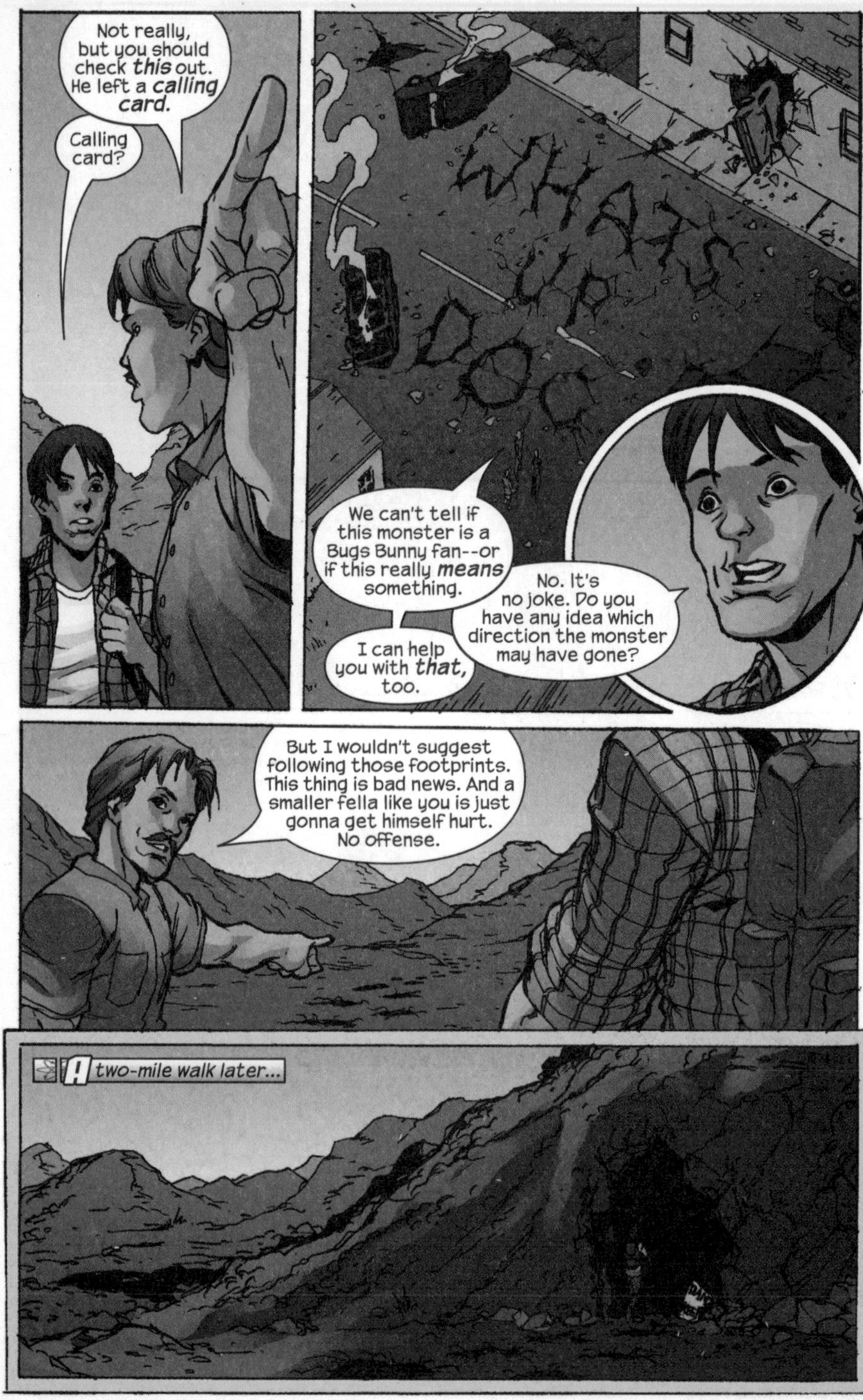

Not really, but you should check *this* out. He left a *calling card.*
Calling card?
WHAT'S UP DOC
We can't tell if this monster is a Bugs Bunny fan--or if this really *means* something.
No. It's no joke. Do you have any idea which direction the monster may have gone?
I can help you with *that,* too.
But I wouldn't suggest following those footprints. This thing is bad news. And a smaller fella like you is just gonna get himself hurt. No offense.
A two-mile walk later...

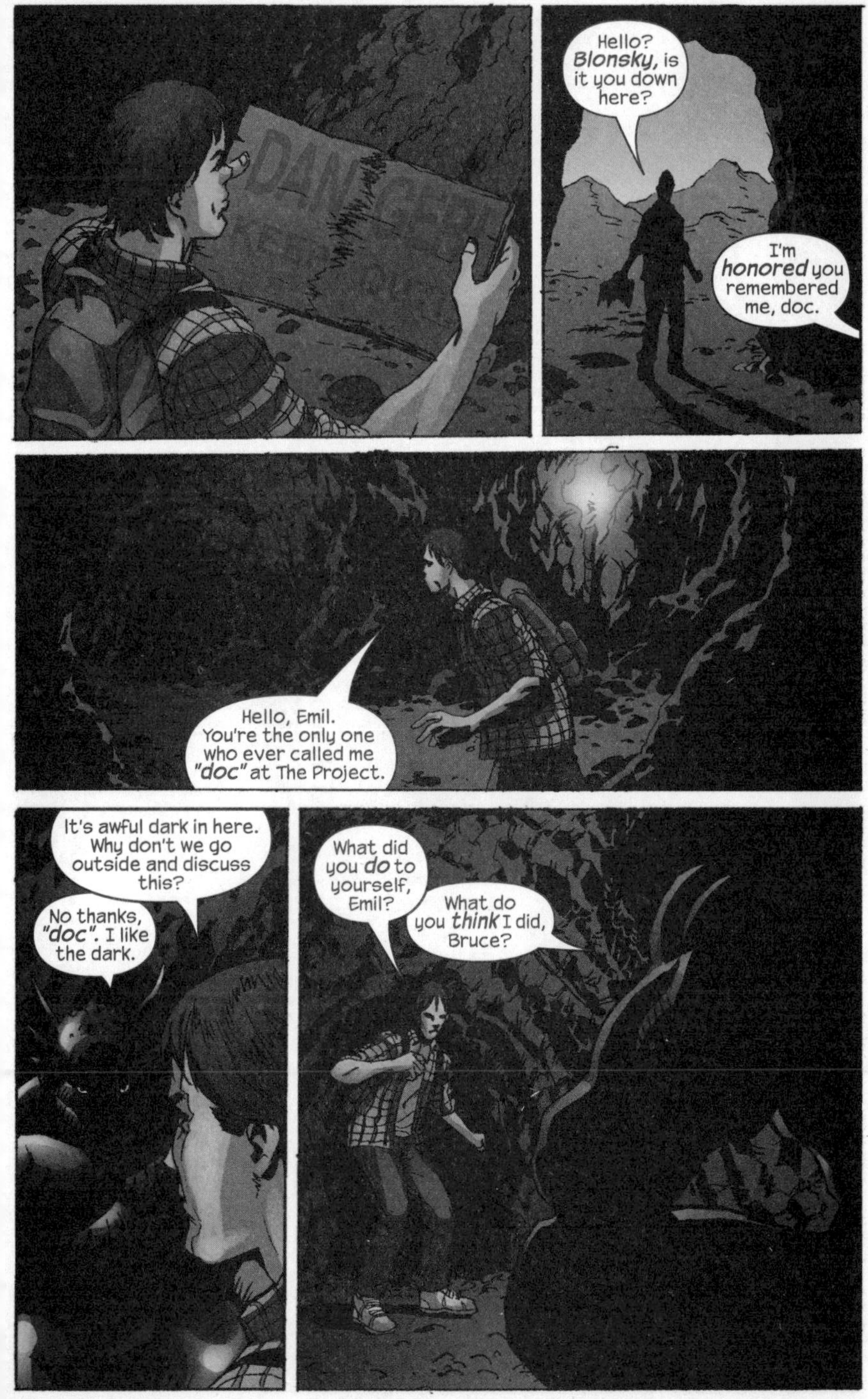
Hello? *Blonsky,* is it you down here?
I'm *honored* you remembered me, doc.
Hello, Emil. You're the only one who ever called me *"doc"* at The Project.
It's awful dark in here. Why don't we go outside and discuss this?
No thanks, *"doc"*. I like the dark.
What did you *do* to yourself, Emil?
What do you *think* I did, Bruce?

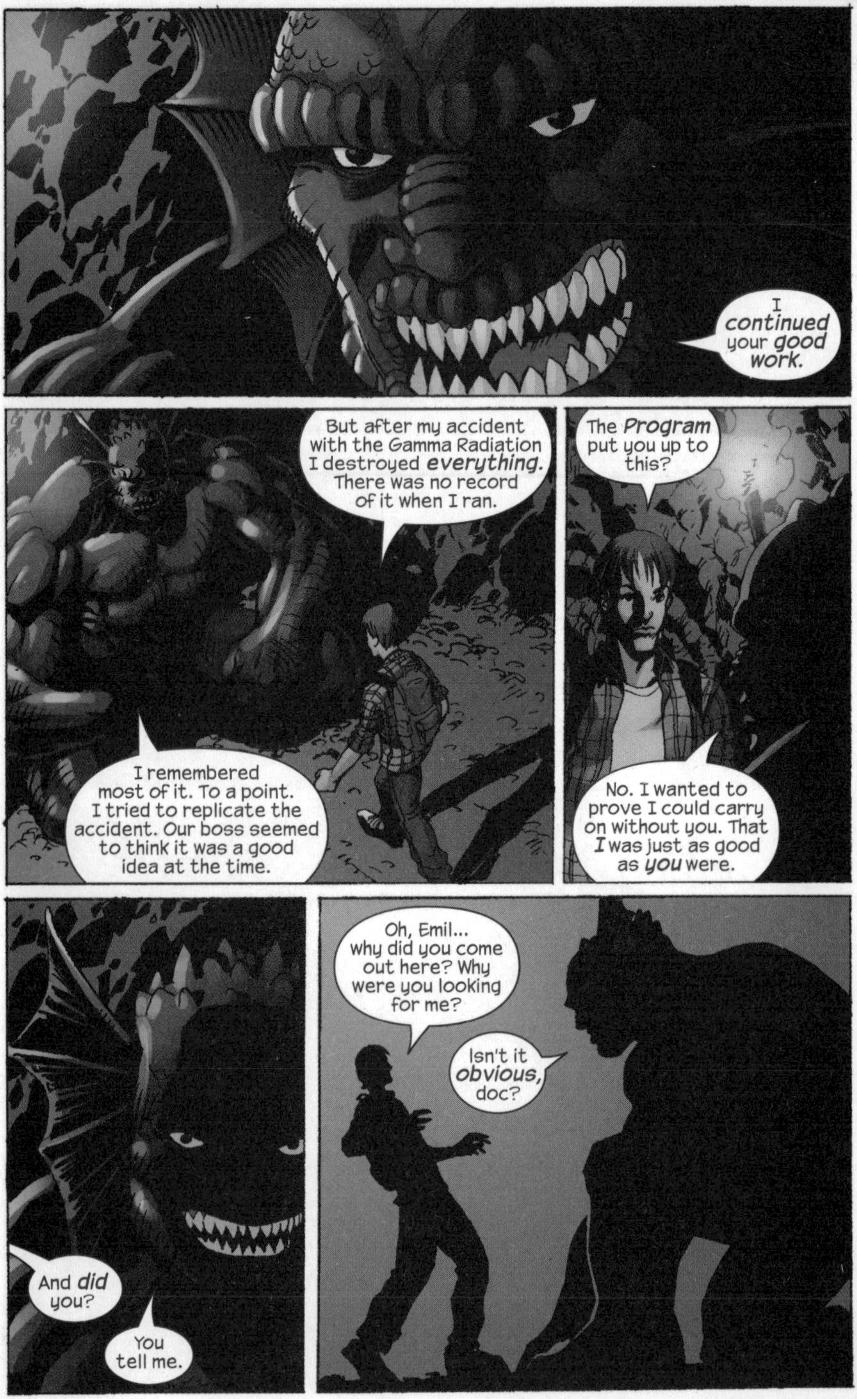
I continued your good work.
But after my accident with the Gamma Radiation I destroyed everything. There was no record of it when I ran.
I remembered most of it. To a point. I tried to replicate the accident. Our boss seemed to think it was a good idea at the time.
The Program put you up to this?
No. I wanted to prove I could carry on without you. That I was just as good as you were.
And did you?
You tell me.
Oh, Emil... why did you come out here? Why were you looking for me?
Isn't it obvious, doc?

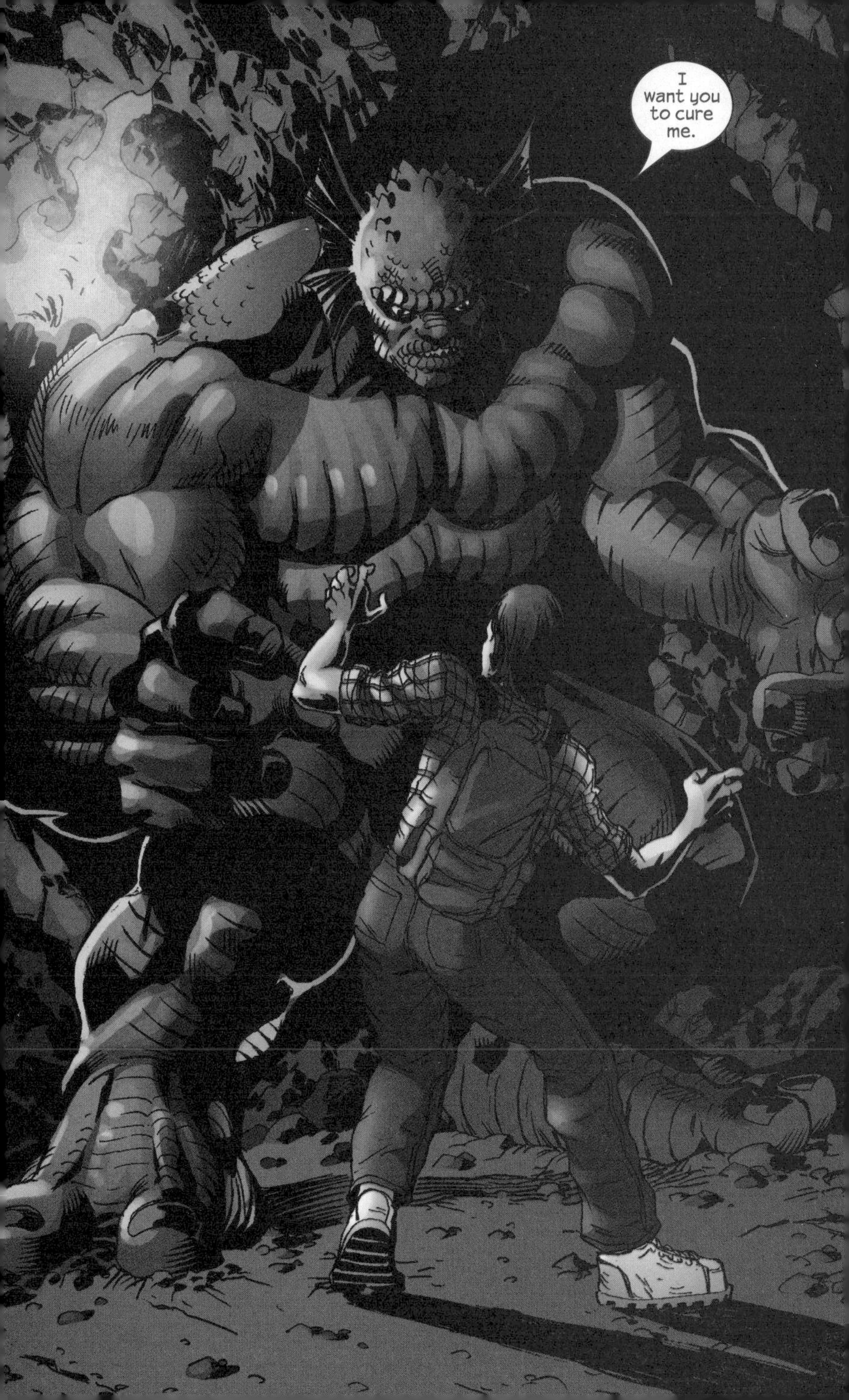
I want you to cure me.

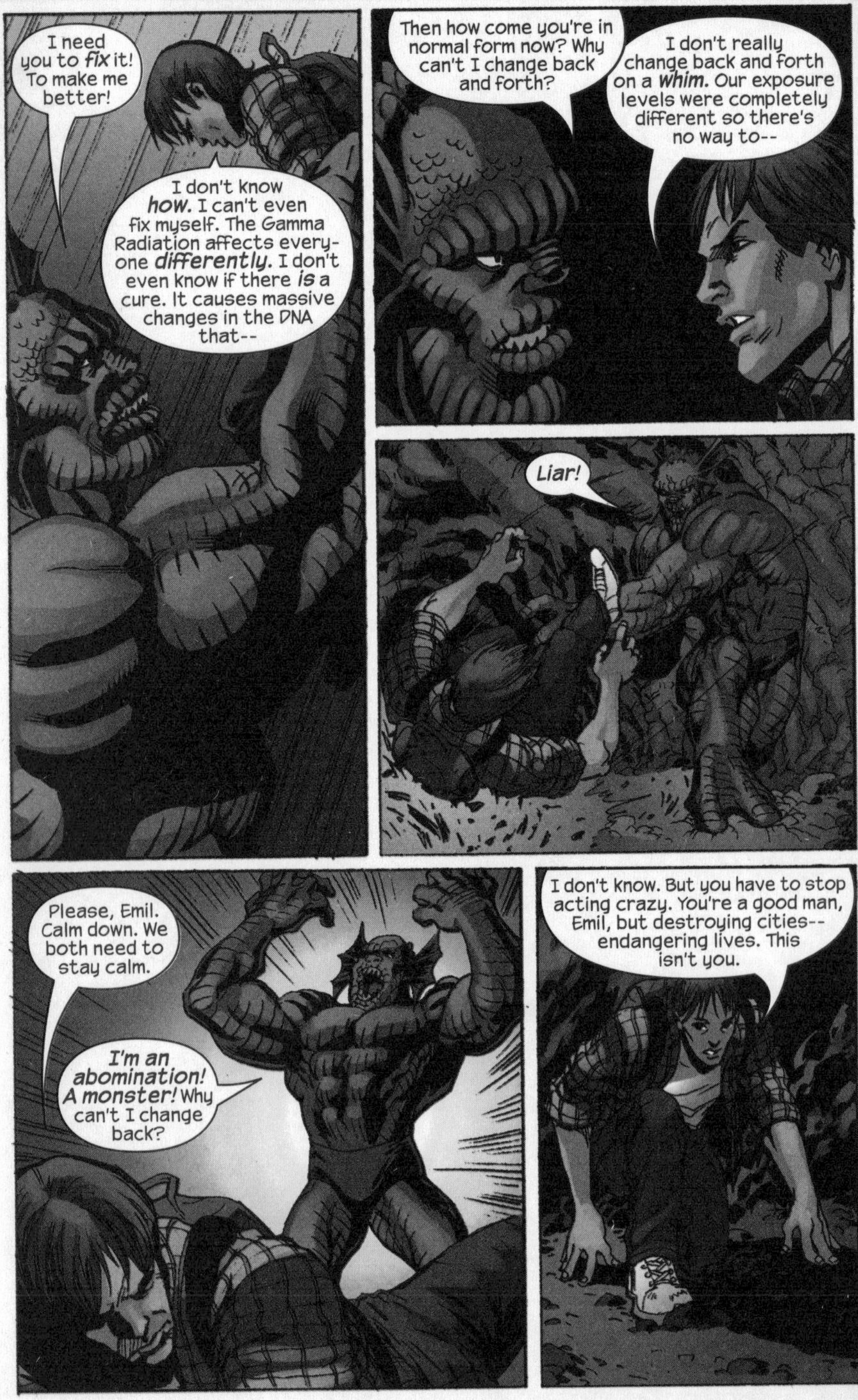
I need you to *fix* it! To make me better!
I don't know *how*. I can't even fix myself. The Gamma Radiation affects every-one *differently*. I don't even know if there *is* a cure. It causes massive changes in the DNA that--
Then how come you're in normal form now? Why can't I change back and forth?
I don't really change back and forth on a *whim*. Our exposure levels were completely different so there's no way to--
Liar!
Please, Emil. Calm down. We both need to stay calm.
I'm an abomination! A monster! Why can't I change back?
I don't know. But you have to stop acting crazy. You're a good man, Emil, but destroying cities-- endangering lives. This isn't you.

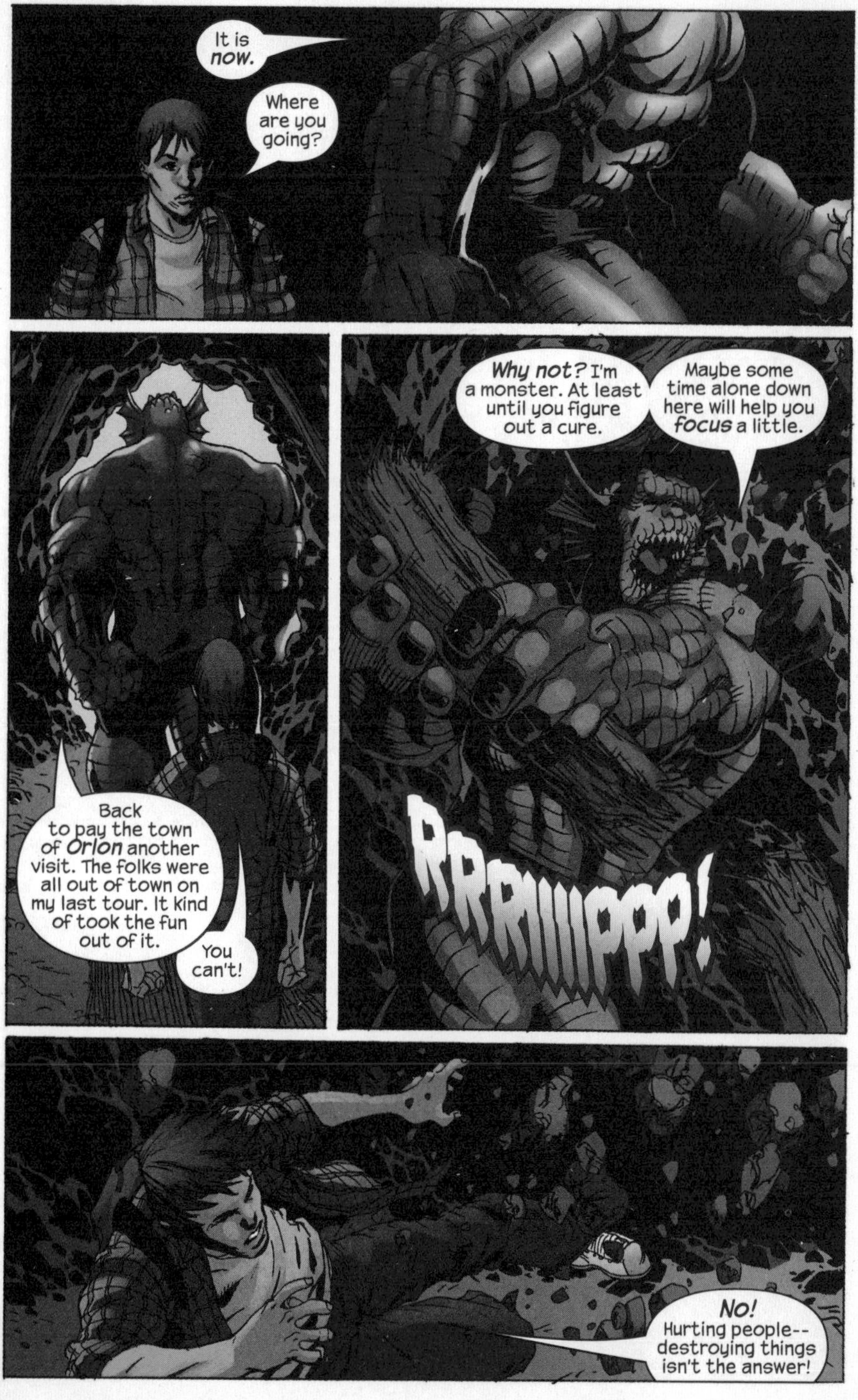
It is *now.*
Where are you going?
Back to pay the town of *Orlon* another visit. The folks were all out of town on my last tour. It kind of took the fun out of it.
You can't!
Why not? I'm a monster. At least until you figure out a cure.
Maybe some time alone down here will help you *focus* a little.
RRRIIIIPPP!
No! Hurting people--destroying things isn't the answer!

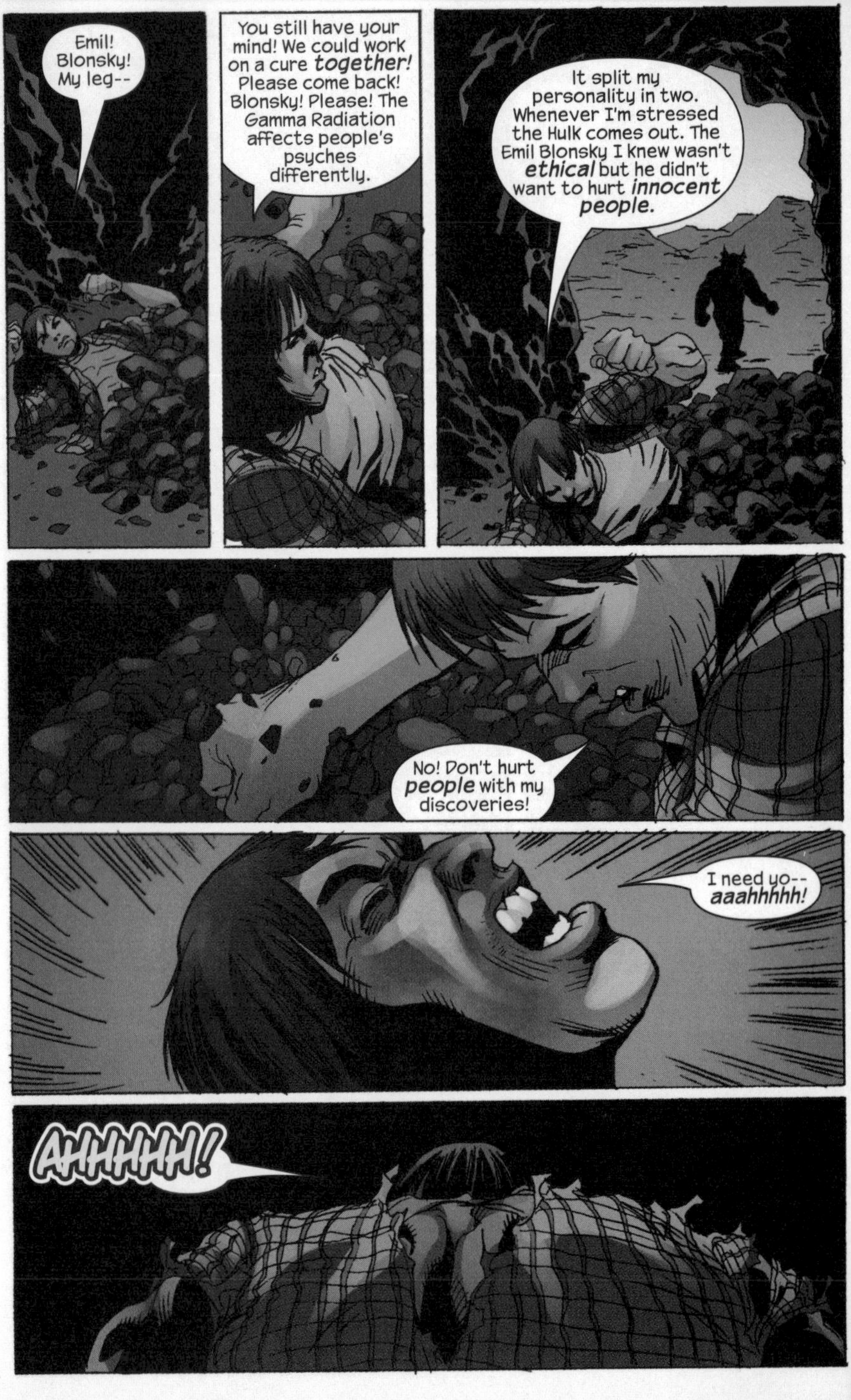

Emil! Blonsky! My leg--
You still have your mind! We could work on a cure *together!* Please come back! Blonsky! Please! The Gamma Radiation affects people's psyches differently.
It split my personality in two. Whenever I'm stressed the Hulk comes out. The Emil Blonsky I knew wasn't *ethical* but he didn't want to hurt *innocent people.*
No! Don't hurt *people* with my discoveries!
I need yo-- *aaahhhhh!*
AHHHHHH!

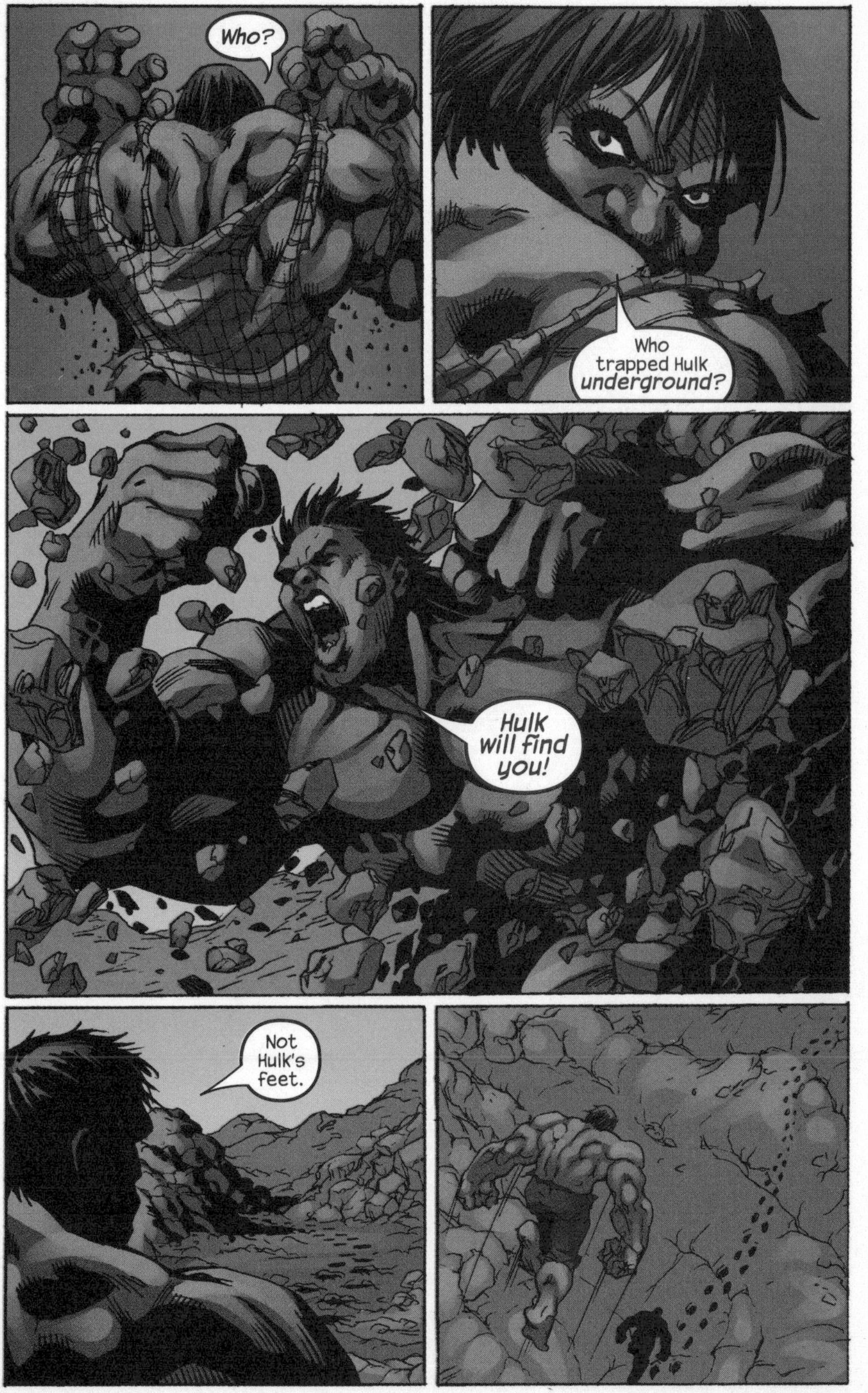
Who?
Who trapped Hulk underground?
Hulk will find you!
Not Hulk's feet.

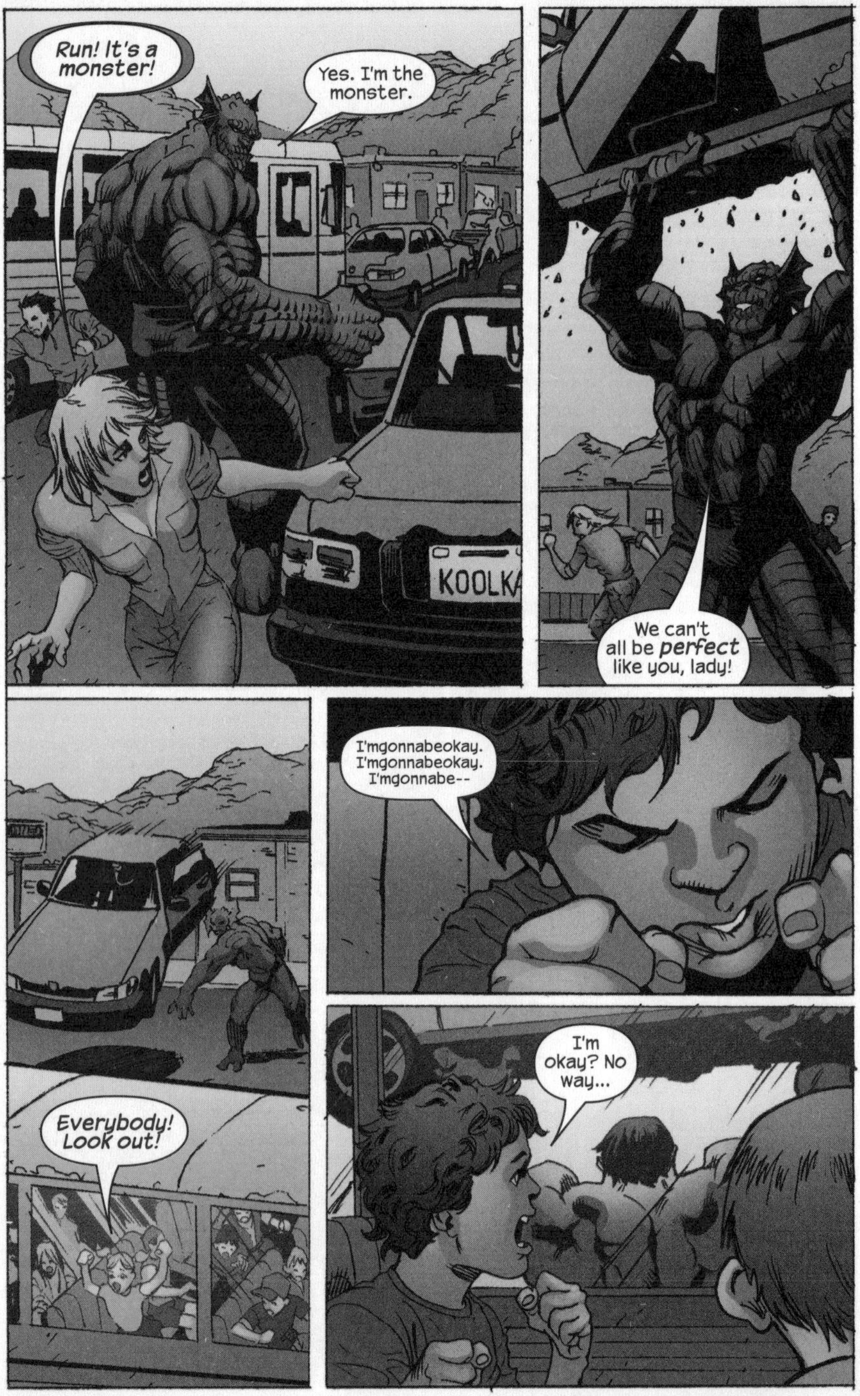
Run! It's a monster!
Yes. I'm the monster.
KOOLKA
We can't all be perfect like you, lady!
I'mgonnabeokay. I'mgonnabeokay. I'mgonnabe--
Everybody! Look out!
I'm okay? No way...

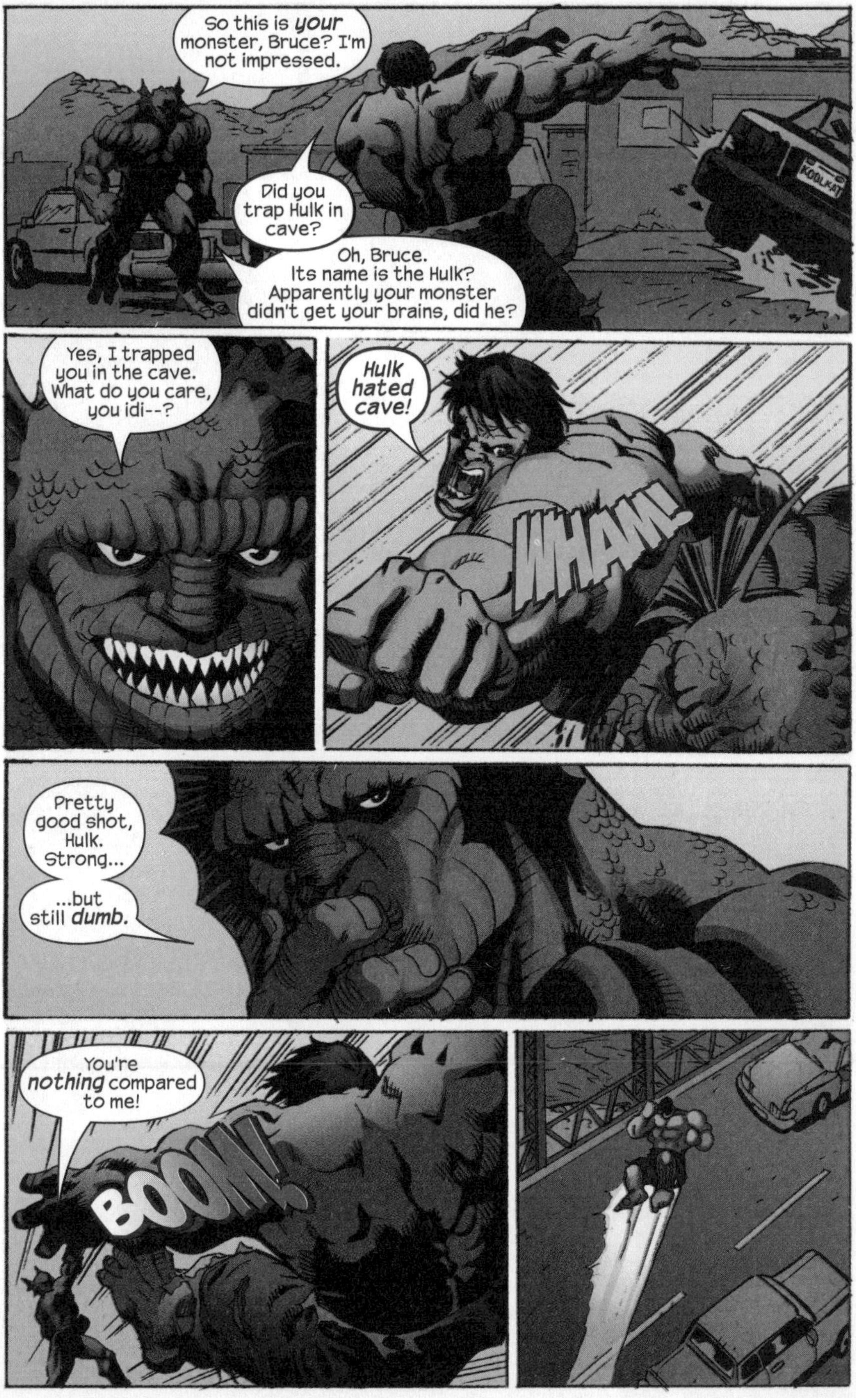
So this is your monster, Bruce? I'm not impressed.
Did you trap Hulk in cave?
Oh, Bruce. Its name is the Hulk? Apparently your monster didn't get your brains, did he?
KOOLKAT
Yes, I trapped you in the cave. What do you care, you idi--?
Hulk hated cave!
WHAM!
Pretty good shot, Hulk. Strong...
...but still dumb.
You're nothing compared to me!
BOOM!

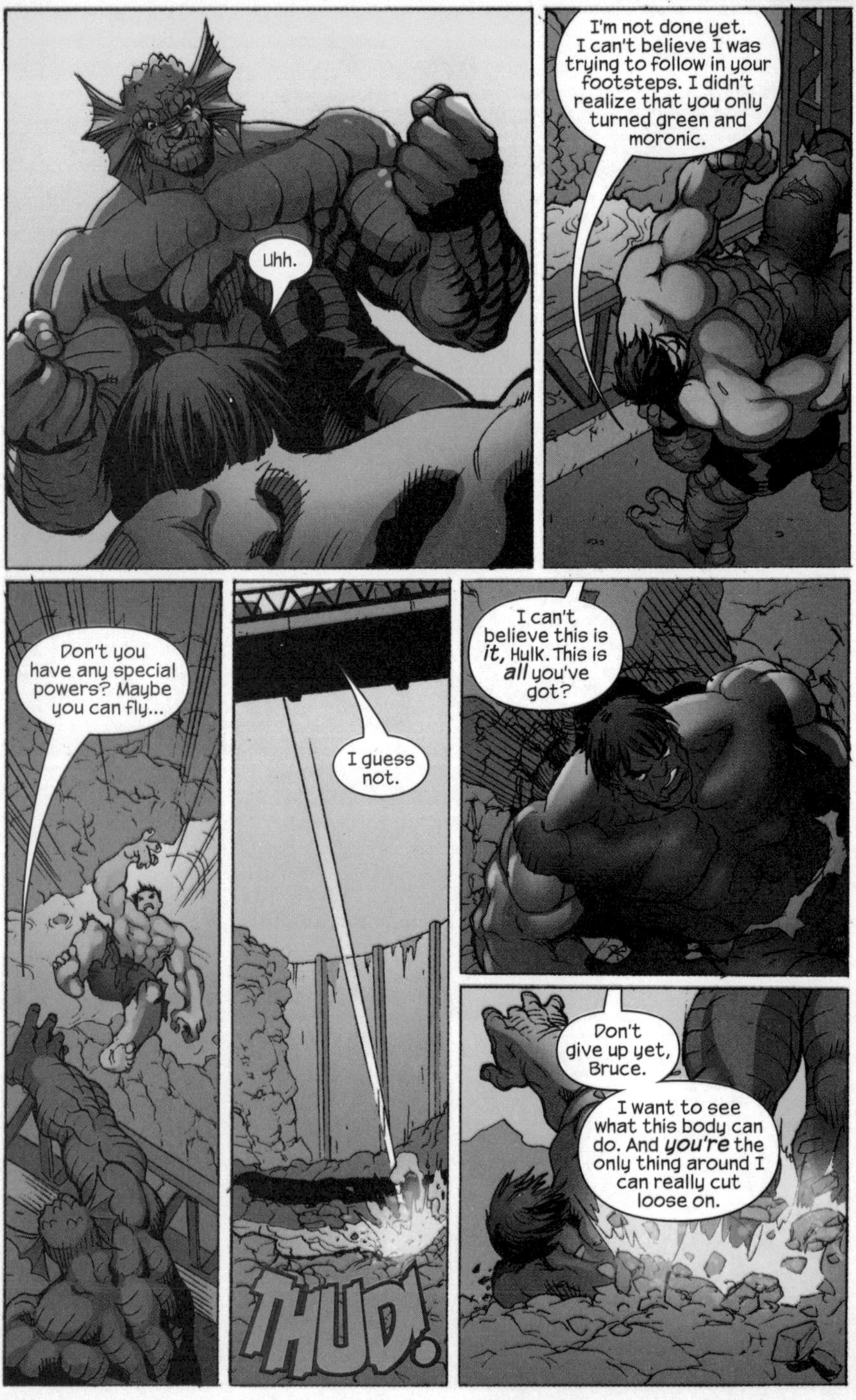
Uhh.
I'm not done yet. I can't believe I was trying to follow in your footsteps. I didn't realize that you only turned green and moronic.
Don't you have any special powers? Maybe you can fly...
I guess not.
THUD!
I can't believe this is *it,* Hulk. This is *all* you've got?
Don't give up yet, Bruce.
I want to see what this body can do. And *you're* the only thing around I can really cut loose on.

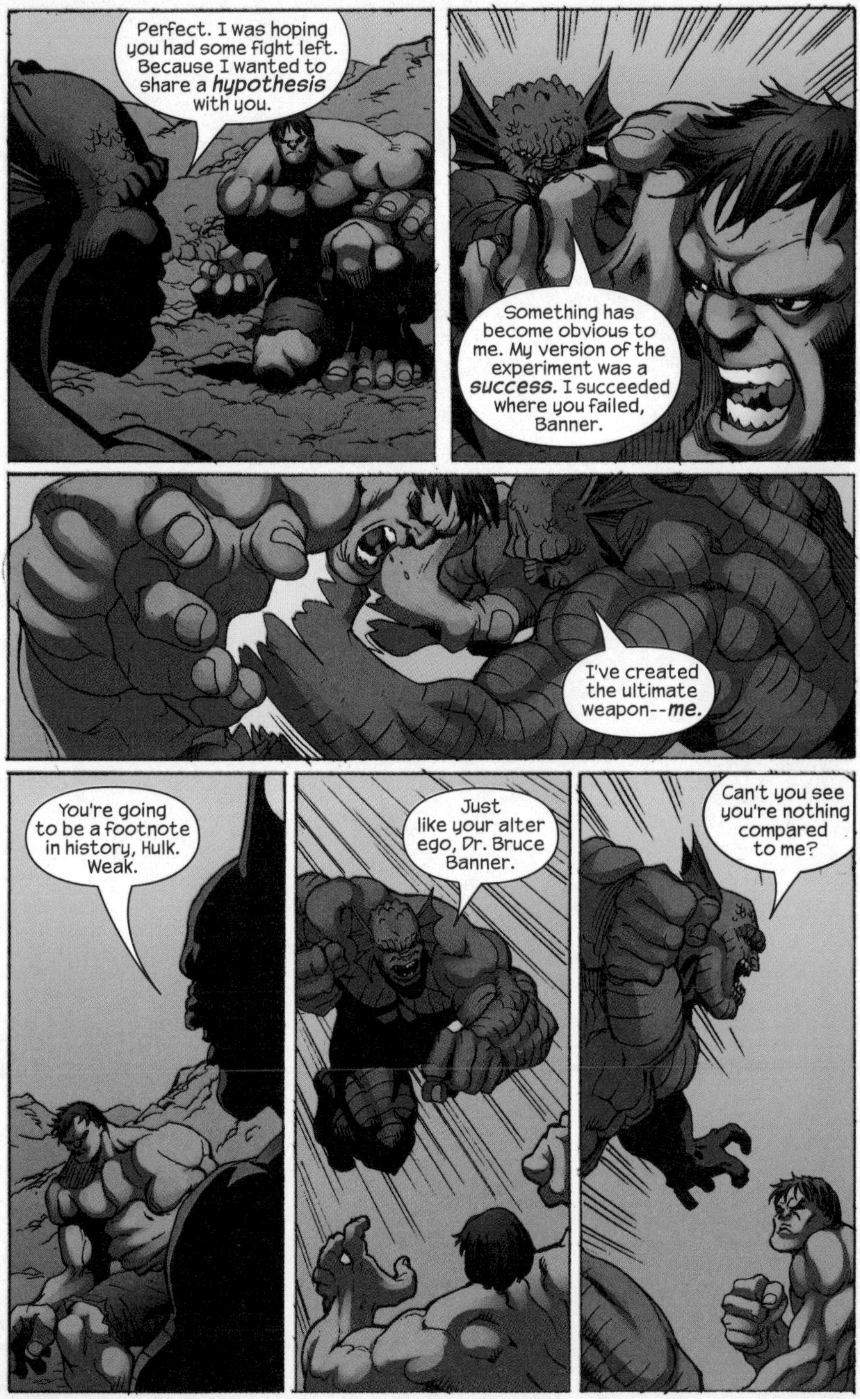
Perfect. I was hoping you had some fight left. Because I wanted to share a *hypothesis* with you.
Something has become obvious to me. My version of the experiment was a *success.* I succeeded where you failed, Banner.
I've created the ultimate weapon--*me.*
You're going to be a footnote in history, Hulk. Weak.
Just like your alter ego, Dr. Bruce Banner.
Can't you see you're nothing compared to me?

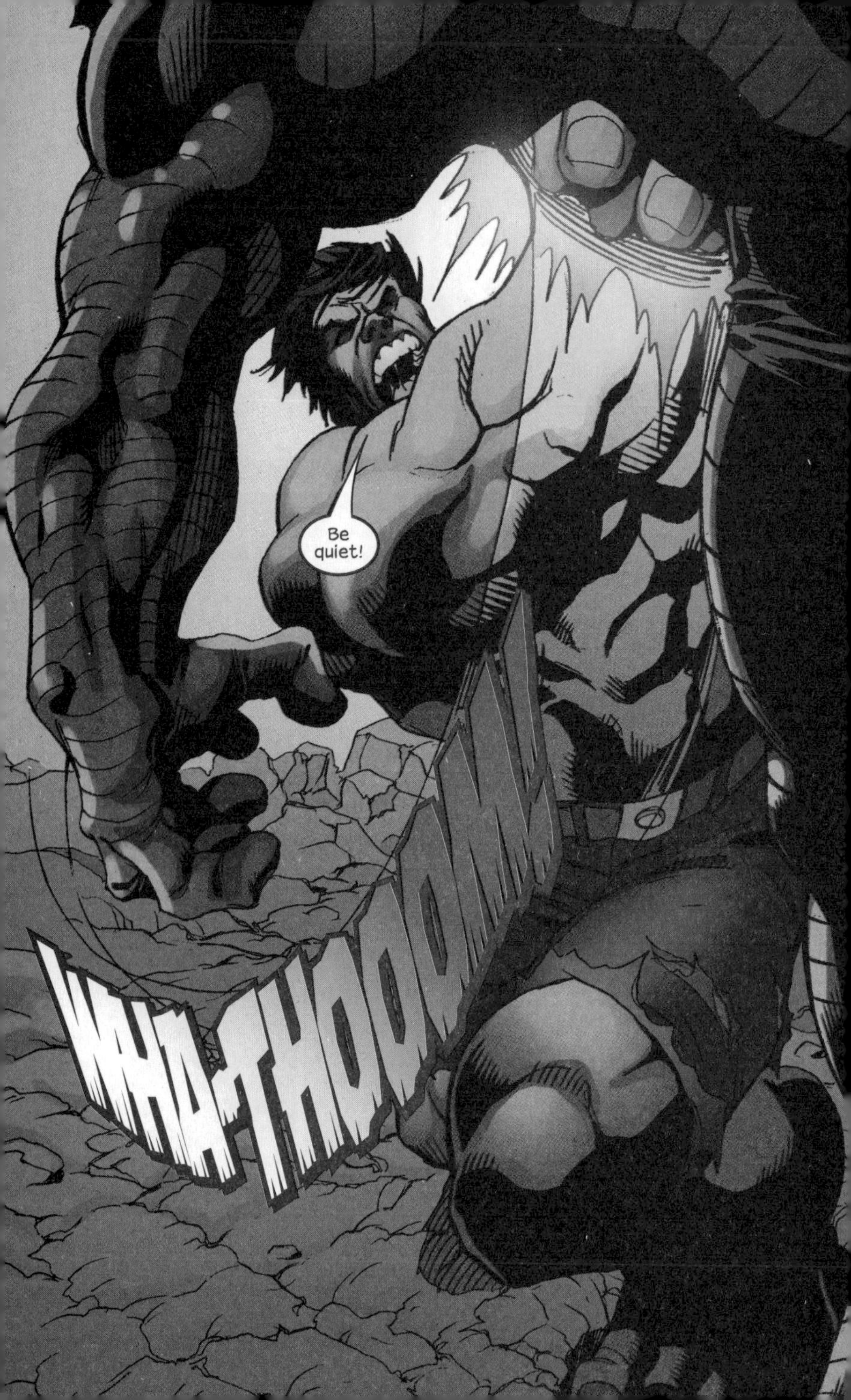
Be quiet!
WHA-THOOOM!!

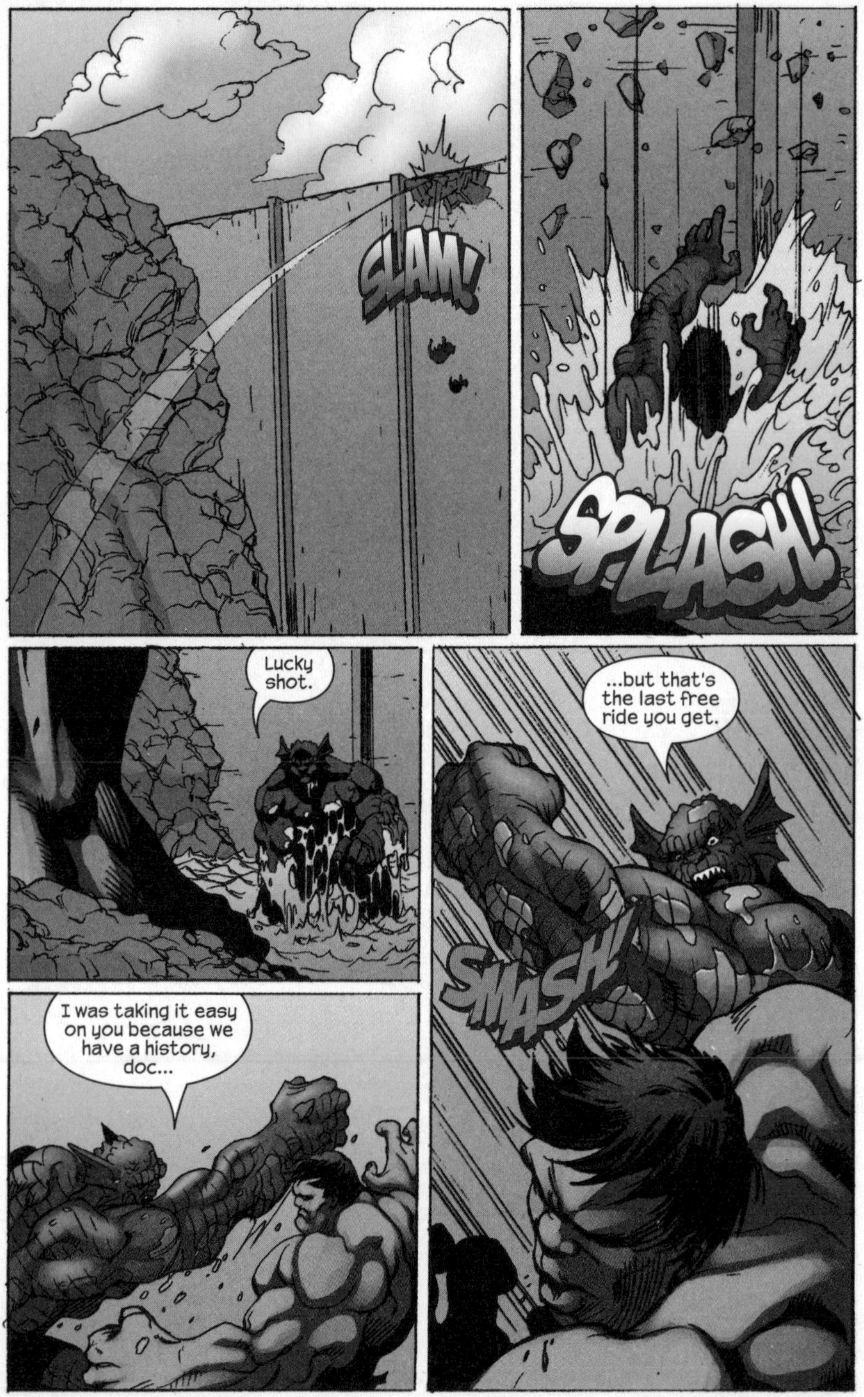
SLAM!
SPLASH!
Lucky shot.
I was taking it easy on you because we have a history, doc...
...but that's the last free ride you get.
SMASH!

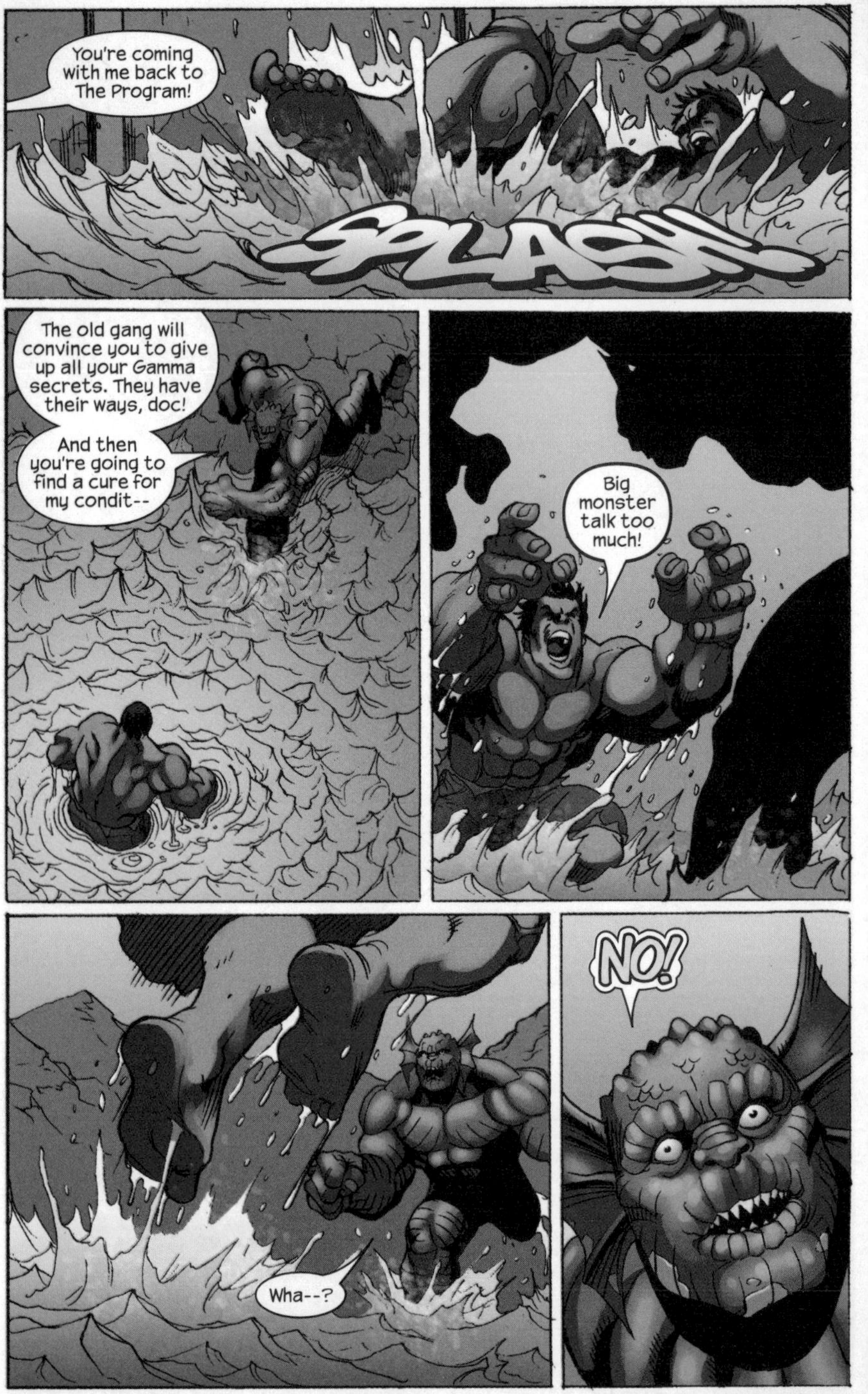
You're coming with me back to The Program!
SPLASH!
The old gang will convince you to give up all your Gamma secrets. They have their ways, doc!
And then you're going to find a cure for my condit--
Big monster talk too much!
Wha--?
NO!

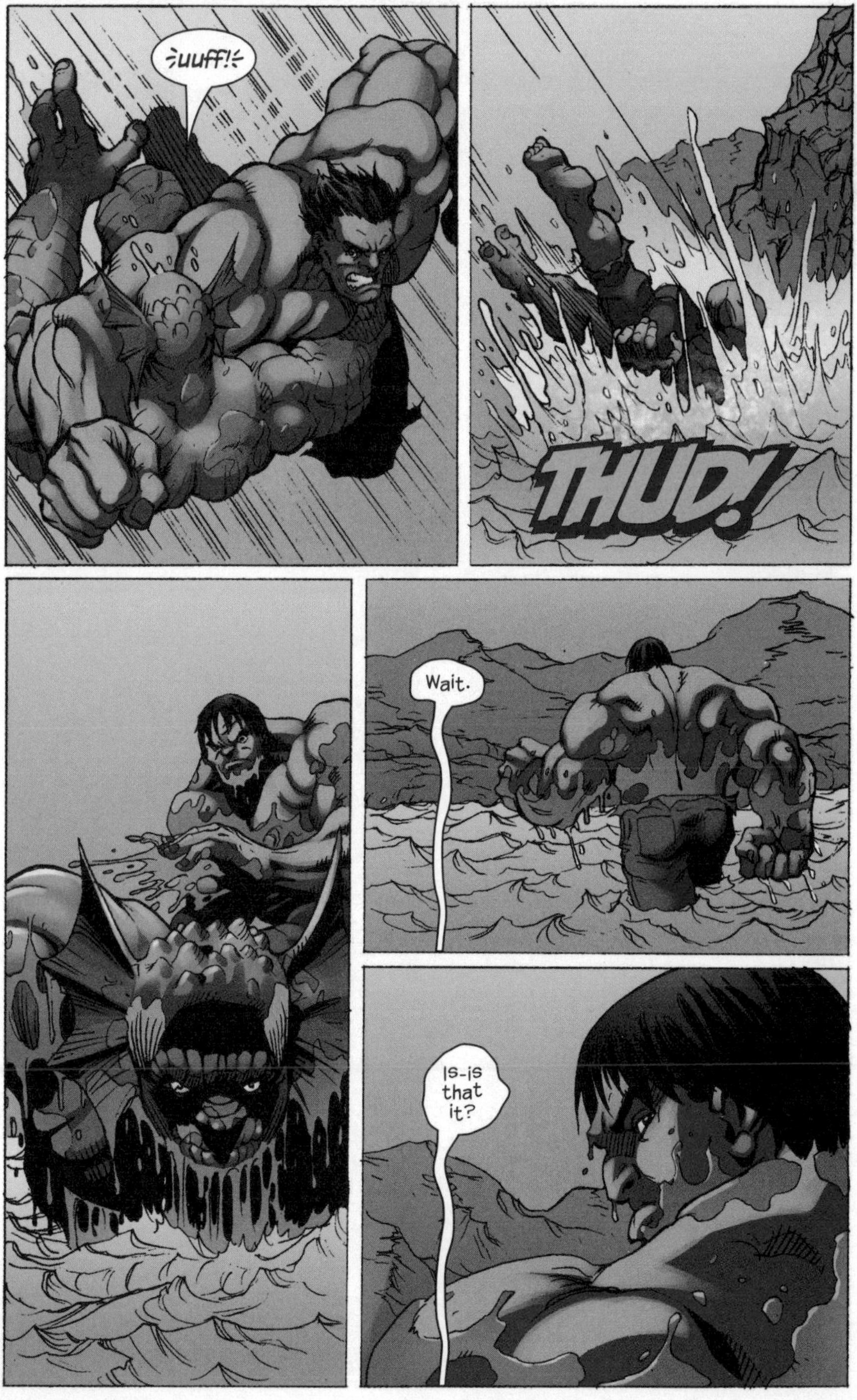
uuff!
THUD!
Wait.
Is-is that it?

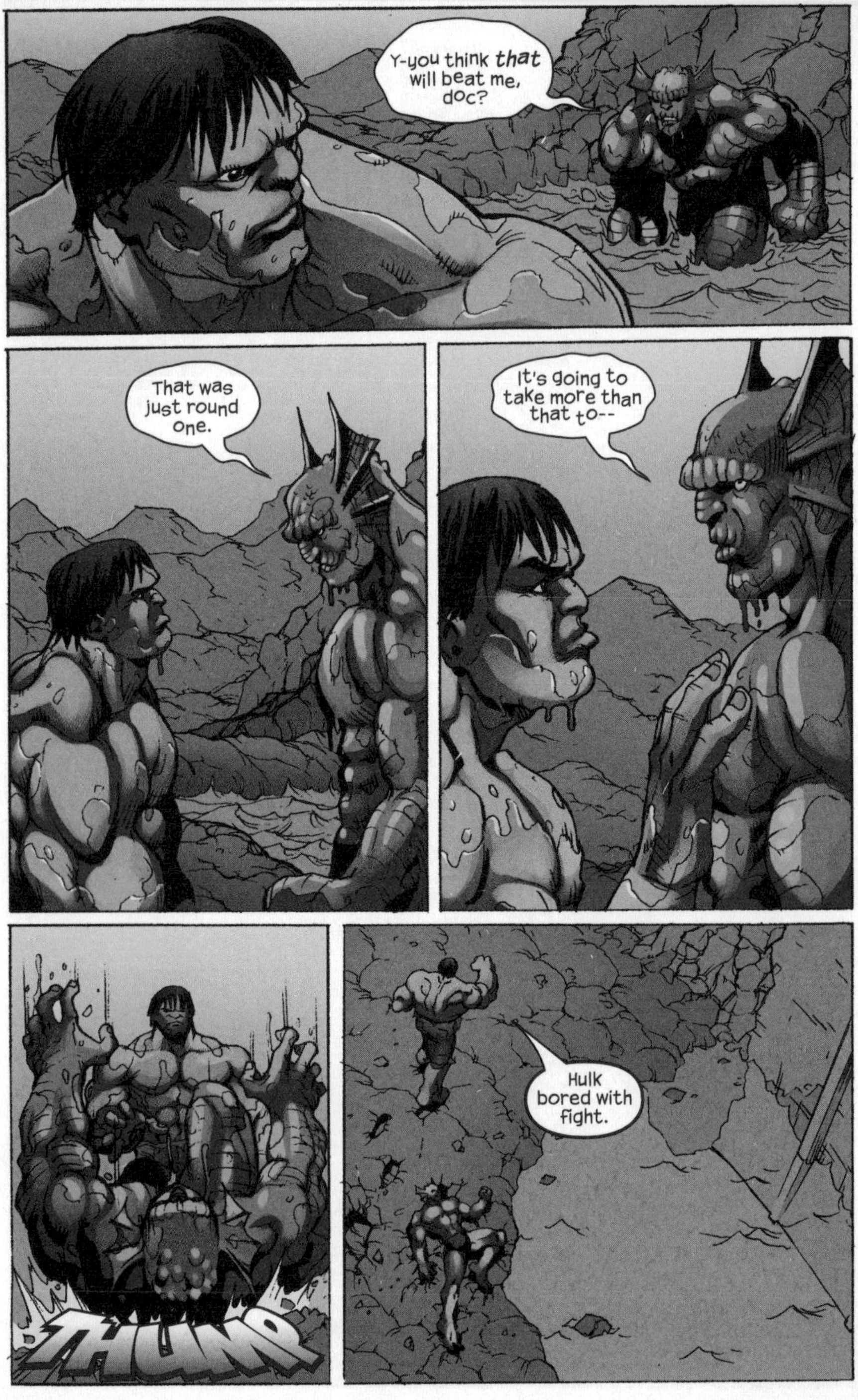
Y-you think *that* will beat me, doc?
That was just round one.
It's going to take more than that to--
THUMP
Hulk bored with fight.

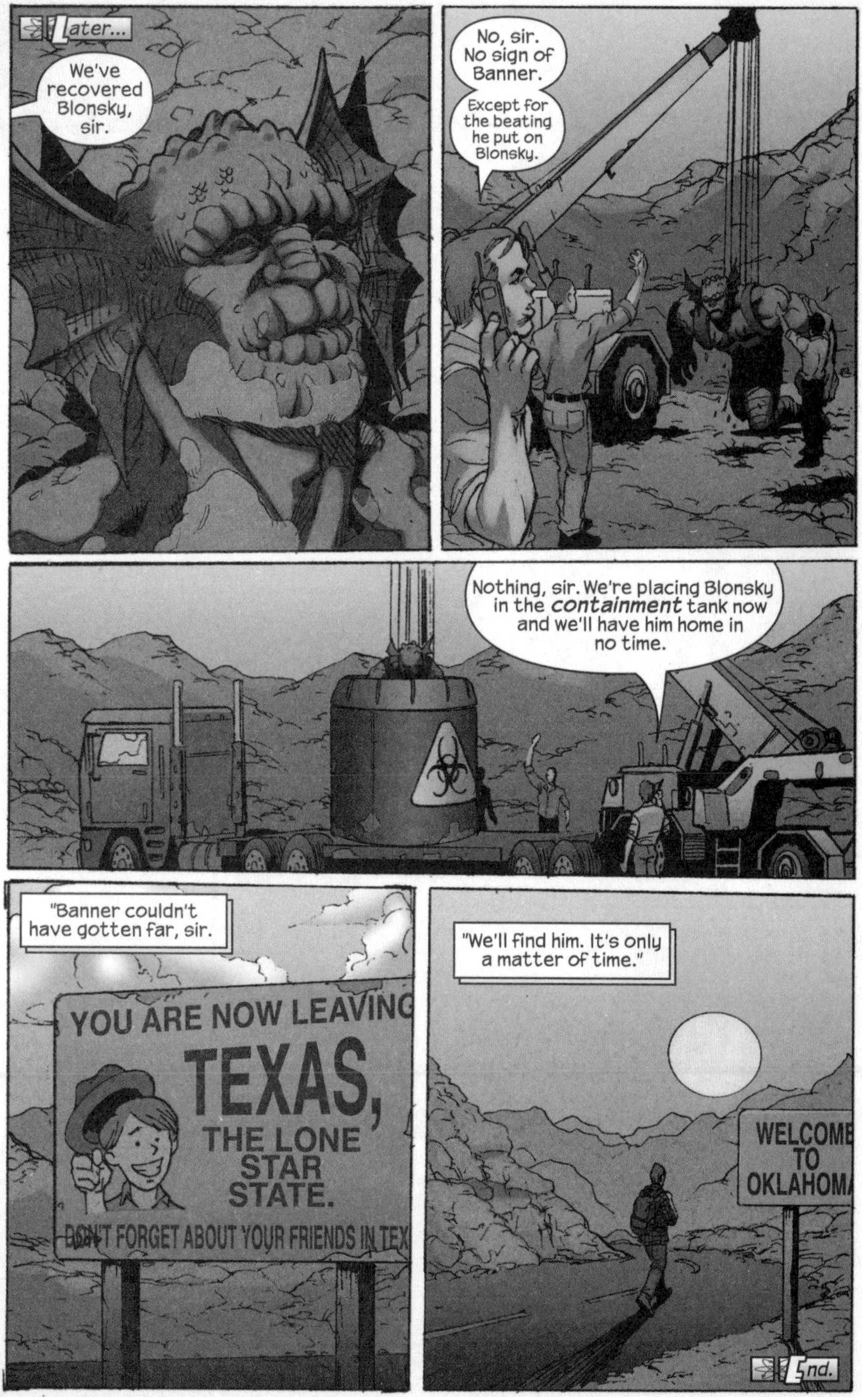
Later...
We've recovered Blonsky, sir.
No, sir. No sign of Banner.
Except for the beating he put on Blonsky.
Nothing, sir. We're placing Blonsky in the *containment* tank now and we'll have him home in no time.
"Banner couldn't have gotten far, sir.
YOU ARE NOW LEAVING
TEXAS,
THE LONE STAR STATE.
DON'T FORGET ABOUT YOUR FRIENDS IN TEX
"We'll find him. It's only a matter of time."
WELCOME TO OKLAHOM
End.

MARVEL AGE BACK PAGE

COLLECT ALL THE MARVEL AGE TITLES!

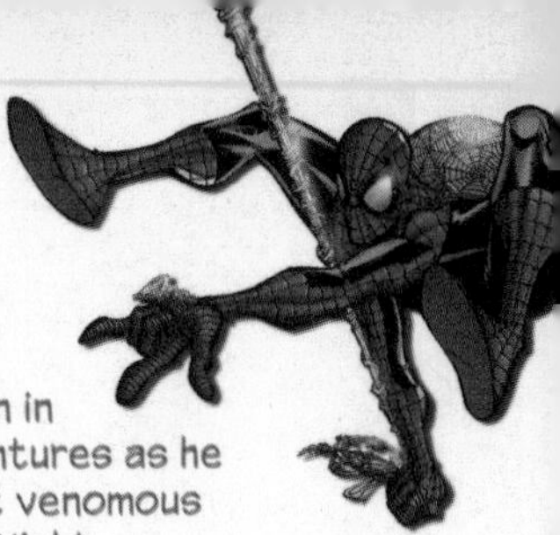

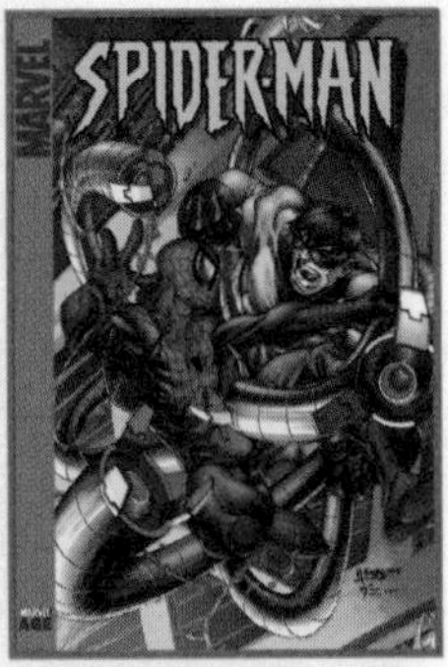
SPIDER-MAN

Catch Spider-Man in his thrilling adventures as he tackles the most venomous villains from the Mighty Marvel Mythos!

- ☐ Marvel Age Spider-Man vol 1 (pictured)
- ☐ Marvel Age Spider-Man vol 2
- ☐ Marvel Age Spider-Man vol 3
- ☐ Marvel Age Spider-Man vol 4

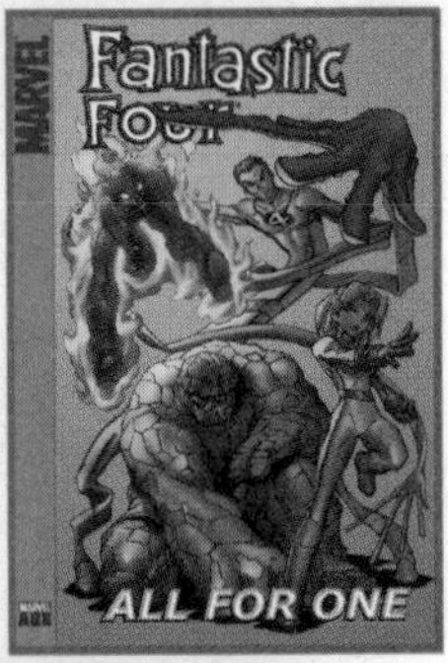
Fantastic Four
ALL FOR ONE

Join Marvel's First Family on their fantastic adventures, from the deepest depths of the ocean to the farthest reaches of outer space!

- ☐ Marvel Age Fantastic Four vol 1 (pictured)
- ☐ Marvel Age Fantastic Four vol 2

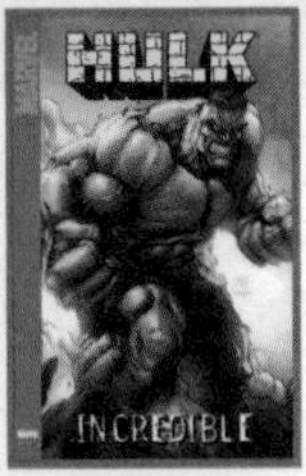
HULK
INCREDIBLE

- ☐ Marvel Age Hulk vol 1: Incredible

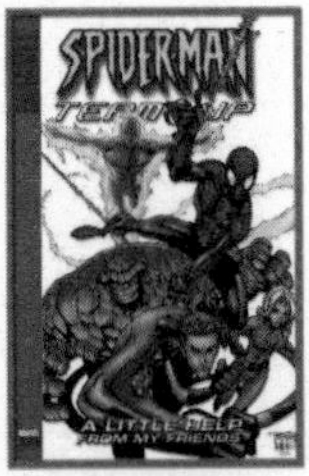
SPIDER-MAN
TEAM-UP
A LITTLE HELP FROM MY FRIENDS

- ☐ Marvel Age Spider-Man Team-Up vol 1: A Little Help From My Friends

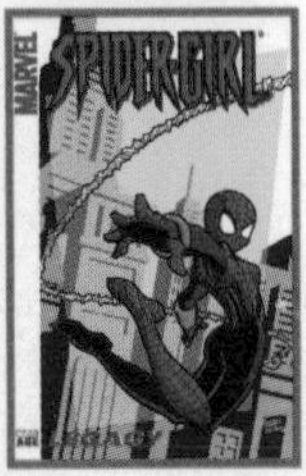
SPIDER-GIRL

- ☐ Marvel Age Spider-Girl vol 1: Legacy (pictured)
- ☐ Marvel Age Spider-Girl vol 2: Like Father Like Daughter

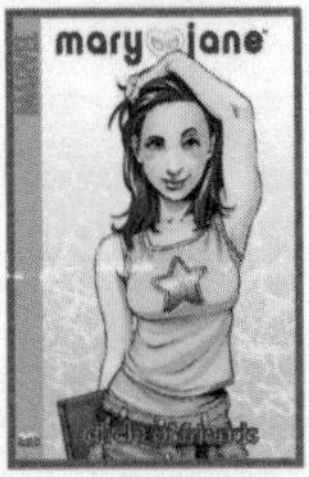
mary jane

- ☐ Marvel Age Mary Jane vol 1: Circle of Friends

Available in bookstores and your local comic shop! Don't miss out!

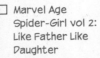